Cézanne's Portrait Drawings

Wayne Andersen

The MIT Press; Cambridge, Massachusetts, and London, England

Library of Congress catalog card number: 69–10529

Set in Linofilm Palatino by Book Graphics Inc.,
and printed by The Murray Printing Co.
Bound in the United States of America by
A. Horowitz & Son
SBN 262 01026 7 (hardcover)

In memory of my father,
Vesti, son of Thor

Contents

Preface   vii

Note on Terms and Abbreviations   ix

A Chronology for the Portrait Drawings

I	1858–1871	3
II	1872–1874	9
III	1875–1880	17
IV	1879–1889	25
V	1890–1900	37
	Notes	41

Catalogue

I	Self-Portraits	47
II	Portraits of Madame Cézanne	71
III	Portraits of Cézanne's Son	115
IV	Portraits of Cézanne's Father	183
V	Portraits of Cézanne's Mother	191
VI	Portraits of Cézanne's Friends	193
VII	Group Portraits of Cézanne's Friends	247
VIII	Portrait Studies for *Les Joueurs de Cartes*	227
IX	Portraits of Unidentified Persons	233

Provenance	239
Concordance of Catalogue Numbers	240
Selected Bibliography	243
Index of Identified Sitters	247

Preface

Paul Cézanne's career spanned almost five decades, from Impressionism, in which he played an important role, to Cubism, which built on his achievement. He left over eight hundred paintings, about four hundred watercolors, and roughly twelve hundred and fifty drawings. Together these should record an extraordinary development, but the over-all picture is clouded by problems in chronology. Only six of the paintings are dated on the canvas (dates for only some eighty-five others can be surmised), none of the watercolors bears a date, and the only date on a drawing is neither correct nor in the artist's hand. Moreover, the external evidence for dating the paintings is not necessarily valid for related drawings, even though in some cases the subject and even the artist's viewpoint are the same. Cézanne had the habit of returning many times to the same landscape motif; he also used the same still-life elements over periods of years, and he occasionally depended on earlier drawings for ideas and studies for later paintings.

Because Cézanne was vitally interested in his own development—more so than in achieving completeness or perfection in a single work—the chronology of his work is especially relevant to art historians who are concerned above all with the artistic process and who are as much interested in the artist and his total achievement as in single objects of art. An understanding of Cézanne's process, his year-to-year struggle to arrive at what he himself called "the right way to see," depends on a correct reconstruction of the steps he took. To prevent his process from being understood as a neat, linear progression through "logical" stages, we are obliged to subordinate our assumptions of stylistic progression to as many external, or nonstylistic, criteria as we are able to establish.

My decision to focus on Cézanne's portrait drawings as a way to a more precise chronology was based on two major considerations: that roughly half the documentation pertinent to Cézanne's chronology concerns portraits and that the many drawings Cézanne made of his son can be dated by estimating the child's age. Since the documentation available is particularly helpful for the sixties and the nineties, and since the portraits of the child extend from about 1874 to the mid-nineties, it has been possible to outline quite precisely Cézanne's graphic development over these four decades and to derive sufficient visual evidence to date with reasonable accuracy the balance of the portrait drawings. This study may be helpful in establishing a more accurate chronology for the balance of Cézanne's graphic work.

This study began in 1959 with my investigation of Cézanne's sketchbook in the Art Institute of Chicago and is a recast of my dissertation prepared at Columbia University. Professor Meyer Shapiro read my manuscript at an early stage and gave me very helpful advice. A William Bayard Cutting Traveling Fellowship from Columbia University for 1961 and 1962 enabled me to study the available Cézanne drawings in European collections. I worked principally in Paris and in the printrooms of the museums in Basel and Rotterdam, and made excursions to other sources of Cézanne drawings.

Dr. Adrien Chappuis permitted me to see his large collection of Cézanne drawings and to reproduce most of the unpublished portraits; he also supplied helpful information in response to my inquiries. In Paris I was assisted by my dear friend Leni Iselin, who proved to be an extraordinary private detective. Cézanne's grandson, Jean-Pierre, put his collection of Cézanne's memorabilia, much of it previously unknown, at my disposal. In London I enjoyed the hospitality of Sir Kenneth and Lady Clark, whose fine collection of Cézanne drawings had not been previously studied. They permitted me to unframe all their drawings in London and at Saltwood in order to examine the versos and determine exact measurements. Dr. John Rewald sent me photographs of unpublished Cézanne drawings and responded to my inquiries. Mr. Harold Joachim, of the Art Institute of Chicago, attended to my needs for photographs and information concerning the Chicago sketchbook and the sketchbook owned by Mr. and Mrs. Leigh Block. Mademoiselle Roselyne Bacou, curator of the printroom at the Louvre, has been very generous with assistance, as have Professor H. R. Hoetink, former curator of the Museum Boymans-van Beuningen, and Dr. Hanspeter Landolt of the Kunstmuseum in Basel. To all these people I am greatly indebted.

I am grateful also to Mrs. Haupt for allowing me to examine her collection of Cézanne drawings and to photograph the unpublished portrait drawings. Although access to these came too late to permit inclusion of them in the discussion, the portraits are reproduced in the catalogue. (I should mention that as the drawings could not be examined outside their frames, their exact coordination with entries in John Rewald, *Carnets de dessins,* cannot be guaranteed.)

To Henry Schaefer-Simmern, teacher and dear friend, I offer thanks for advice and encouragement extended to me over many years. To my friend Sam Surace I owe the realization that I might make as good a scholar as I was a carpenter.

W. A.

Notes on Terms and Abbreviations

Portrait I have reserved the designation "portrait" for drawings Cézanne made of persons he actually knew, even though the drawings were sometimes made from a photograph; therefore, I have not classified his drawings of Delacroix, for example, as portraits; these are more accurately called copies. In differentiating between drawings and watercolors, I have used the simple criterion of apparent intention: if the example appears to be a drawing only heightened by watercolor, I have called it a drawing, whereas if its pencil lines appear to be guidelines for the application of color, I have considered it a watercolor and excluded it. Sometimes the choice appears arbitrary, but I believe this does not create difficulties.

I have catalogued the portraits by subject rather than by sheets; thus, a sheet that holds both a self-portrait and a portrait of Cézanne's son is catalogued twice, with appropriate cross references. This seemed necessary because many original sheets have been divided by dealers and collectors, and because images appearing together on a single sheet are not always exactly contemporary. The recto and verso of a sheet are catalogued separately.

Date The dates I have assigned to the drawings are for the portrait images only and do not necessarily apply to other drawings on the same sheet. I have used the words "circa" and "about" to indicate the possibility that a drawing dates from one year earlier or later than the date I have assigned it; thus, "ca. 1878" means that I believe 1878 to be probable but either 1877 or 1879 to be possible. On the other hand, a date "1877–1879" indicates that I have allowed equal probability to each of the three years. In citing dates assigned by others to a sheet that includes more than one drawing, I have tried, whenever possible, to include only the dates for the portrait drawing on the sheet.

Dimensions In all entries dimensions are given in centimeters; height precedes width.

Photographic Credits Unless otherwise indicated at the catalogue entry, photographs were supplied by the owners of the drawings.

General Abbreviations and Designations

The abbreviation "No.," or a number in parentheses, refers to an entry in this catalogue. The abbreviation "n.r." after an entry number in the catalogue indicates that the drawing has not been reproduced here. The abbreviation "fac." after a catalog entry indicates a facsimile reproduction of the original drawing. Illustrations in the text are referred to as "Figures." In the catalogue, for the sketchbooks known as the first, second, third, and fourth Chappuis sketchbooks (measuring, respectively, 12 × 19.5 cm., 12.6 × 21.5 cm., 15 × 23.8 cm., 21 × 27.3 cm.), I have used the designations "Chappuis I, II, III, IV," following the size of the sketchbooks. Similarly, I have used the designation "Basel III" for the Basel sketchbook measuring 12.5 × 20.5 cm. (These books are inventoried in Lionello Venturi, *Cézanne, son art, son œuvre,* Vol. I, pp. 304–319.) The designations *Carnet 18 × 24* and *Carnet 10.3 × 17* refer to sketchbooks partially reconstructed in Adrien Chappuis, *Les Dessins de Paul Cézanne au Cabinet des Estampes du Musée des Beaux-Arts de Bâle,* Vol. I, p. 27.

Bibliographical Abbreviations

Berthold
Gertrude Berthold, *Cézanne und die alten Meister,* Stuttgart, 1958.

Chappuis
Adrien Chappuis, *Les Dessins de Paul Cézanne au Cabinet des Estampes du Musée des Beaux-Arts de Bâle,* 2 vols., Olten, 1962.

Chappuis, 1938.
Adrien Chappuis, *Dessins de Paul Cézanne,* Paris, 1938.

Chappuis, 1957.
Adrien Chappuis, *Dessins de Paul Cézanne,* Lausanne, 1957.

Chappuis, Album.
Adrien Chappuis, *Album de Paul Cézanne,* 2 vols., Paris [1966].

Correspondance
Paul Cézanne, *Correspondance,* ed. John Rewald, Paris, 1937.

Hoetink
Rotterdam. Museum Boymans-van Beuningen. *Franse Tekeningen uit de 19ᵉ eeuw: catalogus van de verzameling,* prepared by H. R. Hoetink, 1968.

Neumeyer
Alfred Neumeyer, *Cézanne Drawings,* New York, 1958.

Reff, "Studies"
Theodore Reff, "Studies in Cézanne's Drawings," unpublished Ph.D. dissertation, Harvard University, 1956.

Rewald, Carnet I, II, III, IV, or V
Paul Cézanne, *Carnets de dessins,* preface and catalogue raisonné by John Rewald, 2 vols., Paris, 1951.

Schniewind
Paul Cézanne Sketchbook Owned by the Art Institute of Chicago, introductory text by Carl O. Schniewind, 2 vols., New York, 1951.

Venturi
Lionello Venturi, *Cézanne, son art, son œuvre,* 2 vols., Paris, 1936.

Vollard
Ambroise Vollard, *Paul Cézanne,* Paris, 1914.

A Chronology for the Portrait Drawings

Figure 1 Sheet from the *Carnet de jeunesse,* fol. 10. Pencil. 1857–1860 (the ink drawing, ca. 1865–1866). Louvre, Paris.

Figure 2 Sketches on a letter to Zola dated July 9, 1858. Ink.

Figure 3 Sheet from the *Carnet de jeunesse*, fol. 50 verso. Pencil. 1857–1860. Louvre, Paris.

Cézanne's sheets of youthful drawings of the late fifties contain many sketches of heads, ranging in style from the classicism of Ingres to brutal caricature in the spirit of Daumier (Figs. 1, 2). Among them are remarkable drawings (Fig. 3) rendered in sweeping contours and bold parallel hachures that look ahead to the graphic style of the artist's maturity. They belie Cézanne's academic training and demonstrate his early reluctance to draw in a schooled manner. The frankly asserted crudeness of these drawings, which are often juxtaposed on the same sheet with themes of violence or of sentimentality, is the stylistic trademark of Cézanne's portraits of the sixties, which are characterized by the combining of a brutal technique in the rendering of the image with great sensitivity for the human subject. In 1865 Cézanne's Aixois fellow painter, Antoine Valabrègue, wrote to Zola that Cézanne, in using his friends as sitters for portraits, had crucified them one by one.[1]

We know that Cézanne was interested in portraiture in the early sixties, for upon arrival in Paris he undertook a portrait of Zola, but the earliest of the extant drawings of this decade that can be described as portraits date from 1866. In a letter to Zola written in the autumn of that year (241),[2] Cézanne made sketches of two portrait paintings on which he was then working: one is of his sister Rose reading to her doll, and the other, a large painting of his friends Marion and Valabrègue standing side by side out of doors. For the latter there are also studies on a sheet in Basel (242) and a small oil sketch (241a).

Contemporary with these are two portrait studies of Valabrègue, a sketch of Marion, and one of another of Cézanne's artist friends, Armand Guillaumin. The strongest evidence for grouping these drawings is their relative consistency with Cézanne's predilection at this time for strong contrasts of dark and light. The portraits of Valabrègue (234), for example, as well as the portrait drawings of Guillaumin (226) and Marion (229), are drawn with two kinds of contour lines: one is loose and light and delineates the general shape of the heads and the position of the features; the other, which is heavy and dark, expresses and reinforces the contours of the dark areas. These contrasting graphic traits are indicative also of the duality of the young Cézanne's temperament as reflected in his style, that is, of marked sensitivity bolstered by aggressive exuberance.

According to a recollection by Monet, who was in close touch with him during these years, Cézanne placed a black hat and a white handkerchief beside his models at the Académie Suisse to define the poles between which he could establish the values of his drawing.[3] This method of working might explain why he intensified the coat collar of the upper portrait drawing of Valabrègue (234) with India ink, for the broad black band next to the white collar projected the full range of values that he intended for the final painting. The same sheet also bears a rough sketch of a standing male from the back. After indicating the general shape of the figure and before attending to details, Cézanne darkened three small areas on the drawing, the hair and the shadow cast by the coattail on each leg. The spotting here, too, seems to reveal the wish to establish the extreme poles of dark-light values, and the same kind of visual thinking is evident in the ink sketch of Marion and Valabrègue in the letter to Zola. Having determined the general appearance of the figures in the landscape setting, Cézanne completed his sketch of the painting he had in mind by contrasting a white with a black hat. The spotting in blacks to establish poles of value might be recognized, therefore, as peculiar to Cézanne's graphic process in the mid-1860's. To this period belongs the only drawing on which he wrote the name of a color intended for the painted version; significantly, the color was "blanc."[4]

Cézanne's preoccupation with contrasting qualities shows that he did not yet have a unified graphic style that was obedient both to his inclination toward forceful dramatic imagery and to his wish to reproduce the true and the natural. He relied instead on the power of contrasts and a distribution of black to unify his drawings. The ink sketch of his father reading a newspaper (198), for example, is remarkable for its logical though unsophisticated use of contrast to achieve a unified form.

Cézanne seemed to believe that strong contrasts of value favored the expressive and abstract over the natural image; in many of the portrait drawings of this period his shift of attention from the profile to the back of the head, for example, is marked both by a change from a fine to a heavy line and by a greater degree of expressive abstraction. When delineating Valabrègue's face, he thought first of achieving a likeness and traced the profile with a light and searching line, but in rendering the back of the head, the hair, beard, and ear (when he was no longer guided by a likeness), the movements of his hand became more energetic. Where the lines border the face, hair, and beard, they properly serve as outlines, yet they also set up abstract formal relationships with distant lines or areas. The lower portrait is especially rich in such abstractions. The shape of the lower edge of the beard is the converse of the hairline above it, the ear tilts back in line with the beard, and the flatness of the top of the head is repeated at the lower edge of the beard; perceived together, these abstractions relate to the rectangularity of the face. The upper portrait, more completely rendered after an equally abstract beginning, owes much of its expressiveness to the visual excitement of these relationships, which have been intensified by strong contrasts.

These stylistic peculiarities can be used to determine the dates of a small group of studies for Cézanne's painted portrait of his Aixois friend and fellow painter, Achille Emperaire (Fig. 6), which has been variously dated from 1866 to 1870. Estimates have depended, first, on Cézanne's attempt to enter the portrait at the Salon of 1870[5] and, second, on the stylistic affinity between these drawings and some of the studies he made at the Académie Suisse.[6] More recently, the date has been advanced to 1868–1870,[7] as Cézanne scholars have paid attention to the greater naturalism in Emperaire's expression in comparison with that in the 1866 painted portraits; to the wider range of values and more sensitive coloring; and to the linear, moving strokes that have replaced the early palette knife patches. Preference for the earlier year is supported by biographical data, which indicate that Cézanne was at Aix during most of 1868 (returning to Paris either in mid-December 1868 or, at the latest, January 1869),[8] but the style suggests a date closer to 1870.

Of the five drawings of Emperaire now known, only three can be considered studies for the painted portrait. A full-length study, now in Basel (215), is a quickly executed charcoal drawing that differs sufficiently from the painting to be placed as a preliminary idea. Here the viewer's eye level is on a line with Emperaire's hands, whereas in the painting it is aligned with his eyes. The study must have been made with Emperaire's chair placed on a platform, perhaps a model's stand, but for the final painting the chair is at floor level. In the same sequence as this sheet is the drawing of Emperaire in the collection of Chappuis (218). The tilt of the head to one side and slightly back is comparable with the first study, even though reversed, and the viewer's line of sight is equally low. The third drawing, a charcoal in Basel (217), which corresponds very closely to the painted portrait, was singled out by Venturi as the principal study. In many respects the Chappuis drawing shares this distinction, for its general attitude is very close to that of the painting, in which Emperaire's head also tilts slightly downward and to one side. The construction of the eyes in the painting is based as much on one study as on the other; in the Chappuis drawing they are wide open, and in the Basel drawing, half closed, These studies, then, form a chronological sequence with the painted portrait.

Figure 4 *Louis Auguste Cézanne.* Ca. 1866. Collection J. V. Pellerin, Paris. (Photo Bulloz.)

The series of drawings of Emperaire does not mark a distinct break in style with the drawings of the mid-sixties. Cézanne's love of strong contrasts lasted until the end of this decade.[9] Emperaire's black and white socks in the painted portrait and the black shadow cast on a white cheek in the Basel charcoal (217) establish poles for the intermediate tones, but the entire series also shows a marked increase in the use of modulated values with a corresponding lessening of emphasis on line. This seems to have resulted largely from Cézanne's greater interest in color—in the drawings, many gray tones seem equivalent to hues—and from a greater degree of differentiation in his images, reflecting a more careful scrutiny of the model.

This direction is particularly evident in the sensitive modulation of both contours and surfaces in the Basel charcoal (217), but the dark shadow cast by the nose, the stark white triangle on the right cheek, and the isolated band of neck indicate that this head was envisioned as a painting intensified by black and white paint. The tonal drawing alone shows an interest in the modulating quality that light can give to a variable surface and seems to be a result of the direct observation of a play of natural light across the face of the sitter. This type of observation differs from that of Cézanne's former period, in which he sought in nature for the strong contrasts that he had found in the works of earlier artists and had employed in studio painting.[10] On the other hand, when Cézanne emphasized shadows in this drawing and retraced the mustache until it became an isolated figure, spatially unstable in its detachment from the face, he was observing not only his model but also the peculiarities of his drawing, which prompted him to seek some unique expressive or abstract quality. At such moments he ignored the over-all unity of the image and, as Professor Schapiro has remarked of Cézanne's art as a whole, made his probing and searching a visible part of his drawing.[11]

The rectangular construction of Emperaire's face in the studies, especially in the Basel charcoal (217), recalls the portrait drawings of Valabrègue (234) and Guillaumin (226) but also prefigures the rectangularity of the painted portrait of Emperaire (Fig. 6), which has surprising frontality and strong horizontal-vertical contrasts of folds in the sleeves and in the front of the coat. Yet in each case, and especially in the drawings, Emperaire's face is set within sensitive shapes of hair and beard and is rendered in a way that points toward understanding of a greater variability of contour and surface, the essential prerequisite for Cézanne's mature style of interrupted outlines and infinitely modulated surfaces. This achievement depended on Cézanne's willingness to submit his manner to corrections suggested by natural appearances. In Emperaire's coat there is still an artificial life of writhing folds and contours that results from a mannerism imposed on form, but very little of this quality appears in the face. Only the shadow cast by the nose and by the left half of the mustache, especially as it appears in the Basel charcoal, seems severely abstract and to be included merely for dramatic effect. There is as much difference between the style of this painting and that of the 1866 portraits—for example, the large portrait of Valabrègue, with which Cézanne assaulted the Salon that year (Fig. 5)—as between the drawings of Emperaire and those of Valabrègue. It is almost certain, then, that these images of Emperaire can also be dated after 1867—sometime between 1868 and the Salon of 1870.

During the late 1860's Cézanne also developed the idea of a group portrait, with one sitter speaking and the others listening. The first reference to this project occurs in correspondence between Cézanne's friends Marion and Morstatt, dated May 1868: "Cézanne projette un tableau auquel il fera servir les portraits. L'un de nous, au milieu d'un paysage, parlera, tandis que les autres écouteront."[12] Two of Cézanne's sketches of about 1868 are concerned with this treatment of a genre scene as a group portrait (243, 244). Although it seems likely that Cézanne had in mind Manet's *Déjeuner sur l'herbe*, I believe that an illustration of a company of satyrs, which Cézanne may have copied that year (243a), was the most direct source.[13] In any case, as Chappuis has already noted, the idea of a group of friends engaged in conversation led toward the group portraits of Paul Alexis and Emile Zola, *Zola dictant*, and *La Lecture chez Zola*.[14] The date of these paintings falls between mid-September 1869, when Zola and Alexis met in Paris, and August 1870, when Cézanne and Zola left for Aix.[15]

The three studies for *Zola dictant* form one of the few sequences that demonstrate Cézanne's early process of constructing a composition. The earliest study (246) is small in conception; its com-

Figure 5 *Antoine Valabrègue.* Ca. 1866. Wildenstein Gallery, Paris. (Photo Bulloz.)

Figure 6 *Achille Emperaire*. 1868. Bernheim-Jeune, Paris.

position, fundamentally horizontal-vertical, is elementary and is placed within a close-fitting frame. The contours, which are impulsive and searching, lack force, the curtain is meager, and the tonal drawing serves only to set off the figural elements from an essentially uncharacterized ground. Yet there are also some energetic lines and expressive touches, and it is remarkable that in so crude a sketch the heads of both figures fully indicate their actions: Zola is intent on his reading, and Alexis is listening, his hand poised and ready to write.[16]

In the Basel drawing (247) the space is more open. Cézanne first placed Zola in a standing position; he then drew him in a seated position, in profile, and moved him away from Alexis into a space of his own. While increasing the spatial intervals, Cézanne was also attentive to the unifying relationships: breaking the horizontal-vertical structure, he made Alexis lean forward and then paralleled this movement with a curtain. To unify mass and space, he enlarged the curtain and increased its bulk and added to the weight of the figures; he augmented the recession of the table into the picture plane by shading the void beneath it, and he turned Alexis' leg to follow the same direction.

The conception is largest in the third and final study (248). The structure for the final painting has now been determined: the floor line, the table, and the wall molding are horizontal and parallel, while Alexis and Zola form a strong diagonal across the large space. The values have been established with dominating blacks and whites; the tone of the curtain, the scribe's coat, and the wall behind Zola follow the diagonal formed by the figures and set off the whites in a reciprocal relationship. Alexis is dark against a light background, Zola light against dark; sustaining this logical alternation of values, the table, which in the previous studies was light, is now dark against a light floor. This attention to forceful contrasts is accompanied by an assertive expression in the lines and in the poses, which are more energetic. The curtain is awry; Alexis is seated below a normal level of sight, and his legs are turned diagonally; Zola is very tense. There are no essential changes in the final painting: Zola's glasses have been omitted; Alexis has been turned slightly more toward Zola, resulting in a distorted viewpoint that makes him appear to be seated in air; his head has been lowered onto his shoulder; and the entire figure is more plastic.

To understand Cézanne's graphic development during these years it is important for us to recognize the degree of recapitulation that occurs in this sequence of studies for *Zola dictant*. The first study has stylistic affinities with the drawings of about 1866, the second drawing is loose but more expansive, the third shows the wide tonal range of the drawings of 1869–1870. If we observe, in addition, Cézanne's tendency to become increasingly naturalistic toward 1872 (as seen, for example, in a painted portrait of Gustave Boyer, Fig. 7), then the stylistic differences between *Zola dictant* and *La Lecture chez Zola* do not present an insuperable proble. It is true that Cézanne's juxtaposition of the natural and the artificial in *Zola dictant* has made the suggested date of 1869–1870 rather difficult to accept. In its dramatic and mannered style it contrasts with the more natural appearance of *La Lecture chez Zola*. But the two paintings differ in conception: the setting for *Zola dictant* is indoors, whereas *La Lecture chez Zola* is posed out of doors—although this difference may indicate only a change in Cézanne's mood or attitude toward the idea. Moreover, *La Lecture chez Zola* is unfinished, and there is a great difference in the treatment of the clothing of the two figures; Alexis' right leg, for instance, is rendered in a style very similar to that of *Zola dictant*. It is sufficiently similar, I believe, to allow the assumption that the two works date from about the same time.

A portrait drawing (209) that has previously been considered a self-portrait and assigned to the mid-seventies can be dated between 1870 and the autumn of 1872, when Cézanne moved to Pontoise and thence to Auvers. I have elsewhere reidentified this drawing as a portrait of Gustave Boyer, another of Cézanne's boyhood friends.[17]

Cézanne's desire to achieve a strong and robust image is apparent in this drawing. Using a soft lead, he proceeded from light lines to dark, expressive lines that restated the contours until their many repetitions began to act as color. In the final process, heavy and rapidly drawn lines, some forming crude tonal hatching, intensified the expression and character of the image, recessed the eyes into darkly shaded concavities, and exaggerated the shape of the nose to emphasize its character. Here and there the aggressive rendering gouged and scuffed the paper, and the right eye was accidentally blurred.

This drawing shows the same degree of plasticity as the painted portraits of Boyer (Fig. 7, for example), robust images that are defined by powerful contours and developed into fully three-dimensional masses by vigorous but carefully studied tones. Although Figure 7 has some structural affinities with the charcoal drawing of Emperaire (217), especially in the placing of the ear far to the left, surrounded by dark hair, Cézanne had now overcome the naïve flatness of the earlier portraits by a mature handling of tones consistent with a three-dimensional form. Although the drawing of Boyer is clearly later than the portraits of Emperaire, it does not yet reveal an Impressionist influence, nor can it be connected on any stylistic grounds with the portrait drawings of 1872–1875.

Figure 7 *Gustave Boyer.* 1870–1872. Metropolitan Museum of Art, New York, H. O. Havemeyer Collection.

Figure 8   *House at Auvers*. Pencil. 1872–1874.

Figure 9   *Jas de Bouffon, Aix-en-Provence*. Pencil. 1874.

Of the drawings that can be securely dated to Cézanne's stay with Pissarro's circle at Pontoise and Auvers, from the autumn of 1872 to the spring of 1874,[1] the largest group consists of portraits. They include the earliest self-portrait, two drawings of Pissarro, and two of Dr. Gachet, who was Cézanne's host at Auvers, a charcoal sketch of Cézanne's father (probably made on a visit to Aix), and a sheet with portraits of Cézanne's wife and infant son, who was born in 1872. The only other drawings of this period that can be dated with solid evidence are two landscape sketches—one is a view of Cézanne's family home, the Jas de Bouffon at Aix (Fig. 9)— that Cézanne drew in a letter to Zola written shortly after leaving Auvers in 1874.[2] These are helpful in defining Cézanne's graphic style at this time, as are several landscape paintings, two of which are dated on the canvas, and seven datable still-life compositions in oil and pastel.[3]

The impact of Pissarro's Impressionism on Cézanne's romantic imagery appears as a transitional quality in the style of his drawings as well as of his paintings that can be dated 1872–1874. The landscape paintings dated 1873 (Fig. 10) show a sincere effort to understand Pissarro's brushstroke and color; in the foliage, where Impressionist technique can best imitate the texture of nature, short and varied brushstrokes differentiate the leaves, while the surfaces of the roofs and their soft contours, reinforced sometimes by long lines, are rendered in a fashion consistent with Cézanne's style of the late sixties. In these landscapes, the shadows cast by the roofs are forcefully drawn and the darkest values are often angular patches of shadow cast by one roof on a lower one, demonstrating Cézanne's continuing interest in high-contrast chiaroscuro. Most landscapes of this period show this contrast between the strokes differentiating trees and those defining contours of surfaces—a transitional characteristic of curving outlines juxtaposed with surfaces that are painted with an Impressionist touch. The only two landscape sketches (Figs. 8, 9) that can be assigned with certainty to these years show that this quality continues into 1874. The chronology of a number of portraits and of other drawings within this period depends largely on the degree to which they show the same transitional character.

The first indication of Impressionist influence on Cézanne's graphic style is not so much in his touch as in his use of a soft drawing medium. It is probable that Armand Guillaumin was chiefly responsible for Cézanne's adoption of soft media during his stay at Auvers. Guillaumin's pastels reveal his special gift for equating soft media with the Impressionist style, and the one pastel we have by Cézanne, the still life of flowers in a vase drawn in Dr. Gachet's studio, is very close in style and touch to those of Guillaumin. Although Cézanne had used a soft medium —charcoal—in the sixties, his drawings were then in line with the current academic use of charcoal for achieving strong chiaroscuro and fine gradations of tone. The charcoal portrait of Achille Emperaire (217), for example, dramatically rendered in harsh contrasts and a broad range of values, does not really suggest the Impressionist style that Cézanne developed in the early seventies.

In the portrait etching of a young girl that Cézanne made at Auvers (256), one sees the process by which he began to subordinate his vigorous and expressive linear technique to the Impressionist tonal style. This etching can be compared with a pastel portrait by Guillaumin of the same child (256a). Although in Guillaumin's example there is a clear separation of the figure from the ground, the image is rendered by soft tonalities and is pervaded by the light of the white paper; the light across the child's face appears to be both in front of and behind the graded tones that define the image. Starting with a white ground, Guillaumin established the substance of his image with progressively darker tones overlying the lighter ones and achieved an effect of emanating rather than reflecting light—the image seems to be infused with light rather than physically defined by contrasting values. This procedure, which required fine lines, was counter to Cézanne's baroque inclinations toward strong visual and emotional effects and reversed his customary progression from a dark ground to a highlighted figure. He made the tight contour as strong a line as repeated furrows of the engraving tool would permit and then laced within it dark and heavy features—the eyeballs are intense black circles, and the eyebrows, the median line of the nose and the nostrils, the mouth and cheekbone, and the lines beneath the eyes all record strong, tightly controlled movements. Over this image of harsh contrasts, Cézanne cut a screen of diagonal, zigzag lines through which the image appeared. Despite his apparent understanding, in Guillaumin's terms, that the light was to emanate from the image rather than to reflect from it, he did not achieve the quality of ambivalence in the figure-ground illumination that in Guillaumin's portrait gives the effect of natural fusion of object and light. Cézanne's image is a result of a generalizing and concentrating manner of seeing that yet remains consistent with his previous manner. The only difference in his image of this period is that it has an Impressionistic surface, evincing his willingness to adopt the Impressionist style, which was becoming increasingly tonal.

Of three portrait drawings rendered in soft media, a self-portrait in charcoal (1), the earliest self-portrait drawing, exhibits most clearly Cézanne's transitional style. Like the drawing of Boyer (209), it is a full form and shows a trace of the romantic attitude, especially in the stare of the eyes, but the rendering reveals Cézanne's effort to counter his recognizably curving, erratic line, which at that time may have seemed anachronistic. Over a preliminary image modeled with charcoal smudge, Cézanne retraced the contours with a harder medium—perhaps a conté crayon—in determined and somewhat mechanical strokes, which show that, instead of a spontaneous act, this was a deliberate check on the impulsive flow of his hand. This drawing has the transitional character I have discussed in that it shows the juxtaposition of an earlier style with a later one: tonal gradation, carried over from the past, with straight parallel strokes that relate to the Impressionist subordination of modeling to cohesion of the picture plane (achieved by an over-all system of strokes and a dispersal of color and light). The rapid hatching in the background, on the collar, the beard, and the hair is an antiromantic device acting against those qualities that are suggestive of space, such as the white image emerging from a dark ground, and suggests surface differentiation by hue rather than by tone. The dispersal of the hatching indicates changes in color rather than in the scale of dark and light values. Although some zigzag hatching appeared earlier in the drawings of Achille Emperaire, it was there the result of a rapid and abbreviated modeling stroke that served to establish a scale of values rather than to unify the picture plane.

Similar graphic traits characterize the charcoal portrait of Dr. Gachet painting (222). The top edge of Gachet's cap shows lines familiar from the late sixties, but the contour as a whole has the angular quality characteristic of this period. Cézanne probably sketched Gachet with the same kind of flowing lines that he used in the portrait drawing of Boyer and other earlier drawings, and then reworked the image, emphasizing parts of the contour with dense lines. After smudging the drawing here and there to develop a scale of tones, he imposed on the image the straight, angular lines and the parallel hatching that give the drawing the appearance of having been constructed.

In the third example, the charcoal portrait of his father (199), probably dating from Cézanne's return to Aix in 1874, we see that, even in the soft medium, Cézanne's feeling has not lessened for a solid form and a clearly stated figure-ground structure, or even for the dramatic illumination often characteristic of his art before his years at Auvers. He uses the soft medium much as he did

Figure 10 *House at Auvers.* 1873. National Gallery of Art, Washington, Chester Dale Collection.

Figure 11 Copy of an etching by Delacroix, *Hamlet Contemplating the Skull of Yorick.* Pencil. 1873.

in the late sixties, but more solidly; the background is laid down with the same kind of stroke that Guillaumin used in the pastel portrait of a young girl described on page 10: the eyes and the mouth, the indentation at the bridge of the nose, and the cheekline at the nostril are strongly impressed, much like the corresponding lines in Cézanne's etching of the young girl and in the charcoal self-portrait (1), with which this drawing shares many traits. Final support for the date of this portrait is its close stylistic relationship to the sheet of drawings of Cézanne's wife and son (30) executed when the child was about two years old: on the evidence of the son's age the sheet can be dated about 1874.

Each of these charcoal drawings is characterized by a strong separation of figure and ground. This seems to indicate a continuation in Cézanne's process of a romantic desire for physical amplitude, although the general flatness of the planes and the many repetitions of straight, parallel lines are antiromantic. The contours suggest vigor as much as corporeality; the tones, while still somewhat generalized, are keyed more to visual impressions than to systematic chiaroscuro. The brittle angularity of the lines is the result of a wish to unify the picture plane; hence, the transformation of the curvilinear quality of the contours into broken lines is consistent with his general style. Like the curves of his more energetic drawings of the same time, these broken lines have vitality.

In relation to Cézanne's earlier style, this development seems intrinsically logical, but a response to the graphic style of Delacroix may also have contributed to it. According to Dr. Gachet's son, a painter named Armand Gautier brought a Delacroix lithograph, *Hamlet Contemplating the Skull of Yorick,* to Auvers in 1873,[4] and Cézanne copied it in charcoal (Fig. 11). The graphic character of the copy corresponds exactly to that of the charcoal portrait of Dr. Gachet (222): the contours are blocky, essentially straight lines breaking in angular curves; the surfaces are rendered quite flat by repeated diagonal strokes of conté crayon; and although there is a full range of tonal differentiation, the corporeality of the figures is not stressed. In both Delacroix's painting and lithograph of this subject, the two principal figures are rendered in the strongest darks and the most effective tonal contrasts, whereas the background is horizontally aligned, less detailed, and unified by its own scale of values. Cézanne was sensitive to the formal structure of the older artist's conception; even the general flatness and rectangularity of Hamlet's face are keyed to the harmony of the whole.

Cézanne's renewed interest in Delacroix in 1873 points to certain formal motivations in his process that are simultaneous with his first real interest in Impressionist content and technique and thus helps to explain the graphic peculiarities of both the charcoal self-portrait (1) and the charcoal portrait of Dr. Gachet (222). This interest also explains other peculiarities of Cézanne's graphic style during these years, when he apparently looked again to engravings and lithographs for suggestions. The earliest of his youthful drawings of the late fifties had been chiefly copies of graphic illustrations, etchings, or lithographic reproductions. At that time he had imitated these techniques, but after 1861 his manner of drawing was for the most part attuned to that of his painting; with few exceptions, his drawings of the sixties and the beginning of the seventies do not exhibit a particularly graphic quality. After 1872 he began once more to study modes of drawing carefully. The copies of Delacroix's lithograph, for instance, show his response to the strokes, texture, and tonal quality of the lithograph crayon. Thus, the occurrence of closely spaced, parallel hatching in Cézanne's drawings at this time may depend as much on these graphic models as on an independent evolution of his style in relation to Impressionism.

There is one characteristic of Cézanne's graphic style at this time that seems to have developed without extrinsic influences. Before 1872 parallel zigzag hatching in his drawings was determined perhaps completely by the natural movements of his hand and arms when stressing the darker values of a surface. In the portrait drawings of Valabrègue (234), for example, the hatching only indicated dark local color; in those of Emperaire (217, 218), it developed a complex scheme of tones—lights and darks, highlights and deep shadows—following the traditional method of rendering a portrait image. Then in the drawing of Boyer (209) appeared what Professor Schapiro has called in a different context the "unstable spotting" characteristic of a number of Cézanne's paintings done shortly before 1875.[5] In the drawing, however, this trait seems to have appeared earlier; by 1873 it had become a device for constructing a firm and solid form, evident, for instance, in the groupings of parallel lines in the Coquiot self-portrait (1). In the Morley self-portrait of 1874–1875 (2), discussed on page 17, these groups of parallel lines have become shorter and more compact and are involved in a more expressive play of dark and light, suggesting that Cézanne's system of spotting was a kind of generalization of traditional chiaroscuro.

It seems necessary to distinguish, then, between the kind of parallel hatching that develops an image in a painterly fashion and that which is formally constructive. The first belongs to Cézanne's process in the sixties and up to 1872; the second depends to a large extent on stylistic developments that occurred at Auvers. In one portrait drawing of Emperaire (217) an area of diagonal parallel strokes at the right side of the face offsets, in a traditional fashion, the frontal plane of the head from the side. In other drawings—in the background of the earliest study for *Zola dictant* (246), for example—there are also parallel diagonal lines that indicate light or color projected for the painting, but like the tones in a black-and-white photograph, these lines represent color, while not always revealing the particular color they will have in the painting. In the drawings of about 1870, such as V. 1211, flat areas have been established by a relatively uniform diagonal hatching. In every case these are peripheral areas that never have specific character. It follows that, from at least 1870, Cézanne juxtaposed two modes of drawing: an expressive linear mode used especially for developing the form and character of human figures, and a rather structural planar mode that was applied to background elements such as trees, buildings, areas of sky or grass, and at times even to clothing. It was not until 1873, and probably after Cézanne's acquaintance with Delacroix's lithograph, that the second mode of drawing was applied to the entire composition, even to the characterization and construction of a human face.

The two drawings of Pissarro (230, 231) probably date from the early winter months of 1874, when the two painters made portraits of each other. (Pissarro's painted portrait of Cézanne in a heavy winter coat and fur cap dates from 1874 (Fig. 12);[6] both of the drawings Cézanne made of Pissarro show him also in a winter coat, with a heavy neck scarf.) The style of the drawings reinforces the date of 1874. The profile portrait of Pissarro (230) is characterized by a combination of crisp lines and a few soft curves; even the beard is submitted to a certain angularity in its internal articulation, and the coat collar is drawn with straight lines that break at angles. Overlying some softer tones are many short, parallel, diagonal strokes that seem to derive from the etching technique Cézanne was learning at this time. The etching he made of Guillaumin (227) shows similar parallel and regularly spaced lines, and his portrait etching of the young girl (256) is dominated by parallel hatching, though more rapidly executed and reminiscent of Cézanne's ink drawings of the sixties. The second sketch of Pissarro (231) seems exactly contemporary with the first. The loose contours of the hair and the reinforcement of those of the coat by heavy lines tending toward angularity compare with the charcoal portrait (222) of Dr. Gachet, where the heavy, broken contours and long diagonal lines serve to indicate tones.

A portrait drawing of an unidentified male (258), presumably a fellow painter, seated out of doors can be related to the drawings of Pissarro. Although sketchlike and therefore somewhat difficult to date, its essentially graphic traits of curvilinear, broken contours and abbreviated tonal hatching are very close to those of the portrait etching of Guillaumin (227). In the latter, Guillaumin's hat was scrubbed with a burin on the lower side of the brim to produce a shadow tone very similar to the pencil scrubbing on the hat brim of the portrait drawing. Also important is the correspondence between the areas of accented contour lines in the etching (at the cuffs of the sleeves and trousers, the coat pocket, and the collar) and some segments of the outlines in the drawing that are also loose and suggestive of movement. But this stylistic affinity with the etching of Guillaumin does not permit the dating of the drawing more precisely than 1873–1874.

The pencil drawing of Dr. Gachet (223), which has on its verso the composition of Cézanne's Auvers friends seated out of doors (245), should also be dated 1873–1874.[7] Although it is delineated by loose, erratic, and curved lines, like those in the drawing of Boyer (209), the hatching shows certain qualities and a pattern of tonal distribution not present in Cézanne's art before 1872. The hatching on the hair and coat is as hurried as the contour lines, but its distribution is not associated with a chiaroscuro that would create space and define forms (for which purpose tonal draw-

Figure 12 Camille Pissarro. *Portrait of Cézanne.* 1874. Collection Robert von Hirsch, Basel. (Photo Bulloz.)

ing served in the portrait drawings of Emperaire); instead, it indicates contrasting values of local color that suggest light and movement, not corporeality. Typical of early Impressionist tonal drawings, the tones here reflect a fall of natural light rather than a formal construction of a systematic chiaroscuro. The strokes are arbitrary, like those on the forehead and the coat lapel in the Coquiot self-portrait drawing (1), and the contours have a crisp, angular, and abstract quality similar to those in the charcoal drawing of Dr. Gachet (222).

Cézanne's adoption of a quiet and carefully considered system of graphic strokes is simultaneous with the first appearance of nonromantic genre elements in his drawings, objects of common use that are presented without emotional or symbolic overtones. Among the first to appear are a child's spoon and a grandfather clock on a sheet of drawings of Madame Cézanne and her son (30). The drawings were made when the son was perhaps one or two years old. The head of the child at the center of the sheet is very close in attitude to the child in an oil painting of Cézanne's wife and infant son that Venturi assigned to Cézanne's stay at Auvers (V. 233). The other two studies of the child's head share important stylistic traits with the portrait drawings of Pissarro.

The studies of Madame Cézanne on this sheet, while suggesting some affinity with the charcoal portrait of Dr. Gachet (222), are also related to V. 226, a painted portrait of her that Venturi dated 1871–1873. I agree with Venturi that the touch in that painting suggests the influence of Manet, but of greater significance, in my view, is that the painting quality depends on Cézanne's soft-media techniques in the manner of Pissarro and Guillaumin. Its style exemplifies his adaptation of an Impressionist touch for the sake of lightening his form and animating his canvas by visual means rather than by provocative content. It seems reasonable therefore to date this sheet of drawings 1874.

A portrait drawing in Basel of Cézanne's wife (31) is similarly characterized by many short, fine pencil strokes, here and there grouped in small patches of crosshatching. The contour lines, especially of the collar and the hair, are broken and repeated, as they usually are after 1875, but the full form of the head and especially of the hair, defined by expansive, somewhat mannered curves, suggests a date near the drawings of 1874, particularly the profile sketch of Pissarro. The fullness of Pissarro's beard and the graphic quality of his facial features are stylistically akin to the hair and facial details of Madame Cézanne as she appears here.

Figure 12a Camille Pissarro and Paul Cézanne, ca. 1875–1877.

Figure 13 Camille Pissarro. *Portrait of Cézanne*. Pencil. Ca. 1874. (Photo H. Roger Viollet.)

Figure 14 *Self-Portrait*. 1874–1875. Collection Lecomte, Paris. (Photo Bulloz.)

Figure 15 *Madame Cézanne.* 1877. Boston Museum of Fine
Arts. Bequest of Robert Treat Paine II.

A self-portrait drawing in the collection of Derrick Morley (2) signals new refinements in Cézanne's graphic process. The contours here are more controlled but also more sensitive, lighter, and often repeated to animate the image. The spotting of tones in the beard, while indicating its darker color, at the same time creates an expressive pattern of contrasting values. This drawing is probably the first to show a preponderance of such tonal rendering over local color, yet it partly retains the quality of the chiaroscuro that characterizes Cézanne's portraits of the late sixties.

There is little distance between the style of this drawing and that of the profile portrait drawing of Pissarro (230), which I have assigned (p. 13) to the winter of 1873–1874. In addition to their similar linear character, especially in the rendering of clothing and in details such as the eyebrows, both reveal the new understanding of light that Cézanne had gained during the two years at Auvers. This is easily confirmed by a comparative glance at the charcoal self-portrait drawing of 1873–1874 (1), where the use of light is still determined by traditional chiaroscuro. In the Morley self-portrait, both the light and dark areas are active; the darks in the beard and the face are dense spots of hatching, often somewhat rectangular and therefore constructive in an abstract fashion.

Because the date I have assigned to the Morley drawing had earlier been accepted as the date for the portrait drawing of Boyer (209), when it was considered a self-portrait,[1] a brief stylistic comparison of the two works may be useful to determine which traits of the Morley self-portrait correspond to those of the very early seventies. Underlying the stylistic differences that place these drawings on opposite sides of 1873 are others that pull them together. The long erratic lines in the portrait of Boyer that move haltingly yet loosely around the shapes of the hair, beard, bald head, and facial features remain characteristic of some of Cézanne's preliminary sketching well into the seventies. In the beard is a rectangular patch of intense hatching similar to certain areas of hatching in the Morley self-portrait. Moreover, in the background of this self-portrait, the areas of concentrated black lines and the trenchant divisions between black and white recall Cézanne's painting style of about 1870 and even a little earlier. The treatment of the dense shape of hair on the left resembles that in the portraits of Achille Emperaire (217, 218), although in the self-portrait the contour is tighter and is charged with energy equal to that generated by the impassioned hatching of the beard. In its distribution, the hatching shows the result of Cézanne's antiromantic efforts at Auvers.

It is not impossible, then, for the Morley drawing to date from late 1874, after Cézanne's departure from Auvers, but it is unlikely that it was done later than 1875. This limiting date is supported by a drawing of Cézanne's son in Basel (94) that probably dates from 1876, as it portrays the child at about four years of age. There is sufficient correspondence between these drawings, especially in the rendering of the eyes and nose and in the distribution of light across them, to assure us that they are roughly contemporary. The drawing of the child is the more advanced of the two: it is the first to show consistency in carefully spaced diagonal and parallel hatching, with crosshatching only in the hair; some of the details, especially the eyes and eyebrows, are rendered in diagonal strokes over faint descriptive lines—in the Morley self-portrait, this last trait is less pronounced.

The Morley drawing also has graphic characteristics comparable with those of a small sketch of Cézanne's son on a sheet with a sketch of the artist's wife (35), which can be dated about 1877 on the evidence of the child's age. There are regular, closely spaced strokes in this sketch of the son that are similar to those in the shading at the left of the self-portrait, from the ridge of the nose across the cheek. The strokes seem to have been made with the side of the pencil lead. They recall the light tonal strokes of the charcoal portrait of Emperaire (217), but their straightness and regularity compare with the drawings of 1873–1874, such as the earlier portrait sheet of Madame Cézanne and her child (30), for example, which was discussed briefly in Chapter 2. The sketch of the child in No. 35 is the only drawing from the mid-seventies that is shaded in precisely the same manner as the Morley self-portrait. Further similarities between these two drawings exist in the spotting in the child's hair and in the beard of the self-portrait, and in the loose and searching character of the contour lines defining the hair and the chin.

The graphic peculiarities of the self-portrait are also closely related to those of the portrait of Madame Cézanne in No. 35. A few short parallel lines in her hair correspond almost exactly to the five lines at the left ear in the Morley drawing; this grouping also compares with the loose spotting in the beard of the latter. Furthermore, in the sketch of Madame Cézanne faint parallel lines of fine tonal drawing extend diagonally across the face, and to the left of the nose and mouth are tones that appear in similar areas of the child's head on the same sheet—in places these tones were darkened slightly to animate the facial planes. The drawings on this sheet are, therefore, contemporary and, on the basis of the characteristics I have noted, can be assigned to a later date than the Morley self-portrait.

With the support of the drawings just described, it becomes possible to date fairly precisely a sheet in the Budapest Museum containing two portrait drawings of Madame Cézanne, a third female head, and three quick studies of the crouching woman in *Une Moderne Olympia* (32). The presence of the *Olympia* sketches led Venturi to date this sheet 1872, the year generally accepted for the painting. The evidence for this date, however, is not at all reliable, for it consists only of a recollection by Dr. Gachet's son many years later[2] and a faulty reconstruction by Rivière of Cézanne's work at Auvers.[3] Since Cézanne showed the painting in the Impressionist exhibition of April 1874,[4] it is quite possible that he painted it for this event. But since the heads on the Budapest sheet cannot be assigned to such an early date, it is reasonable to assume that the slight, sketchy studies of the crouching nude were already on the sheet when the heads were drawn. The latter can be dated 1875–1877 on the visual evidence of the heads of Madame Cézanne and her child in No. 35, which I have assigned to about 1877. The drawings on this sheet are almost identical in technique with those on the Budapest sheet. All show a combination of long, parallel tonal lines with small rectangular patches of regularized hatching; the definition of the features is similar; and on both sheets Madame Cézanne seems to be the same age and to have been seen by the artist in a similar way.

The drawings on the Budapest sheet (32) are also closely related in style to the Morley self-portrait (2), notably in the areas of rectangular, spotty hatching, in the handling of the light, and in the way the head casts a shadow on the body. The central front-view head compares closely with the portrait of Cézanne's son (94) in Basel (in the treatment of the nose, for example), and, allowing for the differences in paper texture, the hatching on both is very similar. Though these associations, especially with the Morley self-portrait, and through the latter's relationship to the portrait profile of Pissarro (231), the Budapest sheet can be dated closer to 1876 than 1877.

Two portraits of Madame Cézanne that are at the back of the Chicago sketchbook, page XLIX verso and page L verso (38, 39), but belong to the earliest year of its use can be assigned with reasonable certainty to 1876–1878 on other than purely stylistic evidence.[5] Because of the inscription ''Madame Cézanne'' on both portraits, written in her child's hand about 1878, we are certain of the identity, even though there are no photographs of her from these years. If major stylistic distinctions are to be made between these drawings and the Morley self-portrait of only three years earlier, they would be that all the graphic qualities of the earlier portraits have been refined, systematized, and produced with a lighter hand. Perhaps they are a little later than the drawings on the Budapest sheet, but they remain more or less contemporary with three other portrait drawings of Madame Cézanne, which I shall date on visual evidence.

I shall consider first the evidence of two painted portraits of Madame Cézanne, V. 291, 292 (Fig. 15). Since Venturi dated them 1877 on a combination of external and stylistic evidence, they are important checks on the stylistic sequence established here;[6] both correspond in physiognomic and stylistic details to all the drawings I have assigned to the mid-seventies. Moreover, the style of Figure 15 helps to explain the peculiarly constructed portrait sketch of Madame Cézanne at the left of page L verso (39) in the Chicago sketchbook. The angularity of the nose in relation to the brow and the faceted tonalities of the painting correspond to the rectangular patches of tone in the drawing; in each example the nose has a rectangular ridge, and the coloring of the eyes in the painting is implicit in the drawing. Although in V. 291 this experimental study of faceted form does not appear in the head, it is evident in the construction of the torso and the hands and in the rendering of the cascade of cloth she holds. Similar traits can be found in the second Chicago portrait of Madame Cézanne on page L verso, especially across the bust, and in the portrait drawing of Cézanne's son in No. 35, discussed earlier, which reveals in its tonal rendering a close relationship to Figure 15. With these drawings I have also compared the Budapest sketches of Madame Cézanne (32), with their straight, angular lines and rectangular patches of tonal hatching.

The Chicago drawing, page XLIX verso (38), has hatching that is sometimes zigzag and sometimes precisely repeated in parallel strokes: it is applied in smaller units than those in the Morley self-portrait (2), with the lines more widely spaced, especially in the area of the bust. The contours of the head and garment are rhythmical—especially the line at the right side of the face and inside the sleeve on the left—but the internal or tonal drawing has a harder character. The juxtaposition here of tight hatching with loose contours in the hair and on the cheek and shoulder is peculiar to Cézanne's graphic style between 1876 and 1879.

Of the other portrait drawings of Cézanne's wife belonging to this group, perhaps the earliest is that on a sheet in Rotterdam (34); this sheet also contains a few little genre sketches in the style of the watercolor study for Cézanne's *Apothéose de Delacroix*, to which I have elsewhere assigned the date 1876.[7] This date is reasonable also for the Rotterdam drawing of Madame Cézanne, which was certainly done after the portraits of her on the Budapest sheet (32) and before those in the Chicago sketchbook (38, 39). Moreover, it is roughly contemporary with the small profile sketch of her in *Carnet 10.3 × 17* (31), which contains drawings exclusively from the first half of the seventies. This sketch has been defaced (probably by Cézanne's son at a young age—oscillating, looping scribbles such as these are typical of a three-year-old child), yet the graphic details are still sufficiently clear to prove its stylistic proximity to both the Budapest and Rotterdam sheets. All three are characterized by many very short, sensitively applied lines rendering the eyelashes and brows and by passages of soft shading, such as those at the nostrils and the corners of the mouth, juxtaposed with a broader application of longer and more regularized parallel lines, similarly closely spaced and sensitively applied.

Two sketches of Madame Cézanne on a sheet in the collection of Benjamin Sonnenberg (33) can be dated about 1877 on the visual evidence I have established: they are stylistically comparable with the lower left image of Madame Cézanne on the Budapest sheet (32). The half-length sketch of the artist's wife sewing was dated 1877 by Venturi, apparently on the basis of its close stylistic correspondence with the painted portraits of that year, especially V. 291. The head of Madame Cézanne can be assigned to the same year, if not a year earlier, judging by traces of the Morley self-portrait style and by the rectangular hatching and angular lines that align it with both the Budapest sheet and the rather schematic sketch of Madame Cézanne on page L verso of the Chicago sketchbook (39), which I have dated about 1876–1878. The conclusion that can be drawn from comparing the style of this head with that at the lower left of the Budapest sheet and the corresponding one in Basel (31) is that the density of the lines and the hatching are not in themselves evidence of an early date. Although the quality of lines in these drawings ranges from very light and narrow to dark and heavy, these variations result from differences in media, the relative hardness of the pencil Cézanne used, or his momentary attitudes or impulses, rather than from a distinct stylistic progression.

Roughly contemporary with these portraits of Madame Cézanne are the head of Victor Chocquet on the Sonnenberg sheet (212) and a second portrait drawing (211) on a sheet, now lost, which should be dated about 1877–1878. They are unusual drawings in some respects—noticeably in the minuteness of the hatching lines, which differentiate the surface of the face—but, in general, their style is related to the other drawings on the Sonnenberg sheet. The differences that do exist are largely due to the fact that Cézanne sketched this likeness of Chocquet from a photograph (211a). The photograph (which I recently associated with this drawing[8]) also explains Venturi's confused date for the Sonnenberg sheet, 1878–1885: he assumed that the sketch of Chocquet was a study for a painted portrait (V. 532), which he dated 1883–1887. Because the same photograph served both this drawing and the later painting, we can date the drawing solely on its stylistic character.

Of the thirty-two drawings of Cézanne's son in the Chicago sketchbook, twenty-seven can be dated 1878, two as early as 1876, and one as late as 1881. The stylistic diversities within this large sampling warn against strictly linear and schematic conclusions about Cézanne's development between 1876 and 1880. On page XLIX (122) the face is circumscribed by a strong contour differentiated at the forehead, cheek, chin, jaw, and other features; the hatching is firm and regular, generally parallel in stroke and angular in disposition. On page XXXIX v. (107) the contour is loose and open, and the strokes, though parallel, are more widely spaced and almost consistently cross-hatched. If in one drawing the face seems structured by a solid composition of dark and light, in the other the effect is ephemeral—the lights and darks are loose and fleeting, and the technique is much more impressionistic. Yet these drawings almost certainly date from the same year. Despite the variety, however, none of the drawings of 1878 corresponds closely to the two portrait drawings of the child that I have dated just one or two years earlier (94 and 97); they also differ markedly from the portrait drawing of the child of one or two years later (126). This difference may be partly circumstantial, as the portraits dating from before and after 1878 are limited in number, but it indicates that by 1878 Cézanne had achieved a wide range in graphic technique, which he was able to use with greater variety of expression and meaning than he had in the earlier seventies. The arguments that follow for dating a number of self-portrait drawings between 1876 and 1880 depend largely on the stylistic evidence of these drawings of the son.

The key to the chronology of Cézanne's self-portraits of the second half of the seventies is a sheet in the collection of Henry Pearlman (6) that contains a self-portrait overlaid by a study for a composition of bathers. Parts of this study were copied on the sheet by Cézanne's son at about the same age as when he drew in the Chicago sketchbook. The lettering at the lower left of the sheet corresponds exactly in character and in degree of motor coordination to that on page L of the Chicago sketchbook. The studies of bathers must have been drawn, therefore, between 1876 and about 1878; the later date is a *terminus ante quem* for the self-portrait.

The Pearlman self-portrait seems more advanced than the lower left portrait of the artist's wife on the Budapest sheet of 1875–1877 (32). In both drawings the patches of hatching are rectangular, but in the self-portrait they are smaller, more evenly and rhythmically distributed, and less suggestive of traditional chiaroscuro. They can, nevertheless, be translated into patches of paint—broad, rectangular brush strokes like those on the painted portraits of Madame Cézanne (Fig. 15) and Victor Chocquet (Fig. 16) of about 1877. The portraits of the artist's son in the Chicago sketchbook are in many ways stylistically related to this drawing: the sketches on pages XXXIX verso and XLVII verso (107, 121), for example, are so similar in graphic quality—even to the peculiar rendering of the eyeballs in diagonal hachures within a circular outline—that the self-portrait must date from the same or about the same time. A date of about 1877–1878, therefore, seems reasonable.

With the Pearlman drawing (6) as a central point, eight other self-portrait drawings can be dated between 1876 and 1881. At one end of this span are the Morley drawing (2), the earliest portrait of

Figure 16 *Victor Chocquet*. Ca. 1877. Museum of Modern Art, New York.

Chocquet, and four images of Cézanne's son; at the other is a self-portrait (10) that can be assigned to about 1880–1881 on the evidence of its stylistic similarity to a portrait of the child on the same sheet and on the evidence of the child's age—about eight years—in this portrait. A second portrait of the child, at age seven or eight (124), is also helpful in fixing the stylistic boundaries of this period.

A self-portrait drawing in the collection of Benjamin Sonnenberg (4), though rendered in a softer pencil (and now smudged), is similar in graphic character to the self-portrait on the Pearlman sheet. As in the latter, the range of graphic qualities includes angular contours of the hair and ear at the left, curving lines of the hair at the right and in the beard, and geometric hatching at the coat collar. In both drawings, the hachures in the beard are grayed and here and there opposed in direction; the eyes are drawn in exactly the same manner. Allowing for the sketchiness of the Sonnenberg self-portrait, it still seems less complex in tonal drawing than any of the 1878 drawings of the child in the Chicago sketchbook. The rather soft and swirling hachures in the beard and the wavy hair at the right bring it nearer to the Morley drawing (2) and suggest a date of about 1876.

The self-portrait drawing in the Gobin collection (5) corresponds also in its intense expression and loose patches of hachures to the Morley self-portrait, but it is a larger image and, like the Sonnenberg self-portrait, depends less on chiaroscuro; instead, it shows a relatively even distribution of hatching that tends to flatten the image. A similar graphic quality, though lighter in touch, shows in at least one drawing of Cézanne's son in the Chicago sketchbook: the horizontally aligned image on page XLVIII verso (121). The looseness of the hatching, combined with a flatness caused by the regularity of the hachures in rectangular groups, seems characteristic of about 1877. A reasonable date for this drawing would be 1877–1878.

Although the self-portrait drawing on page VII verso in the Chicago sketchbook (9) is generally assigned to the first half of the eighties, it is contemporary with the self-portrait on the Pearlman sheet (6). Stylistically, it stands near the Morley drawing (2), with which it is comparable in physiognomic character and in the play of light across the face. The same soft, long, parallel shading lines that appear at the right forehead and down the cheek in the Chicago self-portrait occur in the Morley drawing; they are also found in the child's portrait on the 1877 Clark sheet (97), to which the Morley drawing was compared earlier. The tonal rendering of the child's face on the 1876 Basel sheet (94) and in the portrait drawing of Madame Cézanne of about 1876–1878, on page XLIX verso (38) in the Chicago sketchbook, although more varied in distribution than in the Chicago self-portrait, is also comparable and provides visual evidence for a date of about 1878.

A second, more prominent characteristic that the Chicago self-portrait (9) shares with the Morley drawing (2) is the peculiar hatching that modulates the beard. Although more precisely drawn in the former, these regular, parallel, and curved hachures produce in both a swirling motion that is more pronounced than in the self-portrait on the Pearlman sheet (6) or in the Sonnenberg drawing (4). The Chicago drawing is also characterized by a loose, evenly distributed spotting that is Impressionist and not at all like Cézanne's portrait style of the early eighties, when larger divisions of light and dark prevailed. In this drawing he divided the nose at the mid-line, as he did in the portraits of Madame Cézanne and the child in No. 35; he did not sustain a division of tone across the cheek but joined dark spots on the ridge of the nose with the rest of the tonal spotting to establish a pattern of light and dark that corresponds only loosely to the physical structure of the face.

Among the details, at the left ear of both the Morley (2) and the Chicago (9) self-portraits, there are five almost vertical lines about an inch long. The fifth line in each portrait, counting from left to right, continues downward to define the beard, and in both drawings this contour line is then crossed by repeated hatching. At the same point on the opposite side of the beard, the drawings show a small area of parallel hatching that curves outward; in the Chicago self-portrait, the area of hatching at the right side of the mouth extends downward to the contour of the beard.

There are differences between these two self-portraits, however, that are as great as those between the Morley and the earlier Coquiot drawing(1). There is a logical progression between them from long hachures that heighten shaded areas to shorter ones that differentiate the tones of a surface while serving also to define dark areas. In the Morley drawing the hachures are more precise than before, more uniformly applied, and more evenly dispersed to create an Impressionist surface pattern.

The self-portrait drawing in Budapest (7) seems to date from about the same period as the Pearlman (6) and Chicago (9) drawings, although it shows a greater complexity of tonal modulation, especially in the beard and hair. The distribution of tones is still Impressionist, and, while the contour of the forehead and cheek on the left retains something of the more solid character of Cézanne's contours of the early 1880's, the contour of the beard continues the loose and mannered quality of the Morley drawing and even of the much earlier portrait of Boyer (209). While involved in the rhythm of the beard, the patches of hatching are not unified: they still show the loose spotting that was characteristic of the mid-seventies. The crosshatching throughout this drawing is of the same type that appears in a number of portrait drawings of Cézanne's son of about 1878—for example, the heads on page XXXIX verso in the Chicago sketchbook (107) and a slightly later portrait on a sheet in the Albertina (127). The date of the Budapest drawing must therefore be about 1878–1879.

Of the two self-portrait drawings in Basel, one is at a preliminary stage and is difficult to date (3); the other (8) shares important graphic traits with the Budapest head (7) but should be dated, I believe, about 1877–1879. Aside from its points of correspondence with the Pearlman self-portrait drawing (6), the Basel self-portrait (8) has stylistic traits comparable to those in the portrait drawings of Madame Cézanne in the Chicago sketchbook. The character of the hachures in the self-portrait, however, is more developed, and the complex of features is more unified with the structure of the head. The hachures are precise and tightly grouped as structural components, and the features are strikingly unified within a controlled and almost symmetrical contour. This self-portrait is close in date to the one on page XXI (10) of the Chicago sketchbook, which appears with a portrait of the artist's son that can be dated about 1880 on the evidence of the boy's apparent age.

Cézanne scholars have tended to assign the self-portrait drawings in the Chicago sketchbook to the eighties and to disregard their stylistic affinities in favor of the evidence of Cézanne's apparent age. Underlying this tendency has been an assumption that the graphic style of these drawings is too advanced for Cézanne in the seventies. But scholars have overlooked, I think, the influence of graphic models on Cézanne's style at this time; for example, the hachures in the commercial lithograph in the Ashmolean Museum (Fig. 17), on the verso of which Cézanne sketched his wife and son (30), are parallel and evenly spaced, much like those in Cézanne's drawings of the seventies. His self-portraits in the Chicago sketchbook, especially No. 9, in which parallel hachures are grouped and distributed along contours, are remarkably close in style to commercial lithographs. The essential difference between them is that Cézanne's drawings show less dependence on contour lines—a characteristic that links them in technique to the works of the Impressionists in the seventies.

Figure 17 Commercial lithograph, verso of No. 30. Ashmolean Museum, Oxford.

Figure 18 *Self-Portrait.* 1878–1879. Collection Lord Spencer Churchill, London. (Photo Bulloz.)

Figure 19 *Self-Portrait*. 1878–1880. Neue Pinakothek,
Munich. (Photo Bulloz.)

Three self-portrait drawings (14, 15, 16) that can be assigned on the basis of a combination of external and visual evidence to the years 1881–1883 mark a striking stylistic departure from those of the previous years. The head is narrow, tightly symmetrical, and contained within a firm outline, yet in spite of this structural intensity, which complements the intense facial expressions, the over-all graphic quality is loose and energetic.

Seen side by side, these drawings seem closely related in physical appearance and attitude but somewhat distant in style. The first (14) is from the Block sketchbook. The most dense and constrained of the three, it is also the first portrait drawing to show such broad areas of contrasting values. The second (15) is on a sheet in Rotterdam. While identical to the first in the general conformation of the head, it is agitated by many small and erratically directed groups of hachures. The third drawing (16), in the collection of Walter Baker, shares the traits of the first two but is characterized by a greater degree of abstraction in the disposition of hachures: the area at the upper left side of the head, for example, contains alternately vertical and wavy bands of dark and light hatching that ignore the contour line of the head. In none of these drawings did Cézanne respect the distinction of the beard from the face by more than a few randomly placed hachures.

The only evidence we have for Cézanne's appearance at this time is a pastel portrait by Renoir, of which Cézanne made a copy in oil (Fig. 21). Without this evidence it would be hard to accept that these drawings, in which Cézanne's head seems narrower than usual, could have been executed later than No. 10, with its fleshy face and full round beard, and before No. 20, in which the face is again broad and squarish. But the changed appearance of the head may be due only to the style of Cézanne's beard. Certainly the length and fullness of the beard were not constants, and we should be cautious in using its style as sole basis for classifying or dating the self-portraits. During the sixties the length of Cézanne's beard was for his friends a measure of his confidence and well-being. Cézanne himself made the following remark in a letter to Zola in 1878: "The pupils of Villevieille insult me when I pass; I shall have my hair cut, it is perhaps too long."[1]

Cézanne's greater interest in contours at this time is known. Since many portraits of his son in the Chicago sketchbook, as well as other portrait drawings between 1876 and 1880, are marked by concentration on the facial features within a loosely defined head, it might be expected that a change in his drawing process would cause some degree of change in the appearance of an otherwise fairly constant subject. To achieve greater unity Cézanne tightened the shape of the head and carefully measured the disposition of the features within it. In the Block self-portrait (14) he delineated the head perhaps at the same time as he drew the preliminary lines of the features, with a sequence of relatively short arcs that are much more precisely drawn than in the corresponding contours in earlier portraits. The outline of the head in the Rotterdam self-portrait (15), beneath the rather loosely distributed hatching, has similar carefully placed arcs and also a few straight segments (most apparent at the left side) that tighten the conformation of the head and beard. The same holds true for the Baker self-portrait (16); even though its contours are curved, they are not really loose—as are those in the Gobin drawing (5), for example.

The style of these drawings is sufficiently distinctive to place them in the early eighties. Further evidence enables us to establish a more exact date and to align them with other drawings that date also from the first half of the eighties but differ in style. Renoir's pastel portrait of Cézanne is dated 1880, and as the two artists were in close touch during this and the following year, it is tempting to assume that Cézanne's oil copy of the pastel was made about the same time. Certainly the style of the oil copy, especially the systematic stroke, is consistent with that of this period. Visual evidence can also be derived from a copy Cézanne made of a pastel sketch of a seated woman by Pissarro (Fig. 20), which is dated 1880.[2] The copy is in the Block sketchbook and is stylistically very close to the self-portrait there (14). Cézanne exaggerated the curve of the woman's hood to bring it into linear continuity with the round face. Other traits of the drawing, such as the distribution of darks and lights and the outline of the right shoulder and arm, correspond to the self-portrait and also to the three portraits of Madame Cézanne in the Block sketchbook—especially to the portrait illustrated at No. 53, which shows a geometrical background with emphasized vertical lines and careful hatching.

How early a date, then, can be assigned to this style? Renoir's pastel and Pissarro's gouache provide a possible date of 1880, but this is only a *terminus post quem* for Cézanne's copies. And even though the Block self-portrait drawing (14) and the second drawing on the same sheet are exact graphic translations of Cézanne's painting style of about this time, the paintings themselves are not securely dated. Cézanne scholars have disagreed over the date of the earliest appearance of this style, but the most informed opinions confine it to the span 1879–1881.[3] Examples are Cézanne's self-portrait in the Tate Gallery (Fig. 22), a portrait of his wife in the Bührle collection (Fig. 23), and a portrait of Louis Guillaume in the National Gallery, Washington, D.C. (Fig. 24). It seems unlikely, considering both facture and brushstroke, that any of these paintings could be of an earlier date than 1880. The portraits of Madame Cézanne and of Guillaume have the same background and are much alike in color and style; in each the brushstrokes are subordinated to a forceful unity achieved by tightly controlled and emphatic contours. This method of construction, as the following discussion attempts to show, occurs later in Cézanne's process than the systematized brushstroke of 1878–1880 and depends on the full development of the earlier method. All the datable drawings of Cézanne's son that have this peculiar quality in their contours were executed after 1880. Moreover, both the portrait of Guillaume and the portrait of Madame Cézanne are stylistically related to the Block self-portrait (14) and also to the portrait drawings of Zola in a sketchbook owned by Chappuis, which in my opinion should be dated about 1882 (238, 239).

Louis Guillaume's head (Fig. 24) is contained by a firm, oval line; the chin is shifted to the right in the manner of the Block self-portrait; and the smock the boy wears (rendered in the same fashion as the second drawing on that sheet) contains long and deeply shaded lines of folds, with vigorous diagonal hatching between them. The Bührle portrait of Madame Cézanne (Fig. 23) is a more complete painting. The diagonal brushwork has been partly smoothed by more variable and softer strokes, but the lines are oval, and the facial features, hair line, and curves of the right arm are sharply delineated. Continuity of line was obviously intended here, for the lower outline of the right sleeve continues down a fold in the dress and then along the finger tips in a manner similar to the linear continuities in the portraits of Zola from the second Chappuis sketchbook (238, 239).

Looking again at the Block self-portrait (14), we see that the diagonal hatching is disposed along lines and that sometimes the hatching itself forms strong descriptive lines. The characteristic is even more pronounced in the second sketch on this sheet. The portraits of Zola in the Block book (236, 237) also show emphatic hatching along the vertical lines, and a line of architectural detail in the background continues downward as an outline of Zola's sleeve. This continuation of line is even more exaggerated in one portrait of Zola from the second Chappuis sketchbook (239), where the outline of Zola's head, reduced to a simple pear shape, flows into the triangular partition of his coat. In both No. 238 and No. 239 details peripheral to the head are crowded

Figure 20 Copy of a pastel drawing by Pissarro. Pencil.
1880–1881. Collection Mr. and Mrs. Leigh Block, Chicago.

Figure 21 *Self-Portrait*. 1880–1881. Collection Otto Krebs,
Weimar. (Photo Bernheim-Jeune.)

Figure 22 *Self-Portrait*. Ca. 1881. Tate Gallery, London.

inward to enforce the tight unity of form that Cézanne wished to achieve; in the former the result is an awkward reduction in the size of the arm.

A date of about 1881 seems reasonable for the Block self-portrait (14), but still to be determined is the chronological relationship between the highly constructed, systematized brushwork and the prevalence of tightly controlled and reinforced contours. The paintings just described do not attest to an exact coincidence of these qualities. In fact, the portrait drawings of Zola from the second Chappuis sketchbook, which are notable for their tight and restated contours, are remarkably varied in the direction and length of pencil strokes. There are certain graphic differences between them and the Block self-portrait, but do they warrant assigning these drawings to different years? Certainly the Block self-portrait, with its interrupted and weak contours—especially around the beard—and the loose relationship between the complex of features and the circumference of the head, looks back to the late seventies, whereas the Zola portraits point ahead to the mid-eighties, when Cézanne's hachures are often grouped in broad bands contrasting with white areas, which are themselves expressive.

Several portrait drawings of Zola date from the first half of the eighties; on visual evidence alone, none of them could have been executed before 1879, and the friendship between Cézanne and Zola broke off in 1886.[4] During this period Zola lived at Médan where Cézanne visited him on many occasions (in 1879, 1880, 1881, 1882, and 1885),[5] so that our biographical accounts are of little help in pinpointing the date. But the fact that the drawings of Zola are in sketchbooks containing datable drawings of Cézanne's son, with which they can be compared stylistically, makes it possible to date them with reasonable accuracy. In No. 134, which is in the Block sketchbook, Cézanne's son appears about nine or ten years old, so that the drawing dates from about 1881–1882. The two portraits of Zola in the same sketchbook (236, 237) may also be assigned to this date on the basis of their close stylistic similarity to the drawings of the child. The portraits of the son in the second Chappuis sketchbook (155–159) show him to be a little older than in those in the Block sketchbook: he is perhaps ten or eleven years old, so that the drawings date from about 1882–1883. The same date may be assigned to the portraits of Zola from the Chappuis sketchbook (238, 239), again, because of their correspondence in style to the drawings of the son. Thus, a slightly later date is indicated for the portraits of Zola from the Chappuis sketchbook than for those in the Block sketchbook.

It becomes apparent from these observations that Cézanne's extreme systematization of his hachures into regular and parallel rows was not simultaneous with his hardening of contours, although the latter was implicit in the earlier method and followed it quite closely. Looking back at the portrait drawings of the seventies, we recall that at that period, too, Cézanne's attention to contours lagged behind his adoption of a structuring stroke and a geometric facture.

Let us postulate that, as polarities of his graphic style during the early eighties, Cézanne reached the apogee of his constructive stroke about 1880, after which it became increasingly differentiated while still retaining its formal power; that his greatest interest in contours and confined shapes emerged about 1882 and became less evident during the period 1883–1885 as his form achieved a mature unity.

This hypothesis allows us to place the three self-portraits (14, 15, 16) discussed at the beginning of this chapter only a short distance apart. If we assume as correct a date of about 1881 for the self-portrait in the Block sketchbook (14), then the self-portrait in Rotterdam (15)—because of the firm contour around the head (regardless of the loose and expressively distributed hatching) and the careful disposition of the features within it—would be of about the same date, perhaps a year later. The Baker self-portrait (16) could be dated about 1881–1882, judging only from the broader banding of hachures and from a firmer curve in the beard.

Several other portrait drawings can be assigned to this span 1880–1883. Two of these, dating from 1880–1881, are images of Cézanne's son, one in the collection of Sir Kenneth Clark (130) and the other a lively sketch on a sheet in the Albertina (127). The boy appears to be eight or nine years old, halfway in age between the 1879–1880 portrait sketch in the Chicago sketchbook (126) and the

Figure 23 *Madame Cézanne.* Ca. 1881. Collection Buhrle, Zurich. (Photo Bulloz.)

Figure 24 *Louis Guillaume.* Ca. 1881. National Gallery of Art, Washington.

Figure 25 *Portrait of the Artist's Son.* 1880–1881. Collection R. A. Peto, Paris.

Figure 26 *Portrait of the Artist's Son.* Ca. 1882. Private Collection, Paris. (Photo N. Nandel.)

portraits of about 1881–1882 in the Block sketchbook (134). The contour of the head and face in each drawing is firm and carefully traced; the hatching is very similar to that of the Chicago portrait (126) but more rhythmical, and its distribution of hachures seems more in the style of slightly later drawings. The Albertina drawing strikes a harmonious note with the self-portrait drawing in Rotterdam (15), which is also somewhat angular in construction, loose in distribution of light and dark, and rhythmical in line. Also comparable is the rendering of the eyeballs and the differentiation of the clothing at the neck and shoulder.

This small group of portraits demonstrates a characteristic of Cézanne's tonal drawing peculiar to only a few drawings datable between 1880 and 1882. Here and there across the face are small areas of tonal drawing, groups of parallel lines sometimes crosshatched. Unlike the hatchings of the severe drawings of this period, such as the Block self-portrait (14), these are not constructive, nor are they particularly expressive in character; rather, they correspond to what in painting would be light touches of warm color bringing the subject to life—a characteristic more typical of Renoir's portraits at this time than of Cézanne's.

It may be that the peculiarly soft and lightly expressive tonal drawing of this group represents Cézanne's own reaction to the hardness that his style had assumed between 1878 and 1881; this would again bear out his tendency to counteract a restrictive systematizing of his own style. Comparison of the self-portrait in Rotterdam (15), which is characterized by the type of tonal drawing peculiar to this group, with the Block self-portrait (14), shows that they are convincingly alike in construction, and even in expression. But whereas the Block drawing is constructed with hard curves and controlled parallel hatching, the Rotterdam drawing is rendered with contours of straight, angular lines and free curves and with tonal patches that range from quick, parallel touches to looping oscillations of lines kept intentionally loose.

It cannot be said that the style of these drawings simply represents two stages in a drawing process, one a carefully calculated, decisive graphic image and a final result, the other a preliminary and sketchy rendering. The degree of completion is the same in both, and both are unified by a consistency of style. In the Block self-portrait (14) the hair is controlled by tight curves, the eyes are rendered by precisely placed lines, and the darkness of the eyeball is fairly uniform. In the Rotterdam self-portrait (15) the sketchlike quality is consistent throughout, but there is a difference between this drawing and the sketchy drawings of the mid-seventies in that the freedom of the lines and the distribution of tonal patches in the former are contained within a well-defined oval shape and are in a tight visual relationship with other details.

A number of drawings of this period can be grouped around the portrait drawings of Cézanne's son (134–135) and the portraits of Zola (236, 237) in the Block sketchbook. They all date from 1881–1882: four drawings of Madame Cézanne (49, 50, 52, 53) and one of Pissarro (233), which are also in the Block sketchbook; another portrait of Madame Cézanne (55); and the sketch of Cézanne's son (130) in the collection of Sir Kenneth Clark that was discussed on page 28.

Between the Block and the Rotterdam self-portraits (14, 15), we can place the self-portrait drawing (17) formerly in the collection of Lukas Lichtenhan, now apparently lost. In constructing the head, Cézanne used the same oval shape without clear differentiation between the head and the beard. As in the Block drawing, with which this self-portrait has important affinities, the outline of the beard is precisely determined and judged in relationship to the crown of the head; the hatching of facial tones is also similar in character and distribution.

Of these drawings, the portraits of Madame Cézanne (49, 50, 52, 53) may have been executed as early as 1881. The date 1881–1882 seems reasonable for the portrait of Pissarro at his easel (233), which is drawn in a manner close to that of the second drawing on the Block self-portrait sheet (14). One portrait of Madame Cézanne (52) seems stylistically close to the self-portraits of 1876–1878, especially to the one on the Pearlman sheet (6), but its distribution of light is more complex, and the hatching is more varied and is grouped in larger areas. There is also a greater emphasis on the contour lines, especially in the way the hair is contained in two large areas by rather tight, curving lines.

Figure 27 *Portrait of the Artist's Son.* Ca. 1885. National
Gallery of Art, Washington, Chester Dale Collection.

Belonging to the same span of years is a small group of drawings characterized by curvilinear and rhythmical contours juxtaposed with angular lines and small patches of fine, precise parallel hatching. The denominator of this group is the style of two sheets in the collection of Sir Kenneth Clark: on one there are three sketches of Cézanne's son asleep (144); on the other a sketch of Madame Cézanne, also asleep (62). The drawings are contemporary, and both, I believe, date from 1882–1883.

The rhythmical lines of these drawings seem to depend on an earlier style that must have first appeared somewhat later than the Block self-portrait (14), for example. This drawing provides the first evidence of Cezanne's renewed attention to outlines and of his efforts to unify them with the systematic strokes he used in constructing surfaces—a stylistic control of the rhythmical tendency apparent in his slightly earlier drawings that have loose contours but controlled hachures.

The portrait drawings of Madame Cézanne in the Block sketchbook (49, 50, 52, 53) have something of this quality, but the curves are larger and are structural rather than rhythmically repetitious. More consistent with the Clark drawings (62, 144) is the portrait of Madame Cézanne in the Schiess collection (63), which also has curvilinear and rhythmical contours, accented by areas of precise parallel hatching contrasting with angular lines, such as those on the shoulder. The Schiess drawing shows also a degree of the anatomical distortion that affects Cézanne's portraiture of his wife at this time—a greater roundness of her head and features. The same distortion appears in the three self-portraits executed shortly after 1880 (14, 15, 16), where the curvilinear outline of the profile—especially of the nose, lips, and chin—is drawn in a way that rounds them off.

This manner of unifying a drawing by a system of curvilinear rhythms originates in Cézanne's graphic style about 1870. The curves in the later drawings, however, depend on the discipline of Cézanne's style in the late seventies: they are tightly controlled and are unlike the loose sinuous curves of the earlier period. In a planned rhythm, they represent a slight refinement of the controlled outlines of Cézanne's paintings of 1879–1882. These drawings, then, should be dated 1882–1883, with the earlier date favored for the Clark sheet (62), and the later for three portraits of Madame Cézanne in the second Chappuis sketchbook (58–60). This sketchbook also includes a scattering of portraits of Cézanne's son (155–159) at the age of ten to eleven, dating from 1882 to 1883.

The development of Cézanne's graphic style during the remaining years of the eighties is demonstrated by a sequence of portrait drawings of his son from the age of eleven to about seventeen. A photograph of the child in his confirmation suit, taken in 1883–1884 (148a), suggests that he was about eleven years old when the two portraits of him now in Basel (147, 148) were drawn. These date, therefore, from about 1883 and can be used as a stylistic pivot for other portraits of him of about the same time: the two portraits in the Block sketchbook (134, 135) can be dated about 1882; those in the second Chappuis sketchbook (155–159), about 1883. Following these is a group of drawings that depict the child when he was twelve to fourteen years old (160–167), dating from 1884 to 1886, and three drawings in which he appears to be about fifteen (169–171). Finally, there are the studies for the group portrait with Louis Guillaume (172–175) made in 1888, when he was sixteen.

The stylistic character of the first group, 1882–1884, combines the three principal traits singled out previously: bold, firm contours and broad areas of hatching with indications of a return to chiaroscuro, combined with loose, expressive tonal hachures across the face. There is a greater control of the contours, which are more clearly differentiated and physically descriptive, and the hatching is more abstract than Impressionist—at times it tends to structure the head with rectangular facets (159).

Two portrait drawings of Madame Cézanne also belong to the period 1882–1884 (59, 60). Showing a combination of hard curves with tightly controlled rectilinear lines, they are a little more advanced than the more rhythmically curvilinear portraits of her of about 1881–1882 (48, 49), and they look ahead to the sensitively drawn portraits of the very late eighties (69, for example), which, although less severe, are nonetheless more unified both in form and technique.

Figure 28 *Harlequin.* Ca. 1888. Collection J. V. Pellerin, Paris. (Photo Bulloz.)

Figure 29 *Self-Portrait*. 1885–1887. Collection the artist's
family, Paris. (Photo Bulloz.)

The self-portrait in the Cincinnati Museum (18) almost certainly dates from this period. The execution of its tight curves and carefully placed hachures depends on Cézanne's experience with systematized diagonal hatching between about 1878 and about 1881, and the larger rhythm of curves shows a considerable advance over loose drawings of the late seventies such as the Budapest self-portrait (7). The disposition of the facial features in the Cincinnati head is very precise; the face is uniformly structured, and the unity of the image depends on larger relationships. Stylistically, it stands between the portraits of Madame Cézanne in the Block sketchbook (49, 52), which I have dated 1881–1882, and the two self-portrait drawings in the second Chappuis sketchbook (19, 20), which can be dated 1883–1884.

When compared with the Cincinnati self-portrait (18), the Chappuis self-portrait drawings seem to be of a different style and period. In the former Cézanne appears to be thin and youthful; in the latter he seems fleshy and older, and his image is rendered in an abstract fashion that depends less on lines. Whereas the Cincinnati self-portrait, like the other portrait drawings of 1882–1883, has firm and carefully controlled contours and hatching that is subordinate to the contour lines, the Chappuis drawings show a new kind of unity that brings the contours, internal lines, and tonal drawing together. Neither contours nor hachures dominate in these, nor is there a systematization of stroke or line independent of the natural shape of the head. While the left side of the image is not fully realized in depth—a characteristic of Cézanne's portraits dating back to those of Achille Emperaire (217, for example)—the nose, beard, and mustache have been given three-dimensional form, so that these features stand out distinctly from the rest of the face. This plasticity of the image marks a new stage in Cézanne's development: it corresponds to changes in his painting style about this time, from the essentially planar views of L'Estaque to the remarkably abstract and dimensional landscapes painted at Gardanne in 1885–1886. A date of 1883–1884 for both self-portrait drawings in the second Chappuis sketchbook seems correct.

Contemporary with the Chappuis self-portraits (19, 20) are a few drawings of Cézanne's wife and son on a sheet in the collection of Sir Kenneth Clark (65) that are closely related to them in technique and style; these can be dated about 1885 on the evidence of the child's apparent age of about thirteen years.

The renewed plasticity of Cézanne's graphic style at this time marks the stylistic character of his drawings of his son dating from 1886 to about 1888 (169–175). He seems concerned to fully develop the three-dimensional form of his subject, utilizing loose yet controlled contours in combination with stable hachures. A drawing of his son writing (171), dating from about 1888, is remarkable for the degree of unity in the composition of the articles on the table, the boy, the chair, and the background. The top of the ink bottle is aligned with the boy's right forearm; his hand is in contact with his chin; the light tone of his face passes across his ear and onto his collar; the vertical part of the chair is contrasted with the active arm; and the curved line of the chair back, interrupted as it meets the boy's shoulder, carries across the boy's back and down his left arm. His writing arm is rendered in active curves; his left arm is still. There is a gentleness in the over-all rendering of this image: the curves are not aggressive, as they are in the later drawings of the son (191, for example), and the range of quality in the lines and distribution of hachures indicates that Cézanne's attention to the drawing as a whole allows certain weaknesses in the details, such as the facial features and the left hand.

Cézanne's studies for the painting known as *Mardi Gras* (V. 552), involving sketches of his son (174–175) and his son's friend Louis Guillaume (228), date from 1888. They differ from the other portrait drawings in that Cézanne was using the boys as models for Harlequin and Clown, respectively; the attitudes of the sitters are therefore contrived rather than spontaneous. This may account for the general tightness of the contours, especially in Nos. 174 and 228, and for the special care Cézanne exercised in developing the facial expressions, which are specific. The drawing of Guillaume (228) is achieved in outlines that are comparatively weak for Cézanne in the eighties; the lines describing the larger image of Cézanne's son in No. 174 are fumbling to a surprising degree, and the distribution of hachures is unrelated to the conformation of the face. In the smaller image the features are more stable, the contours more decisive, but the over-all effect lacks the effortlessness that marks the best of Cézanne's drawings.

Aside from an apparent difference in the age of Cézanne's son, there is a marked stylistic distinction between the drawings of Cézanne's son of this period and a large group of his images in the second and third Chappuis sketchbooks (176–196). The latter have been assigned to the eighties by Chappuis, but in my opinion they are of a later date. They are powerful images, rendered in masterful strokes and broad hachures that characterize a fully mature style. They must be placed in the context of Cézanne's portraits in the nineties.

Figure 30 *Les Joueurs de cartes.* 1890–1892. Collection
J. V. Pellerin, Paris. (Photo Bulloz.)

Figure 31 *Les Joueurs de cartes.* 1890–1892. Collection
Stephen Clark, New York. (Photo Knoedler.)

Cézanne's five-month stay in Switzerland in 1890[1] marks a logical break in the sequence of his graphic style of the eighties. On his return to Aix he undertook a series of extraordinary portraits of peasants, the most famous of which are two versions of the composition *Les Joueurs de cartes* (Figs. 30, 31), generally assigned to the early nineties.[2] In 1955 Léontine Paulet, son of one of the models, recalled that his father, Paulin Paulet, was a gardener at the Jas de Bouffan in 1890: "Dans le tableau des *Joueurs de cartes* mon père est representé à gauche et moi au fond."[3] A letter from Alexis to Zola of February 13, 1891, gives further proof that Cézanne was painting at the Jas, "où un ouvrier lui sert de modèle, et où j'irai un de ces jours voir ce qu'il fait."[4] And Gustave Geffroy, in an article of 1894, described "un portrait de Jardinier qui est chez Paul Alexis, une toile trop grande, le vêtement vide, mais une tête solide, bien appuyée sur la main, des yeux ardents qui regardent réellement."[5] This description could fit a number of Cézanne's peasant portraits; a possible choice is Venturi 684, as it was in Paul Alexis' collection and may well have been the portrait given to Alexis by Cézanne shortly before Alexis' departure for Paris in April 1892.[6] Vollard recalled having exhibited "trois grandes toiles montrant chacune un paysan" in 1895,[7] and according to Gasquet, when the writer Joseph d'Arbaud visited Cézanne's studio before 1896, he saw one version of *Les Joueurs de cartes*.[8] The dates 1890–1896 would thus encompass the entire group of these portraits, which number a dozen canvases, four watercolors, and a few drawings of outstanding quality.[9]

It is possible to discern a chronological sequence in the studies for *Les Joueurs de cartes*. Meyer Schapiro suggested that the three-player group, V. 559 (Fig. 31) and 560, is earlier than the version with two players, V. 556 (Fig. 30), 557, 558, basing his opinion on the observation that the single shapes in the two-player version are simpler but the relationships more varied.[10] Such a progression is in accord with the over-all development of Cézanne's art. Even in the late sixties, the two versions of Zola and Alexis showed a progression from a rather literal conception in the first to a greater focus on the single figures, with reduced setting and supporting content, in the second.

If Professor Schapiro's observation is carried further, it would seem that V. 560, with its pictorial setting, is the earliest of the canvases: it shows a natural, rather casual arrangement of the figures and includes details such as a pot on a shelf, a picture hanging on the wall, and draperies.
Next in the sequence would be V. 559 (Fig. 31). Here, the details have been reduced: the pot, shelf, and picture are gone, as is the child, which had provided anecdotal content, and the standing figure has been moved closer to the players. The entire composition is more boldly expressed as a construction. Venturi 563 would thus be later than V. 560 and must have been a study for V. 559. It can be assumed, in fact, that V. 568, although appearing also to be a study, was made after V. 559 and perhaps from it, for at the left of the figure are horizontal and vertical lines that indicate the standing figure in the full composition. There is also a playing card on the table, suggesting

Figure 32   *Madame Cézanne.* 1890–1892. Louvre, Paris. (Photo Service de Documentation Photographique.)

Figure 33 *Self-Portrait.* Ca. 1890. Collection J. V. Pellerin, Paris. (Photo Giraudon.)

Figure 34 *Madame Cézanne.* 1892–1894. Collection Stephen Clark, New York. (Photo Bulloz.)

that the figure was isolated from the larger canvas as an independent study after the composition had been realized. It follows that both V. 1085 and 1086 (252) were made after V. 560, and as studies for V. 559 (Fig. 31). The recently published drawing in the Hanley collection (250), then, is the earliest in the sequence, probably dating from before any of the canvases. It is a study of the man who appears at the left of the three-player composition: he is placed at the right side of the table, which indicates, I believe, that the study was made before the general composition of the three-player version was determined.

In brief, this tenuous yet plausible chronology of the graphic studies for *Les Joueurs de cartes* places the Hanley drawing (250) as the earliest, followed by the studies for the figure on the right (252), and finally by the two drawings for the two-player version (251, 262), which are close in viewpoint to the painting and must therefore be latest in the sequence. Moreover, these drawings are closely related to V. 558, which was almost certainly the last of the three two-player canvases, preceded by V. 557 and 556 (Fig. 30), in that order.

Despite the discernible sequence of the drawings for *Les Joueurs de cartes,* the extent of their chronological separation cannot be determined. It is generally believed that this theme commanded Cézanne's interest for a period of two years (1890–1892),[11] but it can only be guessed that as much as a year might separate the drawings for the first version from those for the second.

The portrait of Gustave Geffroy (V. 692) is securely dated 1895 on documentary evidence.[12] The portrait of Joachim Gasquet (V. 694) and one of his father, Henri Gasquet (V. 695), can be assigned with reasonable certainty to 1896–1897 (the date suggested by Venturi), when Gasquet was in touch with Cézanne.[13] Dating from Cézanne's stay at Lake Annecy in 1896 are a drawing (263), a watercolor, and an oil painting of a young girl, *L'Enfant au chapeau de paille* (V. 700); evidence for this date is a watercolor of Lake Annecy on the verso of the last of these.[14] Traditionally the *Jeune italienne accoudée* (V. 701) has been dated about the same year.[15] On a variety of external evidence I have assigned the small but complete sketchbook, the *Carnet violet-moiré,* which includes a portrait sketch of the artist's wife (86), to 1894–1896.[16] The drawings in this little book are valuable guides to Cézanne's graphic style of the mid-nineties.

A self-portrait lithograph (24) dates from about 1898, as it is generally assumed to have been made for Ambroise Vollard's *L'Album des peintres-graveurs.*[17] A drawing of Vollard, not necessarily a study for his portrait of 1899 (Fig. 35) dates from the same year.[18] To Cézanne's last years, only *La Vielle au chapelet* (V. 702)[19] and a few portraits (in both watercolor and oil) of his gardener Vallier can be assigned on external evidence; Cézanne was reported to be working on a portrait of Vallier in 1905.[20] There are no known portrait drawings that date from after 1900.

This scattering of works datable on external evidence is supplemented by somewhat less reliable but useful photographs of Cézanne dating from 1894: one was taken of him among the rocks of the Barbizon forest;[21] the other shows him with a small canvas *L'Apothéose de Delacroix* on his easel.[22] In the latter there is a full-faced image of Cézanne that helps to establish a date close to 1890 for the painted self-portrait V. 578 (Fig. 33) and a date of about 1892–1894 for another self-portrait V. 579, where he appears to be about the same age as in the photographs. The dates of these painted portraits can in turn be verified by comparing them with the more securely dated self-portrait drawings executed before and after this span. The drawings of 1883–1884 in the second Chappuis sketchbook (19, 20) indicate that V. 578 dates from before the 1890's, whereas the self-portrait lithograph (24) of about 1898 provides a check for V. 579, fixing its date prior to 1895. Further support in the dating of V. 579 is the self-portrait painting in the Robert Treat Paine collection, V. 693, which can probably be assigned to 1898–1900 (surmised by Venturi on the basis of a comparison with the lithograph and with several photographs of Cézanne taken during the year 1902–1906).[23]

Aside from the lithograph, only two self-portrait drawings date from after 1885. On the evidence of age and of stylistic comparisons, No. 22, in the collection of Robert von Hirsch, belongs to the first half of the nineties and No. 23, in the third Chappius sketchbook, to the second half. The von Hirsch drawing can be compared with the studies for the second version of the *Joueurs de*

Figure 35 *Ambroise Vollard.* 1899. Louvre, Paris. (Photo Archives Photographiques.)

cartes: point by point—especially at the back of the head, where firm parallel contour lines are crossed perpendicularly by short hatchings—it corresponds to the pencil studies for the two-player version, which may date from about 1892. The date of this self-portrait drawing must consequently be about 1890–1894. On the evidence of both its style and Cézanne's apparent age, the Chappuis self-portrait (23) dates from 1896–1900. By 1896, as in the portraits of the young girl in a straw hat (263) and Madame Cézanne in the *Carnet violet-moiré* (86), the curves are bold yet are gently drawn, whereas the drawings of the late nineties and of about 1900 employ systems of smaller and looser curves perhaps inspired, as Berthold has pointed out, by the large number of baroque busts Cézanne had copied at this time.[24]

Cézanne's sketch of a young girl of 1896 (263), his portrait drawing of Madame Cézanne in the *Carnet violet-moiré* of 1894–1896 (86), and the drawing of Vollard of 1899 (235) bear many resemblances to one another, especially in the sweeping curves and the slight tonal drawing. Variations between them are aligned with the direction of Cézanne's style during the nineties.

The extreme hardness of the tonal drawing and the emphatically curved contours in the portraits of his son of 1892–1896 (179–196) are more sensitive yet still tightly controlled in the portraits of Madame Cézanne from the same years (70–90); they become more gentle in the late nineties, when Cézanne tends to use generalizing contours with a minimum of tonal hatching. The vaporous drawing of Vollard (235) seems to be a culmination of this development, yet it is as intense in expression and as free in execution as the most exuberant compositions of Cézanne's early years.

Figure 36   Photograph of Paul Cézanne in his studio at
Aix-en-Provence. Ca. 1905.

Notes

Chapter 1

1 *Paul Cézanne, Correspondance*, p. 37.

2 *Ibid.*, p. 97. The letter is not dated, but Rewald believes it was written about October 19, 1866.

3 As told by Henri Matisse to John Rewald. See Rewald, *History of Impressionism*, 2d ed., rev. and enl., New York, 1961, p. 62. Although Cézanne's practice may have been a common one, the fact that Monet singled it out in his recollections suggests that it was very important for Cézanne.

4 Chappuis, Cat. No. 16.

5 See *Correspondance*, p. 112, for a letter of June 7, 1870, to Justin Gabet, a boyhood friend of Cézanne's, in which Cézanne comments on the rejection of his entries. See also John Rewald, "Un Article inédit sur Paul Cézanne en 1870," *Arts*, July 21–27, 1954, p. 8.

6 The earlier date seems to have been prompted by Venturi's erroneous identification of the model in V. 1193 as Emperaire. See the notes at my No. 220.

7 See, for instance, Chappuis, Cat. Nos. 49–51 for the date 1867–1870; and John Rewald, *History of*

Impressionism, p. 247, for the date 1868–1870.

8 The earlier date is substantiated by a letter to Numa Coste of late November 1868 (*Correspondance*, p. 108); the later date, by a letter from Marion to Zola of January 2, 1869, published by Rewald (*Cézanne,* London, 1939, p. 157).

9 See, for example, V. 69, 104 (dated on the canvas 1870), and 1208.

10 Cézanne's enthusiasm over the "astounding contrasts" to be found in nature in full light was almost certainly stimulated by the strong contrasts that he loved in earlier art. See a letter to Emile Zola of about October 19, 1866, in *Correspondance*, p. 97.

11 Meyer Schapiro, *Paul Cézanne*, New York, 1952, p. 20.

12 Alfred Barr, "Cézanne d'après les lettres de Marion à Morstatt, 1865–1868," *Gazette des Beaux-Arts,* ser. 6, XVII, 1937, p. 42.

13 I believe that this composition may also be related to a drawing of five men *sur l'herbe,* now in Basel (Chappuis 53), which has been dated 1870–1877 by Chappuis and 1868 by Douglas Cooper, review of

Chappuis, *Les Dessins de Cézanne au Musée de Bâle,* in *Master Drawings,* I No. 4, 1963, p. 56. See my No. 245.

14 See the notes under Chappuis, Cat. No. 53.

15 For the first date see Venturi 118; for the second, see Lawrence Gowing in Arts Council of Great Britain, *An Exhibition of Paintings by Cézanne,* Edinburgh, 1954, note to Cat. No. 6.

16 This interpretation has been questioned by Jean Adhémar in "Le Cabinet de travail de Zola," *Gazette des beaux-arts,* ser. 6, LVI, 1960, p. 286. See also his notes on this in Paris, Bibliothèque Nationale, *Émile Zola,* 1952, p. 8, Cat. No. 53.

17 "A Cézanne Self-Portrait Reidentified," *The Burlington Magazine,* CVI, 1964, pp. 284–285. See the remarks at No. 209.

Chapter 2

1 Cézanne's presence at Pontoise and his intention to move to Auvers is documented by a letter from Pissarro to Guillemet dated September 3, 1872 (*Correspondance,* p. 117). Proof of the move is in a letter from Cézanne, written at Pissarro's house at Pontoise

and dated December 11, 1872, to Pissarro who was then in Paris. Cézanne wrote that, having missed the train that "should have been taking me to my Penates," he was spending the night with Pissarro's family (*ibid.*). Cézanne's penates were no doubt in reference to his own family in Aix, for there was no train to Auvers. (Cézanne's biographers have therefore overlooked a journey to Aix in 1872.) Further evidence of Cézanne's move to Auvers late in 1872 is given by Dr. Gachet's son, who wrote that Cézanne came to Auvers in that year (Paul Gachet, *Le Docteur Gachet et Murer,* Paris, 1956, p. 103).

2 *Correspondance,* p. 118. Letter dated by Rewald as early 1874.

3 V. 138 and 139 are dated 1873. Landscapes datable on visual evidence are V. 133–136, 141–142, 144–147, 149–151. For the still-life paintings, see V. 179–180, 183, 185, 189, 216, and a small pastel formerly owned by Dr. Gachet, now in the collection of Mr. and Mrs. Dunbar Bostwick, referred to by Venturi, Vol. 1, p. 347, and reproduced in Wildenstein & Co., Inc., New York, *Cézanne, Loan Exhibition,* 1959, No. 58. Almost all of these, including the landscapes mentioned, are listed by Rewald in "A propos du catalogue raisonné de l'œuvre de Paul Cézanne et de la chronologie de cette œuvre," *La Renaissance,* XX, 1937, pp. 53–57.

4 See Berthold, Cat. Nos. 244 and 245.

5 Meyer Schapiro, *Paul Cézanne,* New York, 1952, p. 27.

6 See Ludovico Pissarro and Lionello Venturi, *Camille Pissarro, son art, son œuvre,* 2 vols., Paris, 1939, No. 206.

7 Venturi (Cat. No. 1204) entitled this composition *Déjeuner sur l'herbe;* Georges Rivière (*Le Maître Paul Cézanne,* Paris, 1923, p. 93) called it *Les Brigands;* Chappuis (Cat. No. 59), *Quatre hommes assis sous un arbre;* Douglas Cooper (review of Chappuis, *Les dessins de Cézanne au Musée de Bâle,* in *Master Drawings,* I, No. 4, 1963, p. 55), *Three Men and a Woman.* A fifth sitter has been completely overlooked: to the right of the woman is a large dog, his muzzle behind the woman's shoulder and his ear just to her right. His shoulder, flank, and tail are clearly discernible. This drawing was probably made during Cézanne's stay at Auvers, as the bearded man in the

Barbizon hat looks like Pissarro. Its composition recalls a theme Cézanne projected in the sixties. See the discussion (p. 5) of a genre scene for which Cézanne used portraits of his friends.

Chapter 3

1 See the discussion at No. 209.

2 See Paul Gachet, *Tombeau de Cézanne,* Paris, 1956, p. 24, for this recollection that this canvas was painted at Auvers in 1872. He adds (p. 28) that it was painted a few months before *La Maison du pendu,* which he dates 1873 (p. 24), and also relates (p. 280) that although *Une Moderne Olympia* remained a sketch, Cézanne had wished to carry the painting further. It is plausible, then, that the *Olympia* sketches on the sheet with the portraits of Cézanne's wife (32) were drawn later than the 1872 painting. In any case, for the most exact dating, we cannot depend on Paul Gachet's recollections; for example, his statement that the idea for *Une Moderne Olympia* was stimulated by Dr. Gachet contradicts our knowledge that Cézanne's first version of this theme was painted about 1869–1870, before he knew Gachet.

3 Georges Rivière's recollections given in *Cézanne, le peintre solitaire,* Paris, 1923, have proved unreliable. He assigned the portrait of Boyer (V. 131) to the period at Auvers, although it is clearly earlier, and the portrait of Chocquet to the same period, even though Cézanne's first meeting with Chocquet could not have taken place before late in 1875. See No. 211.

4 "Société anonyme des artistes, peintres, sculpteurs, graveurs, etc.," April–May 1875, at the Nadar Gallery in Paris. See the summarized catalogue of this exhibition in Lionello Venturi, *Archives de l'Impressionnisme,* Paris, 1939, Vol. II, pp. 255–256. See also John Rewald, *History of Impressionism,* rev. ed., New York, 1962, pp. 314 ff.

5 See Wayne V. Andersen, "Cézanne's Sketchbook in the Art Institute of Chicago," *The Burlington Magazine,* CIV, 1962, pp. 196–201.

6 Venturi dated these portraits on the assumption that the wallpaper background was from Cézanne's residence at 67 rue de l'Ouest in 1877. See the remarks at V. 209 and in my article cited below in note 7.

7 Wayne V. Andersen, "Cézanne, Tanguy, Chocquet," *The Art Bulletin,* XLIX, 1967, p. 137.

8 *Ibid.* See also the comments at No. 211.

Chapter 4

1 *Correspondance,* p. 138.

2 For the identification of Cézanne's copy see Theodore Reff, "Cézanne's Drawings, 1875–85," *The Burlington Magazine,* CI, 1959, p. 172. For reproduction of Pissarro's gouache see Ludovico Pissarro and Lionello Venturi, *Camille Pissarro, son art, son œuvre,* 2 vols., Paris, 1939, No. 1356.

3 For a summary of Venturi's evidence and its use or interpretation by others see Reff, "Cézanne's Constructive Stroke, *The Art Quarterly,* xxv, 1962, pp. 214–226.

4 See Cézanne's letter to Zola of April 4, 1886, in *Correspondance,* p. 208, and Rewald's note there concerning the meaning of the letter.

5 Cézanne visited Zola in June of 1879 (see letters of June 5 and September 24, 1879); again in the autumn of that year (letter of September 27, 1879); in January of 1880 (letter of December 18, 1879); in March of 1880 (letter of February 1880); perhaps in early April 1880 (letter of April 1, 1880); perhaps in the summer of 1880 (letters of June 19 and July 4, 1880); perhaps in the autumn of 1880 (letter of October 28, 1880); then in the spring of 1881 (letter of May 20, 1881); in the autumn of 1881 (letters of August 5 and October 15, 1881); possibly in the early months of 1882 (letters of February 28, 1882); probably in the autumn of 1882 (letter of September 2, 1882); then not again until the summer of 1885 (letters of July 3, 6, 11, 15, and 19, 1885). All the letters are from Cézanne to Zola, in *Correspondance*, pp. 162–164, 166, 167, 169, 171–172, 174, 180, 183, 185, 188, 202–205.

Chapter 5

1 Documented by a letter from Paul Alexis to Zola dated February 13, 1891, in which Alexis mentions that Cézanne had spent "l'été dernier, cinq mois de Suisse." See also Georges Rivière, *Le Maître Paul Cézanne*, Paris, 1923, p. 218, where he notes Cézanne's stay at Neuchâtel.

2 For all the canvases, watercolors, and drawings related to these see V. 546, 556–561, 563–568, 684–691, 712–718, 1085–1090, 1092, 1102, 1482, 1483, 1587, and my No. 250. Venturi relates his Cat. No. 391 to this series, but I believe it is a painting of Cézanne's son of ca. 1886–1888. Venturi dates one of the peasant paintings 1886–1890 (V. 546); the card-player series 1890–1892 (V. 556–560, 567, 568, 1085–1088); and the related peasant portraits between 1888 (V. 561) and 1894 (V. 564, 565). A third group of peasant portraits is dated 1895–1900 (V. 684–691, 1087); a fourth group, 1900–1904 (V. 712, 713); and a fifth group, 1900–1906 (V. 714–718, 1092, 1102).

3 See Marcel Provence Archives, 1955, Atelier les Lauves, Aix-en-Provence. See also Gustave Coquiot, *Paul Cézanne*, Paris, 1919, p. 97, where the sitter is called "le sieur Paulet"; Rivière, *Le Maître Paul Cézanne*, p. 217, where he is called "le père Alexandre." For other images of this sitter see V. 556–558, 566, 1482 (my No. 251), and 1088.

4 Émile Zola, *Oeuvres complètes*, Paris, 1928.

5 In *La Vie artistique*, III, 1894, p. 259.

6 See a letter from Alexis to Zola written in January 1892 in John Rewald, *Paul Cézanne*, Paris, 1939, p. 368; and a letter from Zola to Alexis dated March 30, 1892, in Émile Zola, *Correspondance, 1872–1902*, ed. Maurice Le Blond, Paris, 1929, p. 746.

7 Ambroise Vollard, *Souvenirs d'un marchand de tableaux*, Paris, 1937, p. 94. Probably Venturi 684–686, 688. On the wall in the background of V. 688 is a portrait of Madame Cézanne that may be one of the group V. 570–573.

8 Joachim Gasquet, *Cézanne*, nouvelle éd., Paris, 1926, p. 107; also Jean de Beuchen, *Un Portrait de Cézanne*, Paris, 1955, p. 260.

9 See note 2 to this chapter.

10 Meyer Schapiro, *Paul Cézanne*, New York, 1952, p. 88.

11 This opinion has been expressed by Venturi at Cat. Nos. 556–558; Fritz Novotny in *Paul Cézanne*, London, 1961, p. 15 ("about 1890") and Plate 30; Schapiro in *Paul Cézanne*, p. 88; and Kurt Badt in *The Art of Cézanne*, Berkeley, 1965, Figs. 8–16. Badt (p. 122) dates the two-player version as late as 1896, but in my view his evidence is not substantial.

12 See Cézanne's letter to Geffroy dated April 4, 1895, in *Correspondance*, p. 218, and Geffroy's remarks in his *Claude Monet*, Paris, 1924, II, p. 67.

13 This event is described by Joachim Gasquet in *Cézanne* (*Les Albums d'art Druet*, Vol. 1), Paris, 1930, especially in the chapter "L'Atelier," and pp. 91–92.

14 The watercolor (V. 965) is on the verso of V. 1096. For other paintings and watercolors of this child see V. 698, 700, 1096–1098.

15 See the entry at V. 701, where Venturi states, ". . . peint d'après la tradition, rue Gabrielle à Montmartre, d'après un modèle qui serait proche parente du garçon au gilet rouge."

16 Wayne V. Andersen, "Cézanne's *Carnet violet-moiré*," *The Burlington Magazine*, CVII, 1965, pp. 313–318.

17 This was made for the third volume of Vollard's *L'album des peintres-graveurs*, Paris, 1898, which was not published.

18 Chapter VIII of Vollard's book, *Paul Cézanne*, Paris, 1914, is devoted to his experience of posing for Cézanne.

19 See Joachim Gasquet in *Les Mois dorés*, No. 3, 1896, p. 94: "Le peintre vient d'achever une toile . . . toute affaissée dans ses vêtements bleus, . . . une vielle femme, une servante, entres ses vieilles mains presse avec ferveur et resignation les grains d'un chapelet." This description undoubtedly refers to V. 702; it was discovered by John Rewald (*Cézanne, Geffroy et Gasquet,* Paris, 1959, pp. 26, 29) and used as evidence to adjust the date of V. 702 from 1900–1904 to 1896. See also Gasquet, *Cézanne,* Paris, 1930, p. 111; Vollard, *Souvenirs d'un marchand de tableaux,* p. 211.

20 See V. 716. For other studies and paintings of Vallier see V. 715, 717, 718, 1092, 1102, 1524, 1566.

21 The photograph was taken by the son of Karl Bodner. In my article "Cézanne's *Carnet violet-moiré*" (p. 317), I transcribed a name Cézanne had jotted down on page III verso of the sketchbook as "Bodner" and suggested that it might be a reference to the painter Barthélémy-Marc Bodner. It is very likely, however, that the reference is to Karl Bodner.

22 On the date of this painting see Fritz Novotny, *Cézanne,* Vienna, 1937, notes for Pl. 67, where it is dated ca. 1894; Venturi, Cat. No. 245, dated 1873–1877; Sarah Lichtenstein, "Cézanne and Delacroix," *The Art Bulletin,* XLVI, 1964, p. 55 and note 3, dated also 1873–1877; Columbia University, Department of Art History and Archaeology, *Cézanne Watercolors,* New York, 1963, pp. 21–22, where Novotny's date, ca. 1894, is supported. See also Theodore Reff, letter to the editor, in *The Art Bulletin,* XLVI, 1964, p. 425, for a summary of opinions on the date. For more direct evidence see Wayne V. Andersen, "Cézanne, Tanguy, Chocquet," *The Art Bulletin,* XLIX, 1967, pp. 137–139.

23 See V. 1603–1605.

24 Gertrude Berthold, *Cézanne und die alten Meister,* Stuttgart, 1958, pp. 52–57.

Catalogue

I Self-Portraits

1

Self-portrait. Present location unknown. Formerly Collection Gustave Coquiot, Paris.
Charcoal on coarse paper. Probably a fragment from a sheet originally measuring approximately 30 × 50 cm.;[1] present dimensions unavailable.
Literature: Reproduced by René Huyghe, *Cézanne,* Paris, 1957, p. 29.

The technique of this drawing combines the gentle modeling of Cézanne's portraits of the end of the sixties (such as the charcoal portrait of Achille Emperaire (No. 217) with an overlay of structural lines made with a harder medium, perhaps a conté crayon; it provides visual evidence of Cézanne's effort after 1872 to restrain the sensual romanticism of his earlier style. The hard and angular lines seem to be a structural translation of his sinuous, impassioned drawing technique of the preceding year.

With but one other exception, No. 11, Cézanne's self-portraits seem to have been made with the aid of a mirror, which naturally aligned his eyes with those of the viewer. This drawing was probably made from a photograph, since the head is seen from slightly below, and the eyes look past and over the viewer's shoulder. Although none of the known photographs corresponds to it exactly, the pose is close to one reproduced here (1a).

Date: 1873–1874. For discussion see pp. 9, 10, 12, 13, 14, 17, 22.

1 A number of sheets of the same texture used by Cézanne in the seventies and the first half of the eighties were approximately of this size. Many were cut up by Cézanne *fils* and perhaps by some dealers so that the drawings could be sold individually. My examination of the paper type and the deckle edges of a number of these sheets has revealed which drawings of smaller dimensions were once part of these larger sheets. See No. 21 for a full sheet; others are pointed out under their appropriate catalogue entries.

2

Self-portrait. Collection Major Derrick Morley, London; acquired from a dealer in Paris in 1935. Formerly Collection Emile Dunan, Paris.

Pencil on white paper, 14.4 × 15.6 cm., with corners trimmed. Signed "P. Cézanne."

Verso: Framer's instructions in pencil at the upper right corner; the figure "No. 2" in blue pencil written across the center of the sheet. (The same style of lettering and color of pencil are on the verso of No. 209.)

Literature: Léo Larguier, "Collectioneurs et collections: Émile Dunan," *L'Art vivant,* March 15, 1929, p. 232; John Rewald, *History of Impressionism,* rev. ed., New York, 1961, p. 351, dated ca. 1875; idem, *Paul Cézanne,* New York, 1968, Fig. 36, dated ca. 1873.

Date: 1874–1875. For discussion see pp. 13, 17–22.

3

Self-portrait, on a sheet with studies of female bathers.
Kunstmuseum, Basel.
Pencil on white paper (bathers in pencil and ink), 20 × 30.1 cm.
Verso: Six sketches of male heads, copied after old masters (Berthold, Cat. No. 292, dated 1875–1880; Chappuis, Cat. No. 87, dated 1877–1882).
Literature: Venturi, Cat. No. 1251; Melvin Waldfogel, "The Bathers of Cézanne," unpublished Ph.D. dissertation, Harvard University, 1961, p. 155; Chappuis, Cat. No. 98, dated 1872–1877.

Venturi reproduced this sheet but did not identify the portrait sketch. Although the bathers have previously been reproduced (by both Venturi and Chappuis), it was not until Chappuis' study of the Basel drawings that the self-portrait was discussed and dated. Waldfogel suggested its comparison with V. 366, which Venturi dated 1879–1882. Chappuis' date for this drawing appears to have been based on 1872 as the earliest date for the parallel hatching, and 1877 as the latest plausible date for V. 289, the Hermitage self-portrait (generally dated 1873–1875), with which he compared this sketch, pointing out similarities in expression and age. But even if the date for the drawing were certain, the Hermitage self-portrait could hardly support it: the hat brim at the line of the brow is the only point of similarity and can also be found in other oil portraits—V. 287 and 366, for example. Closer comparisons can be made with No. 7, which was unknown to Chappuis, and with Pissarro's oil portrait of Cézanne in the collection of Robert von Hirsch (Fig. 12).[1]

As to the bathers, Chappuis reproduced V. 542 to illustrate the use of this study for Cézanne's painted compositions. The central standing bather in this drawing does not appear in V. 542, however, but in V. 382–386 and 547, with some variations in posture. Waldfogel dated the bathers "1879 or later"; his decision was based on the decorative character of the contours and the light-yielding hatching.

I agree with Chappuis that the bather composition should be dated earlier than 1879. (Reff has suggested a date ca. 1877 for one of the paintings closely related to this composition, V. 385.[2]). The self-portrait may not be exactly contemporary; although incomplete, it can be compared with Nos. 4 and 5 and dated according to the same stylistic evidence.

Date: 1876–1877. For discussion see p. 22.

1 Lucien Pissarro and Lionello Venturi, *Camille Pissarro, son art, son œuvre,* Paris, 1939.

2 "Cézanne's Constructive Stroke," *The Art Quarterly,* XXV, 1962, pp. 215f. Reff suggests that such compositions of alternately standing and crouching or reclining figures in a spacious landscape are still Impressionist.

4

Self-portrait. Collection Benjamin Sonnenberg, New York;
acquired in 1955 from Huguette Berès, Paris.
Soft pencil on white paper, 17.46 × 12.7 cm.
Verso: Blank.
Literature: Wayne V. Andersen, "Two Unpublished
Cézanne Self-Portrait Drawings," *The Burlington Maga-
zine,* CVIII, 1966, pp. 475–476.

This drawing was cleaned in 1962 to remove lines probably
added by Cézanne's son; the reproductions here show it
both before and after cleaning.

Date: Ca. 1876. For discussion see p. 21.

5 fac.

Self-portrait. Collection the estate of Maurice Gobin, Paris. Formerly Collection E. Blot, Paris.
Pencil on white paper, 18.5 × 14.5 cm.
Verso: Blank.
Literature: Paris, Musée de l' Orangerie, *Cézanne, 1936*, dated ca. 1878–1880; Venturi, Cat. No. 1238, dated 1878–1885; Fritz Novotny, *Cézanne*, Vienna, 1937, dated ca. 1880; René Huyghe, *Cézanne*, Paris, 1957, p. 66, dated 1878–1885; Reff, "Studies," pp. 48–49, dated 1877–1878; Maurice Gobin, *L'Art expressif*, Paris, 1960, dated ca. 1880.

Charles Sterling's date in the Orangerie catalogue was based on both the apparent age of Cézanne and the tonal hatching, which he compared with Cézanne's painting technique in the late 1870's. Venturi considered the stroke and facture plausible for a later date, extending into what he called "the constructive phase" of Cézanne's stylistic evolution. Theodore Reff, on the other hand, attentive to the deliberate grouping of fine, distinct lines into small patches, set the date back to 1877 and presented as additional evidence a physiognomic comparison with V. 366, which Douglas Cooper had dated 1877–1878 in his debate with Lawrence Gowing.[1]

The date "late seventies" assigned by Sterling and Gobin cannot be challenged in regard to the expression or the apparent age of the sitter. Venturi's date, however, extends much too far into the 1880's to be supported by either the age or the style. If Cooper's date for the Berne self-portrait, V. 366, were definite, it would help in dating the drawing closer to 1878, as Reff has suggested (although the stroke in the oil painting is more regulated than that in the drawing), but Cooper's opinion is no more securely based on fact than Gowing's. His observation that the painting is "characterized by use of black and gives every indication of having been painted in the North"[2] does not necessarily testify to a date before 1879. The identical palette, including black, can be found in *The Bridge of Maincy* (Louvre), which can be dated 1879, and in Cézanne's portraits of his son, V. 282 and V. 534, which can be dated ca. 1880 and ca. 1882, respectively, on the evidence of the child's age. There is nothing in the style of the Berne self-portrait that would preclude a date as early as 1877; the parallel facture in developed form for the head does not, as Gowing believes, indicate 1880.[3] I have shown in the text (pp. 21–22) that this characteristic appears in the mid-1870's, and that it may have reached its peak about 1876–1877, when Cézanne was most deliberate in his efforts to make Impressionism a stronger "constructing" process.[4]

Date: Ca. 1877–1878. For discussion see pp. 21, 26.

1 Douglas Cooper, "Two Cézanne Exhibitions," *The Burlington Magazine.* XCVI, 1954, p. 349.

2 *Ibid.*

3 Lawrence Gowing in Arts Council of Great Britain, *An Exhibition of Paintings by Cézanne*, London, 1954, No. 23.

4 Using other criteria, Theodore Reff has also made this observation in "Cézanne's Constructive Stroke," *The Art Quarterly*, XXV, 1962, pp. 214–227.

6

Self-portrait, on a sheet with studies of bathers and copies of the bathers by Cézanne's son. Collection Mr. and Mrs. Henry Pearlman, New York; formerly collection Sir Kenneth and Lady Clark, London; acquired in 1934 from Cézanne *fils* through the dealer Paul Guillaume, Paris.
Pencil on coarse white paper, 30.4 × 23.5 cm.; edges slightly irregular, right edge corners cut diagonally; half of a sheet originally measuring approximately 30 × 50 cm.
Verso: Half of a fragmentary landscape sketch, similar to that in No. 118.
Literature: Wayne V. Andersen, "Two Unpublished Cézanne Self-Portrait Drawings," *The Burlington Magazine,* CVIII, 1966, pp. 475–476.

Because the self-portrait had been overlaid with rather heavy, undistinguished bather sketches, and the drawing had been disfigured with scribbles by Cézanne's son, this sheet was put aside shortly after its acquisition by Sir Kenneth Clark. It remained forgotten for twenty-nine years until my discussion of the self-portraits with Sir Kenneth, when it was recalled and found. The drawing has proved very important for the chronology of Cézanne's self-portraits. The fact that it was overlaid by bathers, which in turn were copied by Cézanne's son at the age of about six, places the portrait in the late 1870's—not later than 1878.

This sheet, half a standard sheet of artist's paper, may have been divided by Cézanne *fils,* so that a drawing on the other half of the sheet could be sold separately. Realigning the sheet in regard to the bathers, we find that the upper right-hand scribble by Cézanne's son is a copy of a half-reclining bather—one leg with knee up, the other leg stretched out—the original of which was probably on the other half of the sheet. It is also possible that the child's lettering, "RUVERAS," continued on the other half. The letters can be read in two different ways: as RU VERAS . . . (the child having omitted the letter E in "rue") or as RUVE RAS . . . (the structural similarity of a U and a V may have caused the child to make both letters). No street name in Paris during the 1870's corresponds to either spelling, except "Raspail," which was then, as it is now, a boulevard. Written along the torn edge is the comment, "détacher les 3 sujets," referring to the self-portrait and the two bather studies, which are all marked with the word "tel." This writing is in a later hand and was probably an instruction to a photographer preparing photographic copy.[1]

The fine lines and clean hatchings on the shoulder and upper arms of a bather just below and to the left of the self-portrait are a little misleading, because they have the same quality as the self-portrait drawing, whereas the other bathers are drawn with coarser lines made with a soft, blunt pencil. The position and alignment of the bather, however, suggest that it was executed at the same time as the others. Beneath the heavy, expressive lines that give the bathers substance and define their sensuous contours, there are also studied tonal patches and light, firm lines, which were Cézanne's first graphic responses to his subject. These bathers are studies for the painted compositions, V. 272 and 275, dated by Venturi 1875–1877. The little striding bather appears in the background of the latter.

The self-portrait drawing is accurately translated into paint in the self-portrait in the collection of Emile Hahnloser, V. 280, which dates from 1875–1876. Except for the hat, they correspond in every detail: each area of fine parallel hatching on the beard in the drawing has the shape and character of the light brushstrokes that develop the beard in the painting. Their tonal values are reversed, of course—the dark hachures of the drawing are the light strokes of the painting—proving that Cézanne's tonal drawing was not simply a matter of light and shadow or of local color.

Date: Ca. 1877–1878. For discussion see pp. 20–22.

---

1 For an explanation of these notations on other Cézanne drawings, see Douglas Cooper's review, in *Master Drawings,* I, No. 4, 1963, p. 56, of Adrien Chappuis, *Les Dessins de Cézanne au Musée de Bâle,* Olten, 1962, and Theodore Reff's review of the same work, in *The Burlington Magazine,* CV, 1963, pp. 375–376.

7

Self-portrait. Museum of Fine Arts, Budapest.
Pencil on white paper, approximately 30 × 25 cm.; half a
larger sheet originally measuring approximately 30 × 50
cm.[1]
Verso: Sketch of a landscape motif.
Literature: Julius Meier-Graefe, *Cézanne und seine Ahnen*,
Munich, 1921 (Drucke der Marées-Gesellschaft, No. 7);
Kurt Pfister, *Cézanne, Gestalt, Werk, Mythos*, Potsdam, 1927,
p. 35; Budapest, Museum of Fine Arts, *Exposition Majovsky*,
1935, No. 76; Venturi, Cat. No. 1237, dated 1878–1885; Reff,
"Studies," p. 48, dated 1883–1884.

The wide span of Venturi's date (1878–1885) for this drawing was perhaps meant to allow for the disparity between
Cézanne's apparent age (he could be younger than forty
years) and the stylistic traits (the parallel hatching and
abstract pattern of light and dark around the ear) that
Venturi dates ca. 1885. Reff's date of 1883–1884 is based on
a comparison of this drawing with the oil self-portrait V.
368, which he dates also 1883–1884 (Venturi had dated
V. 368 1878–1882). I believe this drawing is stylistically
closer to the self-portrait in the collection of Oskar Reinhart
(V. 367), which seems exactly contemporary with *The Bridge
at Maincy* (V. 396) of 1879.

Not visible in reproductions of this drawing is the faint
impression of a standing or dancing female figure, three-
quarter view, clothed in a full blouse and long, full skirt.
The figure has apparently been erased. Along the right
margin there is an unidentifiable detail from a drawing
that was on the other half of the original sheet. The other
portion of this sheet may be V. 1221, my No. 32; it is identical in paper type and in style. The measurements given
by Venturi may be only for the portion exposed by a mat.

Date: Ca. 1878–1879. For discussion see pp. 22, 34.

---

1 See No. 1, note 1.

8

Self-portrait, on a sheet with a sketch of a female head.
Kunstmuseum, Basel.
Pencil on light grayish-brown paper, 30.4 × 20.5 cm.; part
of a larger sheet that included V. 844 and its verso, V. 1224,
dated by Venturi 1875–1877.[1]
Verso: Studies of landscapes and miscellaneous figures
(Chappuis, Cat. No. 66, dated 1873–1877).
Literature: Vollard, p. 171; Venturi, Cat. No. 1478, dated
1883–1887; Chappuis, Cat. No. 93, dated 1878–1885;
Maurice Serullaz, *French Impressionists* (*Drawings of the
Masters,* ed. Ira Moskowitz), New York, 1963, p. 25.

Venturi's date, 1883–1887, was probably based on the distribution of hatching, which, according to his chronology,
would suggest a date in the mid-1880's. Chappuis' wide
span indicates his uncertainty in dating Cézanne's loose
contours in combination with carefully applied hatching.
The date that I have assigned is supported by stylistic arguments in the text. These can be supplemented by the fact
that this sheet is part of a larger one that included V. 844
and its verso, V. 1224, both dated correctly by Venturi
1875–1877. The verso of this drawing appears to date from
the same period. Moreover, of the several self-portraits of
the second half of the seventies, this one corresponds
closely to the photograph of Cézanne taken with a group of
artists and friends at Pontoise (8a). The group includes
young Lucien Pissarro, who appears to be between twelve
and fourteen years old (he was born in 1863); to the right of
the boy is Aguiar, a medical student and amateur painter,
who was at Pontoise in the mid-seventies. The photograph
dates, therefore, from about 1875–1877.[2]

The female head can be compared with a similar one on
p. XXVI of the Chicago sketchbook (Schniewind, XXVI).
Chappuis' comparison of the head with V. 89, a portrait of
Cézanne's sister, Marie, is without basis, except that both
women wear a head-scarf.

Date: 1877–1879. For discussion see p. 22.

1 Discovered by Robert Ratcliffe in 1956, and cited by Chappuis, 1957, No. 27;
cf. Chappuis, Cat. No. 66.

2 Identified in W. S. Meadmore, *Lucien Pissarro,* London, 1962, p. 61.

In the reserves of the Louvre there is a small landscape by Aguiar, *Maisons à
Auvers* (see *La peinture au Musée du Louvre, École Française XIXe siècle,* I, No. 2),
which bears a dedication dated 1875. It may have been painted during the previous year, however, for both Cézanne and Pissarro painted this motif from the
same viewpoint, and Pissarro's canvas is dated 1874 (V. 156 and V. P. 295).

9 fac.

Self-portrait. Art Institute of Chicago.
Pencil on white paper; page VII verso in a sketchbook
measuring 12.4 × 21.7 cm. (Rewald, *Carnet II*).
Verso: Landscape sketch (Schniewind, VII).
Literature: Rewald, *Carnet II*, p. VII verso, dated ca. 1885;
Schniewind, Vol. I, p. 13, and Cat. No. VII verso, dated
1880–1882; Reff, "Studies," p. 63, dated 1880's; Neumeyer,
Cat. No. 32, dated 1880–1882.

More than any of the others, this self-portrait drawing has
evoked comments on its mood and expression. Four scholars have dated it in the first half of the eighties: Schniewind
suggests that it should be compared with the views of
L'Estaque from the early eighties; Neumeyer agrees with
Schniewind's date, although his own evidence, based on
overly rigid and linear assumptions about Cézanne's
physical and character growth, seems subjective. Reff's
interpretation of the expression as gentle and timid contradicts Neumeyer's statement that "the eyes have lost their
previous timid expression," but Reff's date, though too
broad to be useful, is based on a study of Cézanne's graphic
stroke, with the conclusion that in the eighties Cézanne's
closely spaced diagonal strokes seemed to impose on his
entire drawing surface "a single graphic system." Although
Rewald's date, ca. 1885, was suggested as a *terminus ante
quem* for the style of Cézanne's beard, it was probably based
on stylistic considerations. I have pointed out on page 26
that the stroke and hatching in this drawing differ considerably from Cézanne's technique of ca. 1885 and belong
to an earlier stage in the evolution of his graphic style.

Date: Ca. 1878. For discussion see pp. 21–22.

10 fac.

Self-portrait, on a sheet with a portrait of Cézanne's son (No. 126). Art Institute of Chicago.
Pencil on white paper; page XXI in a sketchbook measuring 12.4 × 21.7 cm. (Rewald, *Carnet II*).
Verso: Study of a garment, probably a coat (Schniewind, XXI verso).
Literature: Rewald, *Carnet II*, p. XXI, dated ca. 1885; Schniewind, Cat. No. XXI, dated ca. 1880; Reff, "Studies," pp. 12, 63, dated early 1880's; John Rewald, *Post-Impressionism*, 2d ed., New York, 1962, p. 13, dated ca. 1885.

Rewald's date for this drawing, ca. 1885, is substantiated only by his supposition that shortly after 1885 Cézanne's style of beard changed. Schniewind has concluded that Cézanne is somewhat older in this portrait than in the one on p. XXII of the Chicago sketchbook (No. 11), but the weakness in his argument lies in his assumption that Cézanne's attitude of decreasing optimism, security, and happiness provides evidence for chronology. He would have us believe that "the poignant expression of discouragement" and Cézanne's more "careworn eyes" confirm a later date for this portrait than for No. 9, where Cézanne appears to him "sombre, critical," and "uncommunicative," though apparently not yet discouraged.

Date: Ca. 1880–1881. For discussion see pp. 21–22, 25.

11 fac.

Self-portrait. Art Institute of Chicago.
Pencil on white paper; page XXII in a sketchbook measuring 12.4 × 21.7 cm. (Rewald, *Carnet II.*)
Verso: Sketches of a male bather, a hand, and a shoe (Schniewind, XXII verso).
Literature: Rewald, *Carnet II*, p. XXII, dated ca. 1885; Schniewind, Vol. I, pp. 11f., and Cat. No. XXII, dated 1875–1877; Neumeyer, Cat. No. 31, dated 1875–1877.

The surprisingly early date assigned to this drawing by both Schniewind and Neumeyer seems to have been prompted by what I think is a deceptive youthfulness in Cézanne's appearance. The narrow shape of the head and the shortness of the beard, which Neumeyer observed in comparing the portrait with my No. 9, does not accurately describe Cézanne in the mid-seventies. While a recent haircut may be a relevant factor, there is also a degree of distortion in the construction of the head itself. The slightly askew nose, the high position of the ear and of the hair above it, relative to the eyes and the crown of the head, indicate that Cézanne viewed himself with his head tilted forward, but did not succeed in the foreshortening. I have dated the drawing on the basis of its stylistic similarity to a number of portraits of Cézanne's son in the Chicago sketchbook.

Date: Ca. 1878–1880. For discussion see p. 22.

12 fac.

Incomplete self-portrait, on a sheet with a sketch of a woman's head, perhaps of Madame Cézanne. Art Ínstitute of Chicago.
Pencil on white paper; page XXXIX in a sketchbook measuring 12.4 × 21.7 cm. (Rewald, *Carnet II*).
Verso: Two portraits of Cézanne's son (No. 107).
Literature: Rewald, *Carnet II*, p. XXXIX, with a date of 1875–1885 for the entire sketchbook; Schniewind, Vol. I, p. 14, and Cat. No. XXXIX, dated ca. 1889.

This hesitantly executed, somewhat mechanically drawn self-portrait was abandoned by Cézanne before completion, but it is valuable evidence of Cézanne's graphic procedure, since a tonal rendering of the beard had just been started at the left. In dating this drawing, Schniewind inferred from the apparent lack of a beard that Cézanne, at the time of making the portrait, wore a mustache and *barbiche pointue* rather than the full, rounded beard of his earlier years. His date of ca. 1889 was based on a comparison with a photograph of Cézanne (23a).[1] The seven hatching lines on the left cheek of the portrait, however, are the first indication of the round beard shape and preclude a comparison with this phogograph. Schniewind's assumption that Cézanne's life was a gradual decline in physique and character, suggested here by his "emaciated, lonelier" appearance, has been discussed at No. 10.

This is one of two self-portraits (the other is No. 1) where the eyes look outward at an angle rather than straight forward, indicating that the drawings were made from a photograph rather than a mirror.

Date: 1878–1880.

1 On the date of this photograph see No. 13, note 1.

13 fac.

Self-portrait. Art Institute of Chicago.
Pencil on white paper; page XXXVII in a sketchbook measuring 12.4 × 21.7 cm. (Rewald, *Carnet II*).
Verso: Study after an *écorché* (Schniewind, XXXVII verso).
Literature: Rewald, *Carnet II,* p. XXXVII, dated ca. 1885; Schniewind, Vol. I, p. 13, and Cat. No. XXXVII, dated 1886; Chicago, Art Institute, *Cézanne: Paintings, Watercolors, and Drawings,* 1952, dated ca. 1886; Neumeyer, Cat. No. 33, dated 1885–1886; Reff, "Studies," pp. 26, 63, dated "later 1880's to 1890's"; Meyer Schapiro, *Cézanne,* New York, 1952, p. 18, dated "1886 (?)."

Rewald's date of ca. 1885 was based on the style of Cézanne's beard: "alors que l'artiste portait encore une barbe en collier, tandis qu'une photo de 1889 le montre une moustache et barbiche pointue" (23a).[1] Schniewind, following his method of basing the chronology of Cézanne's portraits on increasing despondency, sees in his "expression of bleak hopelessness" here the tragic events of 1886: the death of his father and the breakup of a life's friendship with Zola over the publication of *L'œuvre.* He adds, "The highly developed technique of the drawing would be in favor of this late date." Reff dates this drawing later than any others have: first, on the evidence of style—"the subtle illumination" and the fact that "even the pupils are rendered by closely placed diagonal strokes"; second, on the same assumption as Schniewind's, that the chronology of Cézanne's self-portraits reveals an "increasing loneliness, frustration and dejection."

I would discount the evidence of Cézanne's expression in dating this drawing, since a self-portrait often depends on a momentary mood that cannot be generalized; nor can the rendering of the eyes serve as reliable evidence, since several drawings of Cézanne's son of about 1878 have the same characteristic, though more spontaneously executed (e.g., No. 129). Cézanne does appear older here than in other self-portraits of the Chicago sketchbook, and the subtlety of the tonal drawing makes it seem more advanced, but stylistically it belongs with the other self-portraits in this sketchbook.

Date: Ca. 1880. For discussion see p. 22.

1 Rewald, *Carnets de dessins,* Vol. I, p. 31. The date of the photograph is not as certain as Rewald assumes. Two original prints of it exist, one by the photographer Jules Lavier; the other was made after 1910 by Jules's son, Jacques. On the back of the first print is entered the date 1899, overwritten to read 1889. On the back of the second print, in pencil, is entered the date 1890. I examined these photographs at the home of Jean-Pierre Cézanne.

14 fac.

Self-portrait, on a sheet with unidentified copies: the head and shoulders of a man, part of a second head, and a landscape background. Collection Mr. and Mrs. Leigh Block, Chicago.

Pencil on white paper; page XIV verso in a sketchbook measuring 12.6 × 21.7 cm.

Verso: Sketch of a flower stand with flowers.

Literature: Rewald, *Carnet V,* p. XIV verso; Berthold, Cat. No. 322.

Date: Ca. 1881. For discussion see pp. 25–26, 28, 30, 32.

15

Self-portrait, on a sheet with a copy after Pajou's *Psyche abandonnée* in the Louvre and a sketch of Cézanne's son sleeping in an armchair (No. 150). Museum Boymans-van Beuningen, Rotterdam; gift of D. G. van Beuningen in 1940. Formerly Koenigs Museum, Haarlem; acquired from Cézanne *fils* in 1929.

Pencil on coarse textured white paper, 49.6 × 32.0 cm.

Verso: Blank.

Literature: Rotterdam, Museum Boymans, *Teekeningen van Ingres tot Seurat,* 1933, Cat. No. 1; Basel, Kunsthalle, *Meisterzeichnungen französischer Künstler von Ingres bis Cézanne,* 1935, Cat. No. 171; Basel, Kunsthalle, *Paul Cézanne,* 1936, Cat. No. 126, dated ca. 1880; Venturi, Cat. No. 1479, dated 1879–1882; Amsterdam, Cassirer, *Fransche Meesters uit de XIX* *eeuw,* 1938, Cat. No. 23; Amsterdam, Musée Municipal, *Teekeningen van Fransche Meesters,* 1946, Cat. No. 9; Paris, Bibliothèque Nationale, *Dessins du XV* *au XIX* *siècle du Musée Boymans de Rotterdam,* 1952, Cat. No. 139; Rotterdam, Museum Boymans, *Dessins de Pisanello à Cézanne; Collection Koenigs* (*Art et Style,* No. 23), 1952, Cat. No. 1, dated 1879–1882; U.S. National Gallery of Art, *French Drawings,* 1952, Cat. No. 163; The Hague, Gemeentemuseum, *Paul Cézanne,* 1956, Cat. No. 113; Munich, Haus der Kunst, *Paul Cézanne,* 1956, Cat. No. 133; Zurich, Kunsthaus, *Paul Cézanne,* 1956, Cat. No. 173; Berthold, Cat. No. 163; *Great Drawings of All Time,* ed. Ira Moskowitz, New York, 1962, Vol. III, No. 814; Wayne V. Andersen, "A Cézanne Drawing After Couture," *Master Drawings,* I, 1963, p. 46, note 7; Hamburg, Kunstverein, *Cézanne, Gauguin, Van Gogh, Seurat,* 1963, Cat. No. 27, Fig. 76, dated 1879–1882; Maurice Serullaz, *French Impressionists* (*Drawings of the Masters*), ed. Ira Moskowitz), New York, 1963, pl. 97; Paris, Institut Néerlandais, *Le Dessin français de Claude à Cézanne dans les collections hollandaises,* 1964, Cat. No. 201, dated 1879–1882. Hoetink, Cat. No. 23.

Two characteristics of this sheet suggest that the copy after Pajou predates both the self-portrait and the sketch of the child. The position of the last two sketches seems to indicate consideration for that of the nude, as the sheet is virtually divided horizontally by the axis of the nude at the hips, and it seems unlikely that Cézanne would take with him to the Louvre a large sheet already half used. More likely, the two intimate sketches of himself and his son would have been made on a sheet casually available in the studio. It is not possible to discern whether the self-portrait or the portrait of his son was drawn first.

Date: 1881–1882. For discussion see pp. 25–26, 28, 30.

16

Self-portrait. Collection Walter C. Baker, New York; acquired from Ambroise Vollard, Paris, through Reid and Lefevre Galleries, London.

Pencil on white paper, 33.0 × 27.3 cm.

Verso: Could not be inspected.

Literature: John Rewald, "Paul Cézanne, New Documents for the Years 1870–1871," *The Burlington Magazine,* LXXXI, 1939, p. 167, dated ca. 1880; *idem, Cézanne, sa vie, son œuvre, son amitié pour Zola,* Paris, 1939, Pl. 31, dated ca. 1880; Paul Cézanne, *Letters of Cézanne,* ed. John Rewald, 1941, Pl. 20; John Rewald, *Paul Cézanne,* New York, 1948, Pl. 39; *idem, Paul Cézanne,* 1950, Pl. 27; Philadelphia Museum of Art, *Masterpieces of Drawing,* 1950, Cat. No. 103; Chicago, Art Institute, *Cézanne: Paintings, Watercolors and Drawings,* 1952, Cat. No. 40, dated ca. 1885; Aix-en-Provence, Pavillon de Vendôme, *Exposition pour commémorer le cinquantenaire de la mort de Cézanne,* 1956, Cat. No. 88; Paris, Musée de l'Orangerie, *De Clouet à Matisse,* 1958, Cat. No. 150, dated 1878–1880; Wildenstein & Co., New York, *Cézanne,* 1959, Cat. No. 64, dated ca. 1885; New York, Metropolitan Museum, *The Walter C. Baker Collection of Drawings,* 1960, Cat. No. 160.

Since Rewald first published this drawing in 1939, it has been widely exhibited, often reproduced, and on three occasions dated: Rewald dated it ca. 1880; in the catalogue of the Chicago exhibition it is dated ca. 1885; in the catalogue of the Orangerie exhibition it is dated ca. 1878–1880. Only in the last instance are reasons given for the assigned date: the drawing is compared with Renoir's dated pastel portrait of Cézanne[1] and judged to date from not later than 1880.

Date: Ca. 1881–1882. For discussion see pp. 25–26, 28.

---

1 See the discussion on p. 25.

17

Self-portrait. Present location unknown. Formerly Collection Dr. Lukas Lichtenhan, Basel; acquired about 1928 from Ambroise Vollard.
Pencil on paper; measurements unknown.
Verso: Unknown.
Literature: John Rewald, *Paul Cézanne*, New York, 1948, Fig. 19, dated 1877–1882; Wayne V. Andersen, "A Cézanne Self-Portrait Reidentified," *The Burlington Magazine*, CVI, 1964, p. 283, note 10.

Rewald published this drawing as *Portrait of a Man*. His date was based, therefore, on stylistic criteria, perhaps on a comparison with the self-portraits in the Block and Baker collections (Nos. 14, 16). When in the ownership of Vollard and Lukas Lichtenhan, it was known as a self-portrait; with that title it passed into obscurity.[1]

In rendering this self-portrait, Cézanne treated the hair in a style comparable to that in many of his self-portraits, with one lock of hair on the left and two or three flowing locks on the right. Although the eyes are closer together and more recessed, they bear some resemblance to those in the Morley self-portrait (No. 2).

Date: Ca. 1881–1882. For discussion see p. 30.

18

Self-portrait, on a sheet with sketch of an apple. Cincinnati Art Museum, bequeathed by Dr. Allyn C. Poole in 1958; acquired by Ted Schempff from the Vollard collection in June 1935; sold to Dr. Poole in the summer of that year.
Pencil on coarse, textured, white paper, 17.25 × 22.6–22.9 cm.; deckle edges top and right, torn edges bottom and left; from a sheet originally measuring approximately 30 × 50 cm.
Verso: Blank.
Literature: San Francisco, Museum of Art, *Paul Cézanne*, 1937, Cat. No. 62 (self-portrait only), dated 1878–1885: John Rewald, *Paul Cézanne*, New York, 1948, p. 163 (self-portrait only), dated ca. 1880; Meyer Schapiro, "The Apples of Cézanne," *Art News*, XXXIV, 1968, Fig. 16, dated 1878–1885.

Like a number of Cézanne's drawings, this was torn from a larger sheet. The sketch of the apple was folded back and the self-portrait matted. See No. 21, where an apple also appears with a self-portrait on a sheet of the same type of paper and of the same original dimensions.

Date: 1882–1883. For discussion see p. 34.

---

1   This information was supplied by courtesy of Dr. Lichtenhan.

19 fac.

Self-portrait. Collection Adrien Chappuis, Tresserve (Savoie).
Pencil on white paper; page XL in a sketchbook measuring 21.5 × 12.6 cm. (Chappuis II).
Verso: Sketches of a clock, head of Cézanne's father (No. 206), vase with flowers.
Literature: Paris, Musée de l'Orangerie, *Cézanne*, 1936, Cat. No. 157, dated 1885–1890; Venturi, Cat. No. 1293, not dated; Chappuis, 1938, No. 1, dated 1885–1890; Chappuis, 1957, p. 30, dated 1881–1884; Reff, "Studies," p. 77, dated 1880–1881; John Rewald, *Paul Cézanne*, New York, 1968, p. 163, dated ca. 1885.

In 1957 Chappuis revised his date for this drawing, having found that it compared closely with the oil self-portrait in Munich (Fig. 18). The date of the painting, however, is itself debatable: scholars have dated it variously between 1877 and 1882 (all cited by Chappuis). Chappuis concluded that the drawing seemed later than the painting, despite the facial likeness, and justified an extension of the date to 1884. Robert Ratcliffe supported this opinion: "I believe that the drawing, V. 1293, dates from the early years of the eighties, those years when Cézanne repeatedly elaborated and modified his great discovery: the strokes of the brush or the pencil grouped in parallel hachures, following the same direction. . . ."[1]

Reff saw in this drawing, especially in the rendering of the nose and ear and in the expression of the eyes, a similarity to the Tate self-portrait (Fig. 22), and he agreed with Cooper's argument that the tonality and facture of the painting call for a date of 1881.

Date: 1883–1884. For discussion see p. 34.

---

1   In a letter from Ratcliffe to Chappuis, quoted in Chappuis, 1957, No. 30.

20

Self-portrait. Collection Adrien Chappuis, Tresserve (Savoie).
Pencil on white paper; page XVII in a sketchbook measuring 12.6 × 21.5 cm.
Verso: Portrait of Cézanne's son (No. 156); sketch of a formally attired man meeting a woman, a bather seated at the foot of a tree, and a standing female bather.
Literature: Vollard, p. 54; Venturi, Cat. No. 1287; Reff, "Studies," pp. 27, 77, dated 1880–1881; Aix-en-Provence, Pavillon de Vendôme, *Exposition Cézanne*, 1961, Cat. No. 52.

See No. 19.

Date: 1883–1884. For discussion see pp. 25, 34, 39.

21 detail

Self-portrait, on a sheet with a drawing after a self-portrait by Goya, an apple, a running female bather, and other sketches. Collection Sir Kenneth and Lady Clark, London.
Pencil on white paper, 49.5 × 31.1–31.2 cm., folded in half; one of a number of sheets of the approximate dimensions 30 × 50 cm.[1]
Verso: Two portraits of Madame Cézanne (No. 65), three of Cézanne's son (No. 163), a copy after Pedro de Moya of a youth seen from the back,[2] a sketch of a decorative female figure from an eighteenth-century clock (V. 1474 verso, not reproduced; Berthold, Cat. No. 328).
Literature: Vollard, p. 13; Julius Meier-Graefe, *Cézanne und sein Kreis*, Munich, 1922, p. 20; Venturi, Cat. No. 1474, dated 1883–1887; Bernard Dorival, *Cézanne*, Paris, 1948, p. 130; Reff, "Studies," p. 26, dated "later eighties or nineties"; Aix-en-Provence, Pavillon de Vendôme, *Exposition Cézanne*, 1961, Cat. No. 47, dated 1887–1890; Berthold, Cat. No. 328 for the complete sheet; Meyer Schapiro, "The Apples of Cézanne," *Art News*, XXXIV, 1968, Fig. 13, dated 1883–1887.

Venturi's date of 1883–1887 was probably based on a combination of stylistic and physiognomic evidence. Cézanne appears in this drawing to be about the same age as in my No. 19, which Venturi would have dated somewhat later than I have here (1882–1884), but the style of drawing places it with those he dated close to 1880. The outline of the face on the right side indicates that Cézanne still wore a full beard. The drawing is characterized by many short strokes, which cumulatively construct the form; the emphasis is still on contours.

Venturi did not reproduce the complete sheet; his reproduction was made from the one in Vollard's book. Berthold, who reproduced the sheet for the first time, was the first to mention that the copy after Goya's self-portrait was from an etching that appears as Plate 1 of the *Caprichos*. At the center of this sheet is a similar head, perhaps a free-style caricature of the same model. To the left there is a running female bather in a three-quarter view of the back— a pose Cézanne often used in his bather compositions from the mid-1870's on. The apple in combination with a self-portrait also occurs in No. 18 and on a sheet in Vienna, where two apples with similar dark, outlined shadows appear in combination with the same study of the bather.[3]

Date: 1884–1886.

22

Self-portrait. Collection Robert von Hirsch, Basel; acquired from a dealer in Paris about 1957.
Pencil on paper, 31 × 24 cm.
Verso: Blank.
Literature: Vollard, p. 119; Julius Meier-Graefe, *Cézanne und sein Kreis*, Munich, 1922, frontispiece; Émile Bernard, "La technique de Paul Cézanne," *L'Amour de l'art*, I, 1920, p. 286; John Rewald, *Cézanne, sa vie, son œuvre, son amitié pour Zola*, Paris, 1939, Pl. 46; Venturi, Cat. No. 1476, dated 1890–1895; Reff, "Studies," p. 26, dated "later 1880's or 1890's"; Giorgio Nicodemi, *Paul Cézanne, 76 disegni*, Milan, 1944, No. 1, not dated; John Rewald, *Paul Cézanne*, New York, 1968, p. 197, dated 1890–1895.

Date: 1890–1894. For discussion see pp. 39–40.

1 See No. 1, note 1.

2 Identification by Robert Ratcliffe. See Adrien Chappuis, "Cézanne dessinateur: copies et illustrations," *Gazette des Beaux-Arts*, ser. 6, LXVI, 1965, p. 297, No. 9.

3 Albertina, Inv. No. 24084. Cf. Berthold, Cat. No. 290.

23 fac.

Self-portrait. Collection Adrien Chappuis, Tresserve (Savoie).
Pencil on white paper; page X in a sketchbook measuring 15 × 23.8 cm. (Chappuis III).
Verso: Landscape seen from a cavern.
Literature: Venturi, under Cat. No. 1304, not reproduced; Paris, Musée de l'Orangerie, *Cézanne*, 1936, Cat. No. 154, dated ca. 1882; Chappuis, 1938, No. 47; "Cézanne en Savoie," *Revue de Savoie,* 1955–1956, p. 111; Neumeyer, Cat. No. 34, dated ca. 1895; Chappuis, *Album,* No. X, dated 1890–1893; Theodore Reff, review of Chappuis, *Album, The Burlington Magazine,* CIX, 1967, p. 653, dated ca. 1898.

Date: 1896–1900. For discussion see pp. 39–40.

24

Self-portrait. Bibliothèque Nationale, Paris. There are other impressions elsewhere; a maquette in watercolor was in Vollard's collection.
Lithograph on white paper, approximately 47 × 34.5 cm.
Verso: Blank.
Literature: Vollard, 1914, p. 90; Julius Meier-Graefe, *Cézanne und sein Kreis*, Munich, 1922, frontispiece; Venturi, Cat. No. 1158, dated 1898–1900; Paris, Musée de l'Orangerie, *Cézanne*, 1936, Cat. No. 194, dated ca. 1898.

It is generally assumed that this lithograph was executed for the unpublished third volume of Volland's *L'Album des peintres-graveurs*, Paris, 1898.

Date: 1898. For discussion see p. 39.

25 n.r.

Unfinished sketch of a head, on a sheet with other drawings: a group of three bathers in a landscape, a seated man in oriental costume. Kunstmuseum, Basel.
Pencil on white paper, 19.8 × 25.5 cm., irregular edges.
Verso: Head of Cézanne's son (No. 151).
Literature: Venturi, Vol. I, p. 352, not reproduced; Chappuis, Cat. No. 80, dated 1872–1877.

The sheet on which this sketch appears was described, though not reproduced, by Venturi. Chappuis first noted the partial head and identified it as a self-portrait; his opinion was apparently influenced by the similarity of this sheet to No. 3, which contains bather studies and, to the right, an unfinished self-portrait. Although the few lines that constitute this sketch do not disclose with certainty the identity of the subject, they do indicate that it is not Cézanne himself. The way in which the features are sketched in is characteristic of the 1870's, and there is no question that at that date Cézanne was bald.

Date: Mid-1870's.

26 n.r.

Three male heads; one resembles Cézanne, another, Achille Emperaire. Present location unknown; sold about 1956 through the dealer William H. Schab, New York.
Pencil on white paper, approximately 16 × 24 cm.; page from a sketchbook, probably the *Carnet de jeunesse* (Louvre), which measures 15.2–15.3 × 23.8–24.0 cm.
Verso: Sketch of a landscape.
Literature: William H. Schab Gallery, New York, *Graphic Arts of Five Centuries*, 26, [1960?], Cat. No. 130.

The style of drawing and the composition of these small, unsophisticated heads could not be of a later date than 1861. Although one of the heads resembles Cézanne, it would have to date from at least the mid-sixties when he wore a full beard. Thus I do not believe it is Cézanne, nor do I agree that a second head is of Achille Emperaire. In the so-called *Carnet de jeunesse*,[1] to which this page may have belonged, there are dozens of heads copied from books or magazines—it was Cézanne's practice to make such copies throughout his early years. Although the sketchbook does contain a few later drawings, this page belongs with those from the late 1850's, exactly contemporary with sketches of heads on a letter from Cézanne to Zola dated July 9, 1858.[2]

Date: 1858–1861.

1 Described, catalogued, and partially reproduced by Berthold, pp. 154 ff.

2 Reproduced in Figure 2, p. 2.

27 n.r.

Portrait sketch of Cézanne, on a sheet with a second portrait sketch, perhaps also of Cézanne. Collection the estate of W. W. Crocker, Hillsborough, California. Acquired in Paris about 1935.
Pencil on white paper, 15 × 23.7 cm. The inscription "Cézanne peintre" appears at the lower left.
Verso: Could not be examined.
Literature: San Francisco, Museum of Art, *Paul Cézanne,* 1937, Cat. No. 68, dated 1890–1893; John Rewald, *Paul Cézanne,* New York, 1948, p. 214, without the second head and the inscription; *ibid.,* London, 1965, p. 185, detail.

This little drawing, certainly a likeness of Cézanne in his old age, was acquired by the Crocker family as a self-portrait. Rewald published it as a portrait of Cézanne, but did not agree that it was in his hand; instead, he attributed it to Emile Giraud. In my opinion, too, it is not in Cézanne's hand.

28

Dr. Gachet and Cézanne preparing the acid bath for etching a plate. Collection Paul Gachet, Auvers-sur-Oise.
Pencil on beige paper, 19.5 × 12.8 cm.
Literature: Venturi, Vol. I, p. 347, not catalogued; Paul Gachet, *Cézanne à Auvers,* Paris, 1952, dated 1873.

It is difficult to accept that this drawing is both of and by Cézanne. Certainly the man at the left—although only the lower half of his face is shown below the hat brim—looks like Cézanne, and the man at the right, like Dr. Gachet (compare him with No. 223), but it seems unlikely, if not impossible, that Cézanne would have executed this spontaneous drawing as if he were an onlooker rather than the subject. Although it does suggest Cézanne's style— when compared with the other drawings of Dr. Gachet, examination of the details reveals major dissimilarities. Even in his poorest drawings Cézanne is not schematic and could not be responsible for the mechanical repetition of the short, paired lines that occur four times on the left figure (midway in each sleeve, at the coat button, and at the left shoulder) and twice on the right figure (on the sleeve and at the collar). The pattern of these and other short lines across the figure of Dr. Gachet and the blending of both figures into the table are without parallel in Cézanne's drawings of the early seventies.

29

Portrait of Cézanne. Present location unknown.[1]
Pencil on white paper.
Verso: Unknown.
Literature: Unpublished.

This crude, heavy-handed drawing of Cézanne, obviously contrived after No. 20, appeared on the Paris art market in 1961. In my opinion it is not in Cézanne's hand. For the same hand see Nos. 92 and 197.

1 I am indebted to John Rewald for providing me with the photograph.

Portraits of Madame Cézanne

30

Two portraits of Madame Cézanne, on a sheet with four studies of Cézanne's son (No. 93), a seventh head (perhaps Cézanne's son), a spoon, and a clock. Ashmolean Museum, Oxford, bequest of Dr. Grete Ring in 1954; formerly Galerie Flechtheim, Berlin.
Pencil on paper, approximately 23.8 × 31.3 cm., a sheet from a commercially illustrated book.
Verso: Lithographic reproductions of two studies of the head of a horse inscribed ''Cheval - Horse - Cavallo - Pferd - Caballo.'' See Figure 17, p. 22.
Literature: Venturi, Cat. No. 1222, dated 1872–1873.

The conformation of the child's head, the cloth napkin round his neck, and the presence of his spoon all suggest that he is one or two years of age. There is some similarity between the head of the child just below the spoon and that of the nursing child in the painting V. 233. Although the face of the woman in this painting is difficult to verify, there seems to be little doubt that it is Madame Cézanne

nursing her infant; such an intimate scene would hardly have been posed or derived from some pictorial source, let alone produced from Cézanne's imagination. The child in the drawing seems a little older than in the painting.

Date: 1873–1874. For discussion see pp. 12, 14, 18, 20.

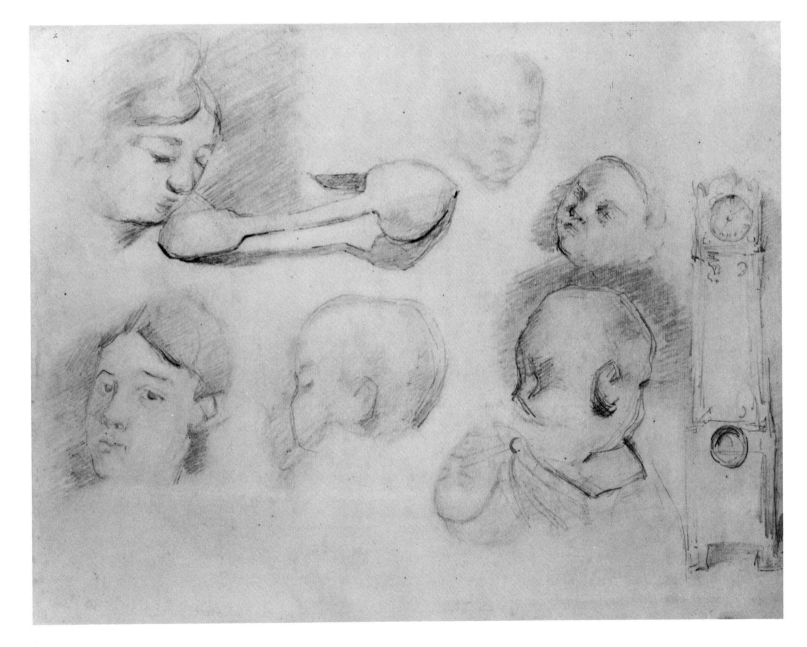

31 fac.

Portrait of Madame Cézanne, on a sheet with a sketch of an erotic theme. Kunstmuseum, Basel.
Pencil on white paper, 17.1 × 10.3 cm.; page from a dismantled sketchbook (*Carnet 10.3 × 17*).
Verso: Sketch of a walking female nude with one arm raised, identified by Venturi (Vol. I, p. 350) and Chappuis (Cat. No. 42, dated 1867–1871) as a study for the *Tentation de Saint Antoine*.
Literature: Venturi, Vol. I, p. 350; Chappuis, Cat. No. 43, dated 1870–1877.

In discussing this sheet, Venturi does not mention the portrait sketch, and he identifies the drawing of the female nude only as a study for the *Tentation de Saint Antoine*.[1] Chappuis follows Venturi's identification of the erotic scene and only mentions the female head, without recognizing it as a portrait of Madame Cézanne. My identification is based primarily on a comparison of this head with that in V. 226, which has the same facial conformation, hair style, eye lashes, etc.; even the neck scarf is identical. The head is also closely related to the upper left portrait in No. 30.

Date: Ca. 1874–1875. For discussion see pp. 14, 19.

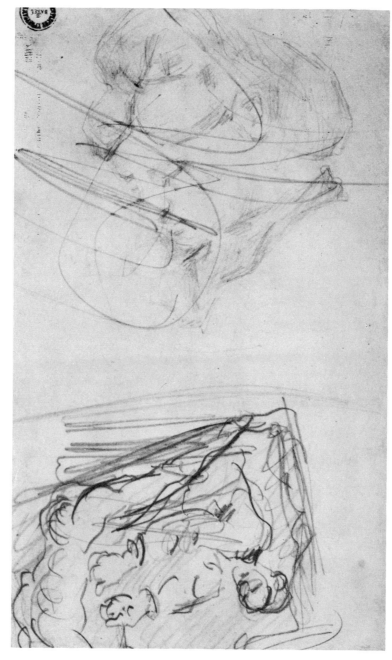

1 The fact that the drawing of the female nude and the drawing on the verso have no evident connection with the *Tentation* has been pointed out by Theodore Reff "Cézanne, Flaubert, St. Anthony, and the Queen of Sheba," *The Art Bulletin*, XLIV, 1962, p. 113, note 7; *idem*, "Cézanne's Drawings," *The Burlington Magazine*, CV, 1963, p. 375.

32

Two portraits of Madame Cézanne, on a sheet with a portrait of Cézanne's sister, Rose(?), three studies for *Une moderne Olympia*, and a dancing nude figure. Museum of Fine Arts, Budapest. Formerly Collections Meller, Budapest, and Paul de Majovsky, Budapest.
Pencil on coarse, textured, white paper, 22.2 × 28.5 cm.; part of a sheet originally measuring approximately 30 × 50 cm.[1]
Verso: Blank.
Literature: Vollard, p. 115; Budapest, Museum of Fine Arts, *Exposition Majovsky*, 1935, Cat. No. 67; Venturi, Cat. No. 1221, dated 1872–1873.

Venturi's date was almost certainly based on an assumption that the studies for *Une moderne Olympia* were for the second oil version, V. 225, which he dated 1872–1873, but which more likely dates from early 1874. The leaping, dancing nude figure in this drawing has gone unnoticed. It is based on another Cézanne drawing, presumed lost

but actually in the Albertina (32a); a detail from it was reproduced by Vollard in 1914. Venturi catalogued the Albertina sheet simply as a *feuillet d'études* (V. 1203, dated 1871–1877), without comment. Its subject was probably copied from an illustration of a cabaret scene. The dancing figure is nude from the waist up and wearing a long dancing skirt, which Cézanne omitted in the Budapest sheet. That this figure appears on the sheet with studies for the nude woman in *Une moderne Olympia* may not be coincidental, for in the right foreground of the Albertina sheet is a gentleman with top hat and umbrella who, along with others, is sitting watching the erotic spectacle. Even though this may not be the same man as in *Une moderne Olympia*, his attitude as he observes the nude woman is strikingly similar. A later version of *Une moderne Olympia*, V. 882, also includes a man in a top hat who is standing with his arms folded, in much the same pose as the gentleman in the cabaret scene, watching the maid reveal Olympia's nude body to him.

Date: 1875–1877. For discussion see pp. 18–20.

1 See No. 1, note 1.

Two portraits of Madame Cézanne, one of her head only,
the other half-length, seated behind a table, sewing, on a
sheet with a portrait of Chocquet (Cat. No. 212). Collection
Benjamin Sonnenberg, New York. Acquired through
Georges Wildenstein and Company, New York, May 1961,
from the collection of Sir Kenneth and Lady Clark, London.
Pencil on beige paper, irregular edges; 19.6 × 23.3 cm.
Verso: Head of Cézanne's son and a coffee pot (No. 99).
Literature: Venturi, Cat. No. 1240, dated 1878–1885;
Mahonri Sharp Young, "Treasures in Gramercy Park,"
Apollo, LXXXV, 1967, p. 181; Wayne V. Andersen, "Cézanne,
Tanguy, Chocquet," *The Art Bulletin,* XLIX, 1967, pp. 137–
139, dated ca. 1877.

The difficulties concerning the dating of this drawing are
many. If, as Venturi suggests, the portrait drawing of
Chocquet is a study for the oil portrait, V. 532, which he
dates 1883–1887, why does he state that the drawing is
contemporary with the sketch of Madame Cézanne sewing,
which he dates about 1877 on comparison with V. 291,
which he also assigns to 1877? Only the third portrait,
again of Madame Cézanne, remains to justify his date of
1878–1885 for the complete sheet, which is impossible.
One might suspect that the span 1878–1885 was suggested
to allow the drawing of Chocquet to correspond with the
oil portrait, V. 532, which he dated rather loosely. To a
second drawing of Chocquet, V. 1241 (210), he assigned the
date 1877–1886 without comment.

Venturi's suggestions that the drawing of Chocquet and
that of Madame Cézanne sewing are studies for V. 532
and 291, respectively, cannot be accepted. The sketch of
Chocquet was actually made from the photograph reproduced here (211a), which was also used in executing the
oil portrait V. 532. (For further information on this, see
No. 211). The oil portrait of Madame Cézanne sewing
(V. 291) is quite different from this drawing: Madame
Cézanne is facing in the opposite direction; only the
lowered head and the position of the hands are similar
—but this is a pose that Cézanne often used.

The table in front of Madame Cézanne and the second
portrait of her on this sheet are linked in an oil painting,
V. 226, where the table has an identical design at
the joints of the legs and the top; the overhang of the top
and side apron are also the same. This does not necessarily
imply that the painting is contemporary with the drawing,
but on visual appearance alone Venturi's date for the
painting, 1871–1873, seems a little too early. Venturi
detected in its color and loose technique the influence of
Manet, whose work inspired Cézanne especially about
1869–1872; but this influence may well have continued
beyond that time. Although the painting does recall
Manet, unlike Cézanne's oil portrait of Boyer (Fig. 7), in
which bold strokes of creamy paint—bright yellow contrasted with black—testify to Manet's style of the sixties,
it looks ahead to Cézanne's style of the mid-seventies and
can be dated without relating it to outside influences. It is
an unfinished painting and shows characteristics of
Cézanne's underpainting methods as well as his graphic
style of the mid-seventies.

Date: Ca. 1877. For discussion see pp. 19, 20.

Portrait of Madame Cézanne, on a sheet with a copy after Michelangelo's *Battle of Cascina,* a nude male figure walking with outstretched arms, and other sketches. Museum Boymans-van Beuningen, Rotterdam.

Pencil on white paper, 31 × 23.8 cm.

Verso: Copy after Puget's *Milo de Croton* and a sketch of four men building a bonfire. (Venturi, Cat. No. 1448, dated 1879–1882; Berthold, Cat. No. 99.)

Literature: Venturi, Cat. No. 1217, dated 1879–1882; Berthold, Cat. No. 258; Neumeyer, Cat. No. 14, dated 1879–1882; Chappuis, Vol. I, p. 124, note 8; Hoetink, Cat. No. 19, dated ca. 1874.

The portrait of Madame Cézanne may be the latest drawing on this sheet, as the walking male figure and the copy after Michelangelo must have preceded the execution of the three little framed sketches. The walking figure has been precisely placed, his feet on the top edge of one frame, his toes stopped just short of the other, his forward hand touching the side of another frame; the figure copied after Michelangelo has been exactly placed between the frames, one leg extending along a margin line. It is much more reasonable to assume that Cézanne marked off the framed areas for quick sketches than that he adjusted the other drawings to fit precisely between them. The appearance of the sheet before the addition of the frames suggests an affinity with No. 39, a page from the Chicago sketchbook, which comprises a walking male, between a complete drawing of Madame Cézanne on one side and a scant, though studied, sketch of her on the other.

The proposed sequence for these drawings is supported also by the placing of the fisherman studies. They undoubtedly represent the same fisherman seen from two views, confirming that they are sketches from nature and not copied from an illustration. Like most of Cézanne's genre sketches, they have been composed and drawn quickly, exhibiting graphic traits that are not always easily associated with those of the more studied and carefully executed drawings. If the center drawings had not been on the sheet previously, Cézanne would not have spaced the two fisherman sketches—made within moments of each other—so widely apart. These framed sketches also remind us that, when Cézanne envisioned his drawings, he sometimes made immediate decisions as to their purpose. Whereas the walking figure and the copy after Michelangelo, and perhaps even the portrait of Madame Cézanne, were studied for their particular structure, character, and expression, the three framed motifs were immediately conceived as tableaux. The termination of the tree top in the lower right frame, the careful composition of the scene with figures, and especially the blank frame, which was no doubt intended to enclose a scene—all confirm that the frames preceded the drawings.

The striding male figure has neither precedent nor sequel in Cézanne's *œuvre.* Its closest counterpart is a standing male bather in an oil painting, V. 881, dating from about 1875–1877. Certain peculiarities in the posture in both examples suggest a posed model: in the drawing, the outward position of the arms is too exaggerated for the stride, and the lack of perspective in the placing of the feet gives the impression that the legs are crossed rather than one behind the other in parallel movement. The attitude of the male bather in the painting V. 881 is also that of a posed model; he stands firm, as if to allow the study of his articu-

lation. Both the painting and this drawing suggest a date in the mid-seventies, when Cézanne was first transforming his earlier academic studies into bathers. I would suggest, for example, that the male figure in V. 881, at one stage of its transformation, served as a source for the bather at the left in V. 728, and that the striding male figure in this drawing could have been one of the many models for the striding bathers with outstretched arms in V. 727 and 729. If this hypothesis is correct, V. 727 and 729 would be of a later date than this drawing and later than V. 881.[1]

The two fisherman sketches show the same subject, first, from slightly behind and then, higher up the river bank, from a quarter front view. (Note the corresponding shift of the tree trunk.) It is a general compositional scheme favored by Cézanne during the seventies: a rise of ground with a figure or a tree, or both, on the left, and spatial recession or minor figures on the right. We can note the same composition in V. 580 and its several versions, in many other bather compositions, and in the little outdoor genre scene on this same sheet, which dates, I believe, from the same outing and was sketched along the same river bank. Cézanne may have regarded these little motifs as independent, self-contained themes but the figures may also have served him for bather models, with the clothing omitted and the anatomy approximated. They date from about 1875–1876.

Date: Ca. 1875–1877. For discussion see p. 19.

1 For other opinions on this figure and the other sketches on the sheet see Hoetink, Cat. No. 19, where Chappuis dates the walking man as early as 1864, and Cooper dates it as late as 1880.

35

Portrait of Madame Cézanne, on a sheet with a portrait of
Cézanne's son (No. 97) and a study of a garment. Present
location unknown. Formerly Collection Sir Kenneth and
Lady Clark, London.
Pencil on beige paper, approximately 22 × 23 cm.
Verso: According to Venturi, who did not see all Sir
Kenneth Clark's drawings, there are other studies of
Cézanne's wife and son on the verso. It is possible, however, that Venturi confused the verso with V. 1240 (No. 33),
which is of the same beige-colored paper and the same
approximate measurements (almost all Venturi's measurements of drawings in the collection of Sir Kenneth Clark
are inaccurate). This hypothesis is also supported by the
fact that, although Venturi mentions the verso of both Nos.
1240 and 1472, he does not catalogue them, thus indicating
that he did not actually know the verso drawings.
Literature: Venturi, Cat. No. 1472, dated 1878–1882.
Date: Ca. 1877. For discussion see pp. 18–19, 21.

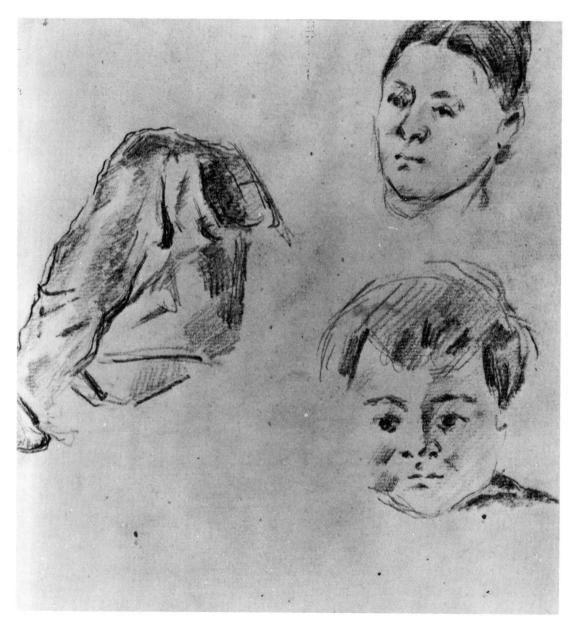

36 fac.

Portrait of Madame Cézanne. Art Institute of Chicago.
Pencil on white paper; page VI verso in a sketchbook
measuring 12.4 × 21.7 cm. (Rewald, *Carnet II*).
Verso: Sketch for the composition *L'Après-midi à Naples*
(V. 223).
Literature: Rewald, *Carnet II*, p. VI verso; Schniewind, Cat.
No. VI verso.

Rewald has tentatively suggested that this drawing is of
Madame Cézanne; Schniewind has simply called it: "head
of a woman in profile." I believe that it is of Madame
Cézanne. The conformation of the lips is the same as in the
oil portrait V. 229; the nose is a little stronger, but it is
similar to No. 33; the hair style conforms to that in oil portraits of the seventies such as V. 229 and 522 (even the
little tendril where the hair is parted compares with that in V.
229, with which this drawing is contemporary).

Date: 1876–1878

37 fac.

Portrait of Madame Cézanne. Art Institute of Chicago.
Pencil on white paper; page VIII in a sketchbook measuring
12.4 × 21.7 cm. (Rewald, *Carnet II*).
Verso: Sketch of a sailboat by Cézanne's son.
Literature: Rewald, *Carnet II*, p. VIII; Schniewind, Cat. No.
VIII, with a suggested date of 1879–1882.

This drawing has not previously been identified. Rewald
catalogued it as "tête aux yeux clos"; Schniewind called it
"head of a youth with eyes closed, possibly a sketch of
Louis Guillaume, the son of a neighbor of Cézanne."
Schniewind's assumption was perhaps based on a comparison of the drawing with a painted portrait of young
Louis Guillaume (Fig. 24). There is some similarity between
the face in this drawing (with its boyishness expressed by
crisp lines and a clear definition of relatively undifferen-
tiated features) and that in the painting, but more apparent
are the differences. The drawing shows the full, round face
characteristic of the portraits of Cézanne's wife of the
seventies and early eighties, a firm, broad nose, and a
characteristic tilt of the head; moreover, the features and
expression are those of a mature person, not of a child. The
break in the hairline occurs at the point where Madame
Cézanne's hair is usually parted, whereas Louis Guillaume's hair is formed with the part at the side and a full,
uninterrupted sweep across the forehead. Schniewind's
identification is understandable, however, for in a number
of portraits Madame Cézanne is rendered in mannish lines;
see, for example, V. 526.

Date: 1876–1878.

38 fac.

Portrait of Madame Cézanne, with the annotation "Madame Cézanne" in the hand of Cézanne's son. Art Institute of Chicago.
Pencil on white paper; page XLIX verso in a sketchbook measuring 12.4 × 21.7 cm (Rewald, *Carnet II*).
Verso: Two portraits of Cézanne's son (122).
Literature: Rewald, *Carnet II*, XLIX verso, dated ca. 1885(?); Schniewind, Vol. I, p. 14 and Cat. No. XLIX verso, dated 1878–1879; Wayne V. Andersen, "Cézanne's Sketchbook in the Art Institute of Chicago," *The Burlington Magazine*, CIV, 1962, p. 197, dated 1876–1878.

Rewald's date of ca. 1885 for this drawing was perhaps influenced by the fact that this and the following drawing are at the back of the sketchbook, which he dates 1875–1885. He writes, "Il est plus difficile de dater le portrait de Madame Cézanne [page XLIX verso]. Tout ce que l'on peut dire est qu'elle a l'air encore assez jeune; en 1885, elle avait trente-cinq ans."[1] He does not consider the annotation by Cézanne's son as a *terminus ante quem* of ca. 1878,[2] although he acknowledges in his catalogue entry that the script is in the child's hand.

See also No. 39.

Date: 1876–1878. For discussion see pp. 18, 21.

1 *Carnet I*, p. 31.

2 See Wayne V. Andersen, "Cézanne's Sketchbook in the Art Institute of Chicago," *The Burlington Magazine*, CIV, 1962, p. 197.

39 fac.

Two portraits of Madame Cézanne, with the words "Madame Cézanne" written by Cézanne's son, on a sheet with a sketch of a walking male figure. Art Institute of Chicago. Pencil on white paper; page L verso in a sketchbook measuring 12.4 × 21.7 cm. (Rewald, *Carnet II*).
Verso: Exercises in lettering by Cézanne's son. See also No. 6.
Literature: Rewald, *Carnet II*, p. L verso; Schniewind, Cat. No. L verso, dated 1878–1879; Wayne V. Andersen, "Cézanne's Sketchbook in the Art Institute of Chicago," *The Burlington Magazine*, CIV, 1962, p. 197.

The style of the portrait drawings on this sheet, as well as the general appearance of the sitter, corresponds to the paintings of Madame Cézanne that can be dated 1877, V. 291, 292 (Fig. 15).

The walking male figure in the center of the sheet is strikingly similar in attitude, dress, and style to the seated man in V. 1202. They both belong to the type of figure composition characterized by V. 231, 234, and 236, in which the outline and tone are severe, and the contrasts harsh; there is no longer the fluidity of the early 1870's. In V. 236 the center figure stands in a similarly relaxed pose, hands in pockets, watching his opponent's *boule*. These paintings date from the mid-1870's, as does this drawing. See also No. 94 for the study of the wrestling men and for the discussion of this style.

See No. 38.

Date: 1876–1878. For discussion see pp. 18–20.

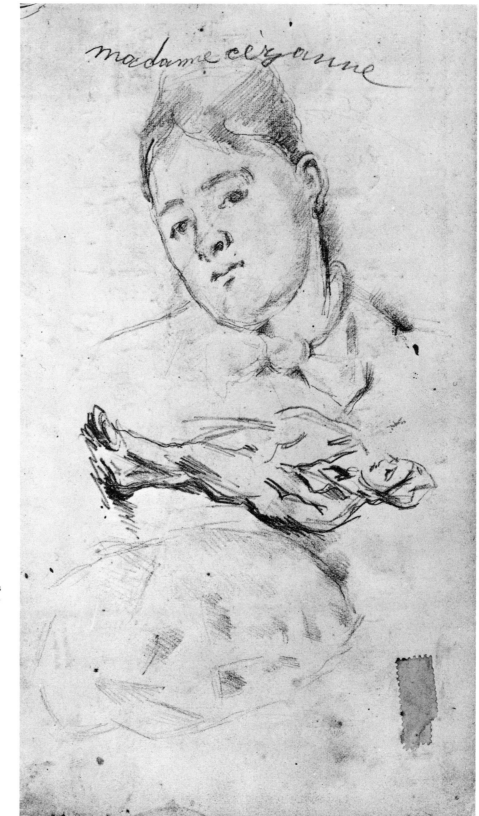

40 fac.

Portrait sketch of Madame Cézanne, on a sheet with a study of a lamp base and an unidentified vessel. Art Institute of Chicago.
Pencil on white paper; page XXVII verso in a sketchbook measuring 12.4 × 21.7 cm. (Rewald, *Carnet II*).
Verso: Miscellaneous still-life studies: a carafe, a pitcher.
Literature: Rewald, *Carnet II*, p. XXVII verso, not reproduced; Schniewind, Cat. No. XXVII verso.

The head has not been previously identified. On comparison with Nos. 39 and 34, it shows, I think, distinct resemblance to Madame Cézanne.

Date: 1876–1880.

41

Portrait sketch of Madame Cézanne, on a sheet with a sketch of Louis-Auguste Cézanne (No. 200). Art Institute of Chicago.
Pencil on white paper; page XIX verso in a sketchbook measuring 12.4 × 21.7 cm. (Rewald, *Carnet II*).
Verso: Study of an *écorché*.
Literature: Rewald, *Carnet II*, p. XIX verso; Schniewind, Cat. No. XIX verso.

Both Rewald and Schniewind identify this image as Cézanne's son.

Date: Ca. 1878–1880.

42

Portrait of Madame Cézanne, on a sheet with a figure study for an erotic theme. Art Institute of Chicago.
Pencil on white paper; page XXXV in a sketchbook measuring 12.4 × 21.7 cm. (Rewald, *Carnet II*).
Verso: Two female heads (No. 43).
Literature: Rewald, *Carnet II*, p. XXXV; Schniewind, Cat. No. XXXV.

Neither Rewald nor Schniewind identifies this image as Madame Cézanne. My suggestion that it is her likeness is based on comparison with Nos. 39 and 34.

The smaller sketch on this sheet is identified by Rewald as "une tête d'enfant"; Schniewind relates it in style and gesture to his Cat. Nos. XXXIII and XXXIV.

Date: 1878–1880.

43

Two heads of a woman, perhaps Madame Cézanne. Art Institute of Chicago.
Pencil on white paper, p. XXXV verso in a sketchbook measuring 12.4 × 21.7 cm. (Rewald, *Carnet II*).
Verso: Head of Madame Cézanne (No. 42).
Literature: Rewald, *Carnet II*, p. XXXV verso; Schniewind, Cat. No. XXXV verso.

Neither Rewald nor Schniewind identifies these heads as Madame Cézanne.

Date: Ca. 1878–1880.

44

Portrait of Madame Cézanne, on a sheet with another female head, probably also Madame Cézanne. Art Institute of Chicago.
Pencil on white paper; page XXXVI verso in a sketchbook measuring 12.4 × 21.7 cm.
Verso: A study of an *écorché*.
Literature: Rewald, *Carnet II*, p. XXXVI verso, not reproduced; Schniewind, Cat. No. XXXVI verso.
Date: Ca. 1878–1880.

45

Portrait of Madame Cézanne(?), on a sheet with a sketch of Cézanne's father sleeping (No. 202). Art Institute of Chicago.
Pencil on white paper; page XXXVIII verso in a sketchbook measuring 12.4 × 21.7 cm. (Rewald, *Carnet II*).
Verso: Two figure studies for an erotic theme, a faint sketch of an unidentified head (No. 256).
Literature: Rewald, *Carnet II*, p. XXXVIII verso; Schniewind, Cat. No. XXXVIII verso.
Date: Ca. 1880.

46

Portrait of Madame Cézanne, on a sheet with a sketch of a milk pail. Collection Sir Kenneth and Lady Clark, London.
Pencil on coarse, textured, white paper, 22.6 × 15.1 cm.; part of a larger sheet measuring approximately 30 × 50 cm.[1]
Verso: A landscape sketch (unpublished).
Literature: Venturi, Cat. No. 1481, dated 1879–1882; Fritz Novotny, *Cézanne*, Paris, 1937, No. 121, dated ca. 1880.

The milk pail appears in three still-life paintings dated by Venturi ca. 1879: V. 337, 338, 340.

Date: 1878–1880.

47 n.r.

One or more portraits of Madame Cézanne, on a sheet with one or more portraits of Cézanne's son (No. 98). Present location unknown. Formerly Collection Sir Kenneth and Lady Clark, London.
Pencil on beige paper; approximately 22 × 23 cm.
Verso: Portrait of Madame Cézanne (No. 35), portrait of Cézanne's son (No. 97), and a study of a garment.
Literature: Venturi, cited at Cat. No. 1472.

A photograph of this drawing was not available to Venturi, who described it simply as "other studies of the artist's wife and son." At No. 35 I have suggested that this drawing could possibly be V. 1240, which is my No. 33. Further evidence of Venturi's uncertainty is that he describes this side of the sheet as "unpublished" in Vol. I, p. 349.

48

Portrait of Madame Cézanne, asleep, head supported by right arm. Present location unknown. Formerly in the possession of Galerie Zak, Paris.
Pencil on paper, 23.5 × 30.5 cm.
Verso: Unknown.
Literature: *Correspondance*, Fig. 26, dated 1880–1882; John Rewald, *Cézanne*, New York, 1946, Fig. 22, dated 1880–1882; *idem, Cézanne*, 1948, Fig. 64, dated 1880–1882.
Date: 1880–1882.

1 See No. 1, note 1.

49 fac.

Portrait of Madame Cézanne. Collection Mr. and Mrs. Leigh Block, Chicago.
Pencil on white paper; page I verso in a sketchbook measuring 12.6 × 21.7 cm. (Rewald, *Carnet V*).
Verso: A female bather in a landscape with an annotation in Cézanne's hand: "Le Barc de Boutteville, La Bodinière."
Literature: Rewald, *Carnet V*, p. I verso.
Date: 1881–1882. For discussion see pp. 30, 32, 34.

50

Portrait of Madame Cézanne, on a sheet with a portrait of
Pissarro at his easel (No. 233) and the head of a peasant
woman. Collection Mr. and Mrs. Leigh Block, Chicago.
Pencil on white paper; page II verso in a sketchbook mea-
suring 12.6 × 21.7 cm. (Rewald, *Carnet V*).
Verso: Sketch of two trees.
Literature: Rewald, *Carnet V*, p. II verso; Neumeyer, Cat.
No. 30.

Both Rewald and Neumeyer have dated the portrait of
Pissarro (Rewald, p. 50, ca. 1880; Neumeyer, 1881), but have
not mentioned the portrait of Cézanne's wife. Both sup-
posed that this drawing dates from Cézanne's later period
of work with Pissarro, in 1880 and 1881, rather than in 1875
or 1877.

Date: 1881–1882. For discussion see pp. 30, 32.

51

Head of Madame Cézanne, on a sheet with a study of a
peasant woman and of a pitcher. Collection Mr. and Mrs.
Leigh Block, Chicago.
Pencil on white paper, in a sketchbook measuring 12.6 ×
21.7 cm. (Rewald, *Carnet V*).
Verso: Sketch of a landscape and of a group of female
bathers.
Literature: Rewald, *Carnet V*, p. III.

Rewald does not identify the head as Madame Cézanne.

Date: 1881–1882.

52 fac.

Portrait of Madame Cézanne. Collection Mr. and Mrs. Leigh Block, Chicago.
Pencil on white paper; page V verso in a sketchbook measuring 12.6 × 21.7 cm. (Rewald, *Carnet V*).
Verso: Sketch of a woman kneeling.
Literature: Rewald, *Carnet V*, p. V verso: *idem, Paul Cézanne*, New York, 1968, Fig. 61, dated 1875–1885.
Date: 1881–1882. For discussion see pp. 30, 32.

53 fac.

Portrait of Madame Cézanne, on a sheet with a landscape study. Collection Mr. and Mrs. Leigh Block, Chicago. Pencil on white paper; page XXXVII in a sketchbook measuring 12.6 × 21.7 cm. (Rewald, *Carnet V*).
Verso: Sketch of the back of a chair.
Literature: Rewald, *Carnet V*, p. XXXVII; *Paul Cézanne*, ed. Fritz Erpel, Berlin, 1958, No. 40, dated ca. 1885.

Rewald suggests that the landscape could be a view from the Jas de Bouffan at Aix with Mount Sainte-Victoire in the background.

Date: 1881–1882. For discussion see pp. 26, 30.

54

Portrait of Madame Cézanne, on a sheet with a study of two chairs. Collection Mr. and Mrs. Leigh Block, Chicago.
Pencil on white paper; page XLVI in a sketchbook measuring 12.6 × 21.7 cm. (Rewald, *Carnet V*).
Verso: Sketch of Cézanne's son (No. 132).
Literature: Rewald, *Carnet V*, p. XLVI.
Date: Ca. 1881–1882.

55

Two portraits of Madame Cézanne sewing, on a sheet with a study of two figures for an erotic theme and a study of a right shoulder and arm. Collection Sir Kenneth and Lady Clark, London.
Pencil on white paper, 31.6 × 24.5–25.0 cm., half of a sheet originally measuring approximately 30 × 50 cm.[1]
Verso: Two sketches of Madame Cézanne (No. 62).
Literature: Venturi, Cat. No. 1477, dated 1886–1890; Aix-en-Provence, Pavillon de Vendôme, *Exposition Cézanne*, 1961, Cat. No. 43, dated ca. 1880.
Date: Ca. 1881–1882.

56 n.r.

Portrait of Madame Cézanne. Collection Mr. and Mrs. Ira Haupt, New York.
Pencil on white paper; page XLII verso in a sketchbook measuring 12.6 × 21.7 cm. (Rewald, *Carnet I*).
Verso: Study after Coustou's *Buste de G. de la Tour* in the Louvre, similar to V. 1395.
Literature: Rewald, *Carnet I,* p. 42 verso, not reproduced.

This drawing is on the verso of a framed drawing and cannot be inspected.

1 See No. 1, note 1.

57

Portrait of Madame Cézanne, head inclined to the right.
Present location unknown. Formerly Collection Werner
Feuz, Zurich.
Pencil on paper, approximately 10 × 13.5 cm. as reproduced.
Verso: Unknown.
Literature: Venturi, Cat. No. 1246, dated 1880–1885.

This drawing is possibly from the same original sheet as
No. 261. For the same paper, see No. 138.

Date: Ca. 1882–1883.

58

Sketch of Madame Cézanne asleep, on a sheet with a copy
after a soldier in Michelangelo's *Battle of Cascina*. Collec-
tion Adrien Chappuis, Tresserve (Savoie).
Pencil on white paper; page XLVIII in a sketchbook measur-
ing 12.6 × 21.5 cm. (Chappuis II).
Verso: Two sketches of soldiers, after Michelangelo's
Battle of Cascina. (Berthold, Cat. No. 256, dated the second
half of the 1870's.)
Literature: Venturi, Cat. No. 1297.
Date: 1882–1883. For discussion see p. 32.

59

Portrait of Madame Cézanne, on a sheet with a portrait of
Louis-Auguste Cézanne (204). Fogg Art Museum, Harvard
University; bequeathed in 1962 by Mrs. Charles Phinney,
Cambridge. Formerly Collections Otto Gerson, New York;
Walter Feilchenfeld, Zurich; Adrien Chappuis, Tresserve
(Savoie), who acquired it in 1934 from Cézanne *fils* through
the dealer Paul Guillaume.
Pencil on white paper; page XLI verso from a sketchbook
measuring 12.6 × 21.5 cm. (Chappuis II).
Verso: Sketch of an interior corner, perhaps in Cézanne's
studio.
Literature: Paris, Musée de l'Orangerie, *Cézanne*, 1936, Cat.
No. 157; Venturi, under Cat. No. 1293, not reproduced.
Date: 1882–1883. For discussion see p. 32.

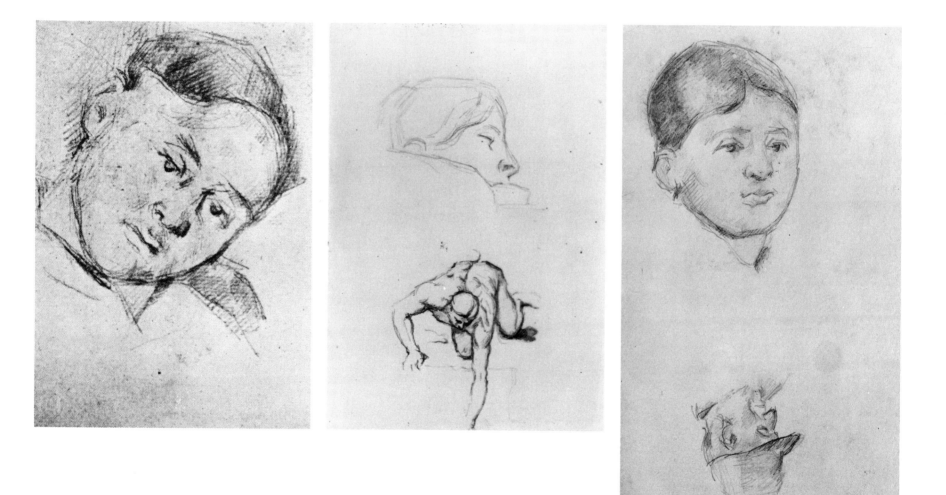

61

Portrait of Madame Cézanne, on a sheet with a sketch of a round object, probably an orange. Collection Adrien Chappuis, Tresserve (Savoie).
Pencil on paper; page XXXIII from a sketchbook measuring 15 × 23.8 cm. (Chappuis II).
Verso: Sketch of a landscape.
Literature: Venturi, Vol. I, p. 307 (description in error); Chappuis, 1938, No. 24.
Date: 1883–1884.

60 detail

Portrait of Madame Cézanne, on a sheet with several studies of a female nude. Collection Adrien Chappuis, Tresserve (Savoie).
Pencil on white paper; facing pages XLIV verso and XLV in a sketchbook measuring 12.6 × 21.5 cm. (Chappuis II).
Verso: Left-hand side: a sketch of a partial figure, seen from the back, and the notation "43 chez Vollard"; right-hand side: an unidentified head and a pitcher.
Literature: Venturi, Cat. No. 1295.

Venturi did not recognize in this portrait a resemblance to Madame Cézanne, but he did point out that the figure studies were of a live model. I would suggest that the figure is Cézanne's wife, who, before meeting Cézanne, was an artist's model. As Cézanne was reluctant to pose nude female models, it is reasonable to assume that he employed his own mistress. We know that she had long hair (see V. 527), and her profession would suggest a well-formed and attractive body. Venturi suggested that his Cat. Nos. 710 and 1096, showing a standing female nude (considerably older in V. 710), were probably modeled by Cézanne's wife; if this is true, it is possible that a number of female figures in Cézanne's bather compositions were also modeled by Madame Cézanne.

This drawing served as a study for a number of paintings, V. 382–386, and 547.[1] Another sketch of this figure appears in Rewald, *Carnet V*, p. XLVII, along with modifications of the pose on both recto and verso of this sheet. The anatomy is closer to that of the painted standing nude, V. 710,[2] and a watercolor, V. 1091.

Date: 1882–1883. For discussion see p. 32.

---

1   Venturi pointed this out with regard to V. 383, 385, 386.

2   See Berthold, Figs. 35, 37, for comparisons of V. 710 with similar poses in bather compositions.

62

Two portraits of Madame Cézanne asleep. Collection Sir
Kenneth and Lady Clark, London.
Pencil on white paper, 24.5 × 31.6 cm.; half of a sheet
originally measuring approximately 30 × 50 cm.[1]
Verso: No. 55.
Literature: Unpublished.
Date: 1882–1883. For discussion see p. 32.

63

Portrait of Madame Cézanne. Collection W. S. Schiess,
Basel. Formerly owned by Adrien Chappuis, Tresserve
(Savoie), who acquired it in 1934 from Cézanne *fils* through
the dealer Paul Guillaume.
Pencil on gray paper, approximately 12 × 15 cm.
Verso: Unknown.
Literature: Paris, Musée de l'Orangerie, *Cézanne,* 1936, Cat.
No. 155, dated ca. 1885; *Correspondance,* Fig. 27, dated ca.
1885; John Rewald, *Cézanne,* New York, 1948, p. 116, dated
ca. 1885; Chappuis, 1957, No. 43, dated ca. 1885.

For this particular head shape see V. 369.

Date: 1882–1883. For discussion see p. 32.

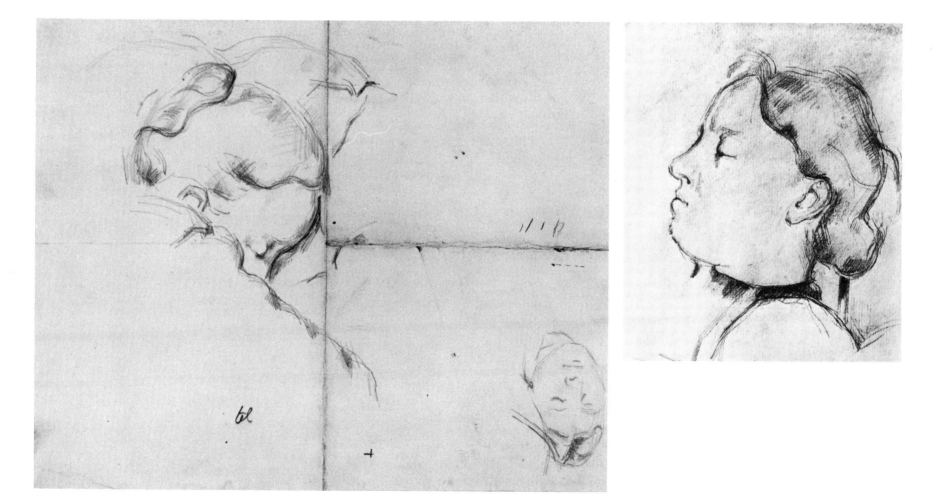

64

Several incomplete sketches, some probably of Madame
Cézanne; one perhaps of Cézanne's son (not catalogued); a
study of the handle of a pair of scissors and a cooking pot.
Albertina, Vienna.
Pencil on paper.
Verso: Two portraits of Cézanne's son (No. 131), a study of
a nude male bather with outstretched arms, a drinking
glass, and a study of a sculptured figure on an eighteenth-
century clock.
Literature: Unpublished.

Three of the heads seem to be of Madame Cézanne: the
uppermost head relates to one in No. 40; the head to the
left of the scissors compares with the lowest head in No. 65,
which also includes an unfinished head similar to some of
those on this sheet.

If the boy at the upper left is Cézanne's son, he would be
between ten and twelve years old—approximately the age
of the child in No. 65.

Date: 1882–1886.

65

Two portraits of Madame Cézanne, on a sheet with a portrait of Cézanne's son (No. 163), a copy after Pedro de Moya,[1] a copy of a sculptured figure on an eighteenth-century clock, and miscellaneous studies. Collection Sir Kenneth and Lady Clark, London.
Pencil on coarse, textured, white paper, deckle edges, 31.1–32.0 × 49.5 cm., folded in half; one of several sheets measuring approximately 30 × 50 cm.[2]
Verso: Self-portrait (No. 21), on a sheet with a copy after a Goya self-portrait, a study of an apple, a running female bather, and other sketches.
Literature: Venturi, cited at Cat. No. 1474; Berthold, Cat. No. 328 (the copy after Pedro de Moya not identified).

See No. 21.

Date: 1884–1886.

66 n.r.

Madame Cézanne asleep, on a sheet with a study of foliage.
Present location unknown.
Pencil and watercolor on paper, 30.5 × 46 cm.
Verso: Unknown.
Literature: Venturi, Cat. No. 1100, dated 1883–1887.
Date: Ca. 1884–1887.

1 Identification by Robert Ratcliffe. See Adrien Chappuis, "Cézanne dessina-teur: copies et illustrations," *Gazette des Beaux-Arts*, ser. 6, LXVI, 1965, p. 297, No. 9.

2 See No. 1, note 1.

67

Portrait of Madame Cézanne, seated in a chair, sewing.
Present location unknown. Originally Collection Ambroise
Vollard, Paris.
Pencil on white paper, 48 × 31.5 cm.; probably one of sev-
eral sheets used by Cézanne that measured approximately
30 × 50 cm.[1]
Verso: Unknown.
Literature: Vollard, frontispiece; Julius Meier-Graefe,
Cézanne und sein Kreis, Munich, 1922, p. 37; Rotterdam,
Museum Boymans, *Dessins d'Ingres à Seurat*, 1933, Cat.
No. 5; Venturi, Cat. No. 1466, dated 1886–1890.
Date: 1885–1888.

68

Portrait of Madame Cézanne, on a sheet with a sketch of a
lady's waist and bustle. Private collection. Formerly Col-
lections O. T. Falk, New York; Mrs. E. F. Hutton, New York
(acquired in 1952 through Fine Arts Associates, New York),
sold at Sotheby's, London, in 1965.
Pencil on white paper, 28 × 21 cm.
Verso: Not examined.
Literature: Fine Arts Associates, New York, *Cézanne*, 1952,
Cat. No. 6; Neumeyer, Cat. No. 35, dated 1880–1885.
Date: 1886–1888.

1 See No. 1, note 1.

69

Portrait of Madame Cézanne. Museum Boymans-van Beuningen, Rotterdam; gift of D. G. van Beuningen in 1940. Formerly Collections F. Koenigs, Haarlem; Paul Cassirer, Berlin; S. Meller, Budapest; Ambroise Vollard, Paris. Pencil on coarse white paper, 48.5–6 × 31.4–32.2 cm., deckle edges. One of several sheets measuring approximately 30 × 50 cm.[1]

Verso: Blank; the indicia "PH/24" in red chalk at lower right corner.[2]

Literature: Rotterdam, Museum Boymans, *Teekeningen van Ingres tot Seurat,* 1933, Cat. No. 6; Haarlem, *Fransche Impressionisten,* 1935, Cat. No. 33; Basel, Kunsthalle, *Meisterzeichnungen französischer Künstler von Ingres bis Cézanne,* 1936, Cat. No. 136; Venturi, Cat. No. 1467, dated 1883–1886; Amsterdam, Cassirer, *Fransche Meesters uit de XIX eeuw,* 1938, Cat. No. 21; Amsterdam, Rijksmuseum, *Teekeningen van Fransche Meesters,* 1946, Cat. No. 14; Paris, Musée du Louvre, *Le dessin français de Fouquet à Cézanne,* 1949, Cat. No. 206; Jacqueline Bouchot-Saupique, *De Fouquet à Cézanne (Art et Style,* 14), Paris, 1950; Paris, Bibliothèque Nationale, *Dessins du XVᵉ au XIXᵉ siècle du Musée Boymans de Rotterdam,* 1952, Cat. No. 141; Washington, D.C., National Gallery of Art, *French Drawings, Masterpieces from Five Centuries,* 1952, Cat. No. 45; François Daulte, *Le dessin français de Manet à Cézanne,* Paris, 1954, Fig. 44; Chicago, Art Institute, *French Drawings, Masterpieces from Seven Centuries,* 1955, Cat. No. 156; Neumeyer, Cat. No. 37, dated 1883–1886; Aix-en-Provence, Pavillon de Vendôme, *Cézanne,* 1961, Cat. No. 97; Paris, Institut Néerlandais, *Le dessin français de Claude à Cézanne dans les collections hollandaises,* 1964, Cat. No. 202, dated 1890–1894; Anne van Buren, "Madame Cézanne's Fashions and the Date of Her Portraits," *The Art Quarterly,* XXIX, 1966, p. 118, dated 1886–1888; Hoetink, Cat. No. 34.

Venturi's date, 1883–1886, was based on comparison with certain painted portraits of Madame Cézanne, especially V. 520, 524, 525. In the catalogue of the Paris, 1964, exhibition, the later date, 1890–1894, is supported both by the apparent age of the subject and by a stylistic comparison with the *Fumeur* (254), which, according to the same source, dates also from 1890–1894.

Date: 1888–1892. For discussion see pp. 32, 40.

1 See No. 1, note 1.

2 This mark appears on other Cézanne drawings. See Chappuis, Vol. I, p. 125, note 30.

70

Portrait of Madame Cézanne. Collection Adrien Chappuis, Tresserve (Savoie).
Pencil on white paper; page VII in a sketchbook measuring 15 × 23.8 cm. (Chappuis III).
Verso: Blank.
Literature: *L'Arte,* September 1935, Pl. 9, Fig. 18; Paris, Musée de l'Orangerie, *Cézanne,* 1936, Cat. No. 160, dated ca. 1888; Venturi, Cat. No. 1303; Chappuis, 1938, No. 32; Raymond Cogniat, *Cézanne,* Paris, 1939, p. 111; Gustaf Engwall, *Cézanne,* Stockholm, 1957, opp. p. 72, dated 1887; Neumeyer, Cat. No. 36, dated 1890; Chappuis, *Album,* No. VII, dated 1890–1891.

Following a suggestion in the catalogue of the Orangerie exhibition of 1936, Neumeyer relates the age, pose, and dress of Madame Cézanne in this drawing to the oil portrait, *Madame Cézanne in the Conservatory,* V. 569.

Date: Ca. 1892–1894. For discussion see p. 40.

71

Portrait of Madame Cézanne. Collection Adrien Chappuis, Tresserve (Savoie).
Pencil on white paper; page IX verso in a sketchbook measuring 15 × 23.8 cm. (Chappuis III).
Verso: Two portraits of Cézanne's son (No. 178).
Literature: San Francisco, Museum of Art, *Paul Cézanne,* 1937, Cat. No. 63, dated 1879–1882; Paris, Musée de l'Orangerie, *Cézanne,* 1936, Cat. No. 156, dated 1885–1887; Venturi, under Cat. No. 1304; Lyon, Musée de Lyon, *Paul Cézanne,* 1939, Cat. No. 65; Wildenstein & Co. Ltd., London, *Homage to Paul Cézanne,* 1939, Cat. No. 87; Chappuis, 1957, Cat. No. 14, dated 1885–1887. Henri Perruchot, *La Vie de Cézanne,* Paris, 1958, reproduction inverted, p. 277; Chappuis, *Album,* No. IX verso, dated 1887–1889; Theodore Reff, review of Chappuis, *Album, The Burlington Magazine,* CIX, 1967, p. 653, dated ca. 1890.

In the Orangerie catalogue this drawing is associated with a painted portrait of Madame Cézanne, dated 1885–1890 by Venturi (V. 523) and 1885–1887 in the catalogue (No. 65).

Date: Ca. 1892–1894. For discussion see p. 40.

72

Portrait of Madame Cézanne(?). Collection Adrien Chappuis, Tresserve (Savoie).
Pencil on white paper, page XI verso in a sketchbook measuring 15 × 23.8 cm. (Chappuis III).
Verso: Unidentified sketch, probably the beginning of a landscape study.
Literature: Venturi, under Cat. No. 1304, not reproduced; Chappuis, 1938, Cat. No. 26; *idem, Album,* No. XI verso, dated 1890–1895, not identified.
Date: 1892–1896.

73

Portrait of an unidentified woman, probably Madame Cézanne, on a sheet with a nude female figure. Kunstmuseum, Basel.
Pencil on white paper, 12.6 × 20.5 cm: page XXVIII from a sketchbook (Basel III).
Verso: Draft of a letter (Chappuis, Cat. No. 165).
Literature: Venturi, Cat. No. 1434; Chappuis, Cat. No. 130, dated 1885–1895.

The nude figure appears also at the left in the paintings V. 282 and V. 547. Madame Cézanne may have been the model for this drawing and for the central bather in these paintings. See No. 60.

Date: 1892–1896.

74

Portrait of Madame Cézanne. Collection Adrien Chappuis, Tresserve (Savoie).
Pencil on white paper; page XLVIII verso in a sketchbook measuring 12 × 19.5 cm. (Chappuis I).
Verso: Copy after Michelangelo's *Bound Slave* in the Louvre. (Berthold, Cat. No. 116, dated 1882–1883.)
Literature: Paris, Musée de l'Orangerie, *Cézanne,* 1936, Cat. No. 162; Venturi, Cat. No. 1280.
Date: Mid-1890's. For discussion see p. 40.

75 fac.

Portrait of Madame Cézanne. Collection Adrien Chappuis, Tresserve (Savoie).
Pencil on white paper; page XII in a sketchbook measuring 15 × 23.8 cm. (Chappuis III).
Verso: A rococo escutcheon (Chappuis, 1938, No. 48).
Literature: Venturi, under Cat. No. 1304, not reproduced; Chappuis, *Album,* No. XII, dated 1878–1882; Theodore Reff, review of Chappuis, *Album, The Burlington Magazine,* CIX, 1967, p. 653, dated ca. 1890.
Date: 1892–1894.

76

Two portrait sketches of Madame Cézanne. Collection
Adrien Chappuis, Tresserve (Savoie).
Pencil on white paper; page XIII verso in a sketchbook
measuring 12 × 19.5 cm. (Chappuis I).
Verso: Blank.
Literature: Venturi, under Cat. No. 1270, not reproduced.
Date: Mid-1890's. For discussion see p. 40.

77 fac.

Two heads of a woman, perhaps Madame Cézanne. Collection Adrien Chappuis, Tresserve (Savoie).
Pencil on white paper; page XIV in a sketchbook measuring 15 × 23.8 cm. (Chappuis III).
Verso: Head of a woman, perhaps Madame Cézanne (No. 78).
Literature: Venturi, under Cat. No. 1304, not reproduced.
Chappuis, *Album,* No. XIV, dated ca. 1894, not identified.
Date: Ca. 1894–1896. For discussion see p. 40.

Portrait of Madame Cézanne. Collection Adrien Chappuis, Tresserve (Savoie).
Pencil on white paper; page XIV verso in a sketchbook measuring 15 × 23.8 cm. (Chappuis III).
Verso: Two female heads, perhaps Madame Cézanne (No. 77).
Literature: Venturi, under Cat. No. 1304, not reproduced; Chappuis, 1938, No. 34; Aix-en-Provence, Pavillon de Vendôme, *Paul Cézanne,* 1961, Cat. No. 53; Chappuis, *Album,* No. XIV verso, dated ca. 1894, not identified.

Neither Venturi nor Chappuis identifies this head as Madame Cézanne.

Date: Ca. 1894–1896. For discussion see p. 40.

Portrait of Madame Cézanne, on a sheet with a study for *Carnaval.* Collection Adrien Chappuis, Tresserve (Savoie).
Pencil on white paper; page LI verso in a sketchbook measuring 15 × 23.8 cm. (Chappuis III).
Verso: Blank.
Literature: Venturi, under Cat. No. 1314, not reproduced; Chappuis, *Album,* No. LI verso, dated 1883–1887.
Date: Ca. 1892–1896. For discussion see p. 40.

Sketch of Madame Cézanne in bed, head resting on a pillow, on a sheet with a study of Cézanne's son (No. 187) and a sketch of an unidentified figure. Collection Adrien Chappuis, Tresserve (Savoie).
Pencil on white paper; page XXXI bis in a sketchbook measuring 15 × 23.8 cm. (Chappuis III).
Verso: Unidentified sketches.
Literature: Venturi, under Cat. No. 1309, not reproduced; Chappuis, *Album,* No. XXXI bis, portrait of Madame Cézanne dated 1877–1882, portrait of Cézanne's son dated 1882–1885.
Date: Ca. 1894–1896. For discussion see p. 40.

81 fac.

Head of Madame Cézanne(?) on a sheet with the address
''Antonio Franchi, Avenue du Maine, 124.'' Collection
Adrien Chappuis, Tresserve (Savoie).
Pencil on white paper; page XXI in a sketchbook measur-
ing 15 × 23.8 cm. (Chappuis III).
Verso: Head of Cézanne's son (No. 183).
Literature: Venturi, under Cat. No. 1306, not reproduced;
Chappuis, *Album,* No. XXI, dated ca. 1880, not identified.
Date: 1894–1898.

104

82 fac.

Portrait of Madame Cézanne(?). Collection Adrien Chappuis, Tresserve (Savoie).
Pencil on white paper; page XV in a sketchbook measuring 15 × 23.8 cm. (Chappuis III).
Verso: Interior scene: a seated woman in a bedroom seen through an open door.
Literature: Venturi, under Cat. No. 1304, not reproduced.
Chappuis, *Album*, No. XV, dated 1890–1894, not identified.
Date: Ca. 1894–1898.

83

Sketch of Madame Cézanne. Collection Adrien Chappuis,
Tresserve (Savoie).
Pencil on white paper, with touches of watercolor at the
upper left corner; page XXXIV in a sketchbook measuring
21 × 27.3 cm. (Chappuis IV).
Verso: Touches of watercolor.
Literature: Venturi, under Cat. No. 1316, not reproduced.
Date: Ca. 1896–1898. For discussion see p. 40.

84

Portrait of Madame Cézanne(?), on a sheet with a small
unidentified head. Collection Adrien Chappuis, Tresserve
(Savoie).
Pencil on white paper; page XLIII in a sketchbook measur-
ing 12 × 19.5 cm. (Chappuis I).
Verso: Drawing of a child writing.
Literature: Venturi, under Cat. No. 1275, neither repro-
duced nor identified.

The smaller head resembles the female head in No. 8.

Date: Mid-1890's. For discussion see p. 40.

85 fac.

Portrait of Madame Cézanne. Collection Adrien Chappuis, Tresserve (Savoie).
Pencil on white paper; page XVII in a sketchbook measuring 15 × 23.8 cm. (Chappuis III).
Verso: Sketch of Cézanne's son writing (No. 179).
Literature: Venturi, under Cat. No. 1304, not reproduced; Chappuis, 1938, No. 36; *idem, Album,* No. XVII, dated 1891–1895.

The verification of the subject as Madame Cézanne depends on the identification of the two drawings that follow.

Date: Ca. 1894–1896. For discussion see p. 40.

86

Sketch of Madame Cézanne, on a sheet with notations in Cézanne's hand. Collection Mademoiselle Edmée Maus, Geneva. Formerly Collection Jean-Pierre Cézanne; sold through Bernheim-Jeune in 1956.
Pencil on white paper; unpaginated sheet in a pocket notebook measuring 10.2 × 6.8 cm. (*Carnet violet-moiré*).
Verso: A landscape sketch and notations in Cézanne's hand.
Literature: Facsimile of notebook printed by Daniel Jacomet for Quatre Chemins-Editart, Paris [1956], unpaginated; Berthold, p. 159, Cat. No. 7; Chappuis, Vol. I, p. 124, note 8, the complete sketchbook dated 1890–1896; Wayne V. Andersen, "Cézanne's *Carnet violet-moiré,*" *The Burlington Magazine,* CVII, 1965, pp. 313–318, dated 1894–1896.
Date: 1894–1896. For discussion see pp. 39, 40.

87

Portrait of Madame Cézanne, on a sheet with a sketch of a female bather entering the water. Collection Robert von Hirsch, Basel; acquired in 1934 from Cézanne *fils.*
Pencil on white paper, with touches of red watercolor on the side of the face; page X from a sketchbook measuring 12.5 × 20.5 cm. (Basel III).
Verso: Touches of watercolor (V. 1412, description in error).
Literature: John Rewald, *Cézanne et Zola,* Paris, 1936, Fig. 45 (without the bather); Venturi, Cat. No. 1411.

Venturi has suggested that the touch of watercolor on the side of the head may have been intended to efface the image. Cézanne may have added the color, however, at the same time that he deepened with watercolor the shadows of the two bathers on the facing page of the sketchbook. Had he wished to destroy the image, he would have applied the color to the features (in the way that he defaced V. 1332, 1333, 1337) rather than to the side of the head, which is usually modeled by dark tones.

Date: Late 1880's. For discussion see p. 40.

88

Portrait of Madame Cézanne. Collection Adrien Chappuis, Tresserve (Savoie).
Pencil and watercolor on white paper; page XXVII in a sketchbook measuring 21 × 27.3 cm. (Chappuis IV).
Verso: Blank.
Literature: Venturi, under Cat. No. 1316, not reproduced.

See also V. 1093.

Date: Ca. 1892–1898.

89 fac.

Portrait of Madame Cézanne. Collection Heinz Berggruen, Paris; originally Collection Mr. and Mrs. John Rewald, New York.
Pencil on white paper, 17.2 × 12 cm.
Verso: Blank.
Literature: Munich, Haus der Kunst, *Cézanne*, 1956, Cat. No. 137; Wildenstein & Co., New York, *Cézanne*, 1959, Cat. No. 65, dated 1885; Theodore Reff, "A New Exhibition of Cézanne," *The Burlington Magazine*, CII, 1960, pp. 114 ff., dated ca. 1895; Hamburg, Kunstverein, *Cézanne, Gauguin, Van Gogh, Seurat*, 1963, Cat. No. 28, Fig. 77, dated ca. 1880.

In Reff's review of the Wildenstein exhibition "A New Exhibition of Cézanne" he disputes the date 1885 for this drawing and suggests a date perhaps ten years later, on the evidence of the age of Madame Cézanne, who, in his opinion, appears to be about forty-five here. He adds, "She is certainly older than in V. 526 (1883–1887) and probably older than in V. 571 (1890–1894)." The date assigned to the drawing in the catalogue of the Hamburg exhibition, ca. 1880, shows considerable uncertainty in the estimation of her age.

Date: Ca. 1894–1896. For discussion see p. 40.

90 fac.

Portrait of Madame Cézanne, on a sheet with a portrait of
Cézanne's son (No. 186). Collection Adrien Chappuis,
Tresserve (Savoie).
Pencil on white paper; page XXIV in a sketchbook measur-
ing 15 × 23.8 cm. (Chappuis III).
Verso: Blank.
Literature: Venturi, under Cat. No. 1306, not reproduced;
Chappuis, 1938, No. 11; *idem, Album,* No. XXIV, dated 1891–
1895, not identified.

Venturi identified both these heads as Cézanne's son.
Chappuis described them simply as "deux têtes." The hair
line and the face of the right figure are without doubt those
of Madame Cézanne; see No. 85.

Date: Ca. 1894–1898. For discussion see p. 40.

91 fac.

Portrait of Madame Cézanne. Collection Adrien Chappuis, Tresserve (Savoie).

Pencil on white paper; page XIII in a sketchbook measuring 15 × 23.8 cm. (Chappuis III).

Verso: Sketch of an unidentified statue.

Literature: Venturi, under Cat. No. 1304, not reproduced; Chappuis, 1938, No. 30, not identified; *idem, Album,* No. XIII, dated "vers 1900."

Venturi described this portrait as unfinished, but it is actually complete and is roughly contemporary with a number of copies of sculpture that show the same omission of the contour on one side.[1] In a photograph of Madame Cézanne (91a) that portrays her at a later age than in this drawing, there is an effect of strong light and shadow; it may have been just such an effect that influenced Cézanne in omitting the contour of the lighted portion of the face. A second photograph (9lb), helps also to identify the sitter; it does not bear a date but, on the basis of comparison with photograph 91a (which was taken at the end of Madame Cézanne's life), is generally considered to be of about 1900. In my opinion it was probably taken during the second half of the nineties.

Date: Ca. 1894–1898. For discussion see p. 40.

---

1 For examples see Berthold, Cat. Nos. 46, 49, 174, and 177.

Portrait of Madame Cézanne attributed to Cézanne. Present
location unknown.
Pencil.
Literature: Unpublished.

This drawing appeared on the art market in 1961. In my
opinion it is not in Cézanne's hand, but rather in the same
hand that executed Nos. 29 and 197.

Four portrait sketches of Cézanne's son on a sheet with two portraits of Madame Cézanne, a seventh head (perhaps of Cézanne's son), a clock, and a child's spoon.
Literature: Venturi, Cat. No. 1222, dated 1872–1873.

See No. 30.

Date: Ca. 1874.

Portrait sketch of Cézanne's son, on a sheet with a study of two men wrestling and a striding female bather. Kunstmuseum, Basel.
Pencil on white paper, 18.2 × 26.2 cm., half of a larger sheet; the other half is lost.
Verso: The lower half of a commercial lithograph from *Le Monde illustré*, No. 37, Paris, 1870.[1]
Literature: Chappuis, Cat. No. 83, dated 1870–1878; Douglas Cooper, review of Adrien Chappuis, *Les Dessins de Cézanne au Musée de Bâle*, in *Master Drawings*, I, No. 4, 1963, p. 56, dated ca. 1876 (he dates the entire sheet 1876–1878).

Chapuis' date extends from the years 1870–1872 for the wrestling men to about 1878 for the sketch of the child. The earlier date is based on Chappuis' attempt to equate the wrestlers with the man embracing a woman in V. 1201, which he has dated 1870–1872. A reasonable comparison could have been made with V. 235, which shows at the left side a pair of men in a similar attitude. Cooper disputes Chappuis' date and suggests about 1876 for the wrestlers and about 1877 for the striding bather; Chappuis, showing considerable uncertainty in the use of stylistic evidence, dates the latter 1872–1876.

As the child appears here to be four years old, the portrait must date from about 1876. The style invites comparison with the drawings in the Chicago sketchbook that are exactly contemporary, especially those on pages II and L verso (No. 39); on the latter page there is a similar combination of styles. The style of the wrestling men here seems related to that of the walking man on Chicago L verso (see the discussion at No. 39).

Since this is half of a larger sheet, the lower part of the child's head is missing. It could be assumed that Cézanne chose to keep the bather study as an examplar for bather compositions: modifications of this pose appear at the left side of some eighteen paintings of female bathers, among the earliest of which are V. 267 and 270, both dating from 1875–1876.

Date: Ca. 1876. For discussion see pp. 17–18, 20–21.

95 fac.

Sketch of Cézanne's son, on a sheet with a drawing of a goblet, notations in Cézanne's hand, and the word "cézanne" in the hand of the child. Art Institute of Chicago. Pencil on white paper; page II verso in a sketchbook measuring 12.4 × 21.7 cm. (Rewald, *Carnet II*).
Verso: Drawings by Cézanne's son.
Literature: Rewald, *Carnet II*, p. II; Schniewind, Cat. No. II; Wayne V. Andersen, "Cézanne's Sketchbook in the Art Institute of Chicago," *The Burlington Magazine*, CIV, 1962, pp. 196–201.
Date: Ca. 1876.

96 fac.

Portrait of Cézanne's son sleeping, on a sheet with a drawing by the child. Kunstmuseum, Basel.
Pencil on white paper (the child's drawing in charcoal), 13.3 × 20.8 cm., probably from a sketchbook.
Verso: Sketch of a male figure, three-quarter view from the back, with outstretched arms, and turned toward a nude woman seated on a divan; study of a roof in watercolor (Chappuis Cat. No. 57, dated 1872–1878).
Literature: Venturi, Vol. I, p. 351, not reproduced; Chappuis, Cat. No. 82, dated 1872–1878.

Both Venturi and Chappuis have judged this to be a female head: Venturi entitled it "tête de femme endormie"; Chappuis called it "tête d'un enfant," but added that "à en juger par la chevelure indiquée près de l'oreille ce dessin représente une fillette."

The lines to which Chappuis refers do not represent hair but indicate Cézanne's characteristic preliminary graphic process. The same repetition of vague contour lines can be seen on and beneath the chin and along the line of the cheek. The solid line below the ear probably defines bedclothes—it seems continuous with the wavy line under the chin, which, by faint traces, passes around the shoulder. The physiognomy can be compared with Nos. 95 and 110: the round face, full lips, and the broad setting of the eyes are characteristic of the child.

The other drawing was probably made by Cézanne's son. It is a composition of streets with houses and a person in each of the upper two. The people were conceived first as "heads," and then their bodies were drawn with two lines extending down to the floor. The child drew the houses in the same manner, i.e., a roof and a "body," with neither the people nor the houses differentiated further. This type of rendering is typical of children at the age of about four years.

The sheet bears an imprint of what may have been the preceding page of a sketchbook. Though confused and indistinct, a composition of three figures can be made out: at the left, a male figure is kneeling on one knee before a central, standing figure who has extended one hand toward the other's forehead. There seems to be another figure on the left, but his pose is not clear.

Date: Ca. 1876.

119

97 detail

Portrait of Cézanne's son, on a sheet with a portrait of Madame Cézanne (No. 35) and a sketch of a garment. Present location unknown. Formerly Collection Sir Kenneth and Lady Clark.

See Nos. 35 and 98.

Date: Ca. 1877. For discussion see pp. 18–19, 21.

98 n.r.

One or more portraits of Cézanne's son, on a sheet with one or more portraits of Madame Cézanne. Present location unknown. Formerly Collection Sir Kenneth and Lady Clark, London.
Pencil on beige paper, approximately 22 × 23 cm.
Verso: Portrait of Madame Cézanne (No. 35), one of Cézanne's son (No. 97), and a study of a garment.

Not examined. See the discussion of the verso at No. 35.

99

Portrait of Cézanne's son on a sheet with a study of a coffee pot. Collection Benjamin Sonnenberg, New York. Formerly Collection Sir Kenneth and Lady Clark, London.
Pencil on beige paper, irregular edges, approximately 20 × 24 cm.
Verso: Two portraits of Madame Cézanne (No. 33), on a sheet with a portrait of Chocquet (No. 212).
Literature: Venturi, Cat. No. 1240 verso, not reproduced.
Date: 1876–1877.

100

Portrait of Cézanne's son; two sketches of a male figure from the back, perhaps fishing; a sketch of a female head; a standing fisherman from the back. All are on the periphery of a sheet with an engraving of an eighteenth-century rococo vase. Collection J. K. Thannhauser, New York. Pencil on white paper, 32.0 × 24.0 cm.
Verso: Drawing of a panoramic view of L'Estaque; the same motif as in Rewald, *Carnet II,* pp. V and XIV, and V. 407.
Literature: Neumeyer, Cat. No. 13, dated "probably 1878."

Neumeyer's date of 1878 is correct in regard to the age of the child, who seems to be about six years old—the age he appears to be in the Chicago sketchbook (Nos. 107 and 111).

The drawings of the fisherman need not be dated earlier than the one of the child. The sketchlike quality of these drawings persists throughout the seventies. A similar fisherman in much the same technique appears on the verso of a Cézanne letter dating from ca. 1878 (V. 1231 and 1232). The elongated proportions of the figure are typical of the later seventies and are especially predominant in the bather compositions after 1875–1876.

Neumeyer's date of 1870–1872 for the view of L'Estaque on the verso is much too early. He related the flowing lines and the general style of the drawing to V. 51, *Melting Snow at L'Estaque,* which dates from early 1871, but the drawing was made from the same point of view as and is stylistically akin to V. 407, for which it may have been a study. The house that appears at the left in both the drawing and in V. 407 was singled out by Cézanne on a page in the Chicago sketchbook and was, in turn, copied by Cézanne's son on the facing page when he was about six—the age he appears to be on the recto of the Thannhauser sheet.[1]

Date: 1878.

1 Wayne V. Andersen, "Cézanne's Sketchbook in the Art Institute of Chicago," *The Burlington Magazine,* CIV, 1962, pp. 196–201.

101

Portrait of Cézanne's son, on a sheet with drawings by a child, perhaps by Cézanne's sister Rose. Kunstmuseum, Basel.

Pencil on white paper, 22.8 × 35 cm. (Four of the child's drawings are in India ink.)

Verso: Many sketches of violent scenes, murders, and rapes (Chappuis, Cat. No. 4, dated 1864–1867, equated erroneously with an unpublished drawing in the collection of Sir Kenneth Clark, in Venturi, Vol. I, p. 349, *Meurtre*).

Literature: Venturi, Vol. I, p. 352, not reproduced; Chappuis, Cat. No. 96, dated 1876–1878.

My suggestion that the several childish drawings on this sheet were made by Cézanne's younger sister Rose (born in 1854) is based on a comparison with a sheet in the Louvre's *Carnet de jeunesse*, fol. 35, which includes several drawings in both pencil and India ink in a similar hand, with the signature "rose cézanne." (The possibility that the name may have been written by Cézanne himself is ruled out by comparing the writing of "Rose" in the *Carnet de*

jeunesse with the name as it appears in a poem written by Cézanne for his sister that, according to Rewald, dates from late 1858.[1]) Both the drawings on the Louvre sheet and those on the Basel sheet were made by a child between ten and twelve years old, and therefore can be assigned to 1864–1866. This date agrees with that suggested by Cézanne's grandson, Jean-Pierre, for the sketchbook now owned by Henry Pearlman, New York, which also contains a few childish drawings not in Cézanne's hand and apparently made by Rose.

Chappuis dates the verso of this sheet 1864–1867, which supports my date for the child's drawings on the recto. Some ten to twelve years later Cézanne used the same sheet for a portrait of his son. The reason that the sheet survived during the intervening time might be that the many studies on the verso served as exemplars for Cézanne's later imaginary compositions. The child's age in this portrait is the same as in the Chicago sketchbook; cf. XLVIII verso (No. 121).

Date: Ca. 1877–1878.

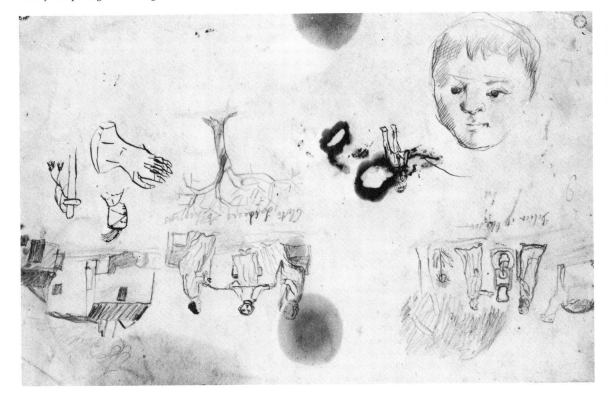

---

1 *Correspondance*, Paris, 1937, p. 48.

102 fac.

Portrait of Cézanne's son, on a sheet with some unidenti-
fiable markings, perhaps made by the child. Art Institute of
Chicago.
Pencil on white paper; page XIII in a sketchbook measuring
12.4 × 21.7 cm. (Rewald, *Carnet II*).
Verso: Sketch of a male figure creeping on all fours; half of a
panoramic view of L'Estaque that continues on the facing
page.
Literature: Rewald, *Carnet II,* p. XIII; Schniewind, Cat. No.
XIII; Reff, "Studies," p. 39, dated "early 1880's"; Wayne V.
Andersen, "Cézanne's Sketchbook in the Art Institute of
Chicago," *The Burlington Magazine,* CIV, 1962, pp. 196–201.
Date: Ca. 1878.

103 n.r.

Sketch of Cézanne's son, worked over by the child himself, and a child's drawing of a man and a woman walking in the rain. Art Institute of Chicago.
Pencil on white paper; page XVI in a sketchbook measuring 12.4 × 21.7 cm. (Rewald, *Carnet II*).
Verso: No. 104.
Literature: Rewald, *Carnet II*, p. XVI; Schniewind, Cat. No. XVI; Wayne V. Andersen, ''Cézanne's Sketchbook in the Art Institute of Chicago,'' *The Burlington Magazine*, CIV, 1962, pp. 196–201.
Date: Ca. 1878.

104 fac.

Portrait of Cézanne's son, on a sheet with a view of L'Estaque and a copy of the portrait by the child. Art Institute of Chicago.
Pencil on white paper; page XVI verso in a sketchbook measuring 12.4 × 21.7 cm. (Rewald, *Carnet II*).
Verso: No. 103.
Literature: Rewald, *Carnet II*, p. XVI verso; Schniewind, Cat. No. XVI verso; Wayne V. Andersen, ''Cézanne's Sketchbook in the Art Institute of Chicago,'' *The Burlington Magazine*, CIV, 1962, pp. 196–201.

Cézanne's son occasionally copied drawings by his father; see especially pages I and IV verso of this sketchbook. Cézanne may have offered helpful advice on this copy, as he was teaching his son to draw. The dark shading of the upper lip, the shadow under the nose, and the careful definition of the eyes are probably not the details that a child of six would select and emphasize, even if the model were immediately adjacent. Yet the awkwardness of the motor tracings suggests that the child was not older than six and was clearly of the same age as when he copied the landscape on p. V of this sketchbook.

Date: Ca. 1878.

105 n.r.

Portrait sketch of Cézanne's son, on a sheet with a land-
scape study. Art Institute of Chicago.
Pencil on white paper; page XXIV verso in a sketchbook
measuring 12.4 × 21.7 cm. (Rewald, *Carnet II*).
Verso: Sketch of a man seated, probably reading a news-
paper.
Literature: Rewald, *Carnet II,* p. XXIV verso; Schniewind,
Cat. No. XXIV verso, dated ca. 1876; Wayne V. Andersen,
"Cézanne's Sketchbook in the Art Institute of Chicago,"
The Burlington Magazine, CIV, 1962, pp. 196–201.
Date: Ca. 1878.

106 n.r.

Defaced sketch of Cézanne's son wearing a hat, on a sheet
with a study of a chair. Art Institute of Chicago.
Pencil on white drawing paper; page XXX in a sketchbook
measuring 12.4 × 21.7 cm. (Rewald, *Carnet II*).
Verso: Two women in a landscape.
Literature: Rewald, *Carnet II,* p. XXX, not identified;
Schniewind, Cat. No. XXX, not identified; Wayne V.
Andersen, "Cézanne's Sketchbook in the Art Institute of
Chicago," *The Burlington Magazine,* CIV, 1962, pp. 196–201.
See No. 116.
Date: Ca. 1878.

107 fac.

Two portraits of Cézanne's son. Art Institute of Chicago.
Pencil on white paper; page XXXIX verso in a sketchbook
measuring 12.4 × 21.7 cm. (Rewald, *Carnet II*).
Verso: A self-portrait sketch (No. 12) and a sketch perhaps
of Madame Cézanne.
Literature: Rewald, *Carnet II,* p. XXXIX verso; Schniewind,
Vol. I, p. 15, and Cat. No. XXXIX verso; Chicago, Art Institute, *Cézanne: Paintings, Watercolors, and Drawings,* 1952,
dated 1877–1878; Yves Taillandier, *Cézanne,* Paris, 1961,
p. 92, the lower image only; Wayne V. Andersen, "Cézanne's Sketchbook in the Art Institute of Chicago," *The
Burlington Magazine,* CIV, 1962, pp. 196–201.
Date: Ca. 1878. For discussion see pp. 20, 22.

108 fac.

Portrait of Cézanne's son on a sheet with the child's drawing of a road crossing over a bridge and the first few strokes
of the letters in the child's name in his own hand. Art
Institute of Chicago.
Pencil on white paper; page XL in a sketchbook measuring
12.4 × 21.7 cm. (Rewald, *Carnet II*).
Verso: A quick sketch of Cézanne's son (No. 109) and a
partial head of a woman, perhaps Madame Cézanne.
Literature: Rewald, *Carnet II*, p. XL; Schniewind, Vol. I,
p. 15, and Cat. No. XL; Wayne V. Andersen, "Cézanne's
Sketchbook in the Art Institute of Chicago," *The Burlington
Magazine*, CIV, 1962, pp. 196–201.
Date: Ca. 1878.

109 n.r.

Portrait sketch of Cézanne's son, on a sheet with a sketch of
a female head, perhaps Madame Cézanne. Art Institute of
Chicago.
Pencil on white paper; page XL verso in a sketchbook
measuring 12.4 × 21.7 cm. (Rewald, *Carnet II*).
Verso: No. 108.
Literature: Rewald, *Carnet II*, p. XL verso; Schniewind, Vol.
I, p. 15, and Cat. No. XL verso; Wayne V. Andersen, "Cé-
zanne's Sketchbook in the Art Institute of Chicago," *The
Burlington Magazine*, CIV, 1962, pp. 196–201.
Date: Ca. 1878.

110 fac.

Portrait of Cézanne's son on a sheet with a study of a landscape motif. Art Institute of Chicago.
Pencil on white paper; page XLI in a sketchbook measuring 12.4 × 21.7 cm. (Rewald, *Carnet II*).
Verso: No. 111.
Literature: Rewald, *Carnet II*, p. XLI; Schniewind, Vol. I, p. 15, and Cat. No. XLI; Meyer Schapiro, *Paul Cézanne*, New York, 1952, p. 27, dated ''1876(?)''; Wayne V. Andersen, ''Cézanne's Sketchbook in the Art Institute of Chicago,'' *The Burlington Magazine*, CIV, 1962, pp. 196–201.

The study of the landscape motif is strikingly similar to the one on the verso of No. 7. Both date from 1878 when Cézanne was painting in the area of L'Estaque.

Date: Ca. 1878.

111 fac.

Portrait of Cézanne's son. Art Institute of Chicago. Pencil on white paper; page XLI verso in a sketchbook measuring 12.4 × 21.7 cm. (Rewald, *Carnet II*).
Verso: No. 110.
Literature: Rewald, *Carnet II,* p. XLI verso; Schniewind, Vol. I, p. 15, and Cat. No. XLI verso; Wayne V. Andersen, ''Cézanne's Sketchbook in the Art Institute of Chicago,'' *The Burlington Magazine,* CIV, 1962, pp. 196–201.
Date: Ca. 1878.

112 fac.

Two portraits of Cézanne's son. Art Institute of Chicago.
Pencil on white paper; page XLIII in a sketchbook measuring 12.4 × 21.7 cm. (Rewald, *Carnet II*).
Verso: No. 113.
Literature: Rewald, *Carnet II*, p. XLIII; Schniewind, Vol. I, p. 15, and Cat. No. XLIII; Meyer Schapiro, *Paul Cézanne,* New York, 1952, p. 27, dated ''1876(?)''; Wayne V. Andersen, ''Cézanne's Sketchbook in the Art Institute of Chicago,'' *The Burlington Magazine,* CIV, 1962, pp. 196–201.
Date: Ca. 1878.

113 fac.

Two portraits of Cézanne's son and a study of an unidentified motif. Art Institute of Chicago.
Pencil on white paper; page XLIII verso in a sketchbook measuring 12.4 × 21.7 cm. (Rewald, *Carnet II*).
Verso: No. 112.
Literature: Rewald, *Carnet II,* p. XLIII verso; Schniewind, Vol. I, p. 15, and Cat. No. XLIII verso; Wayne V. Andersen, "Cézanne's Sketchbook in the Art Institute of Chicago," *The Burlington Magazine,* CIV, 1962, pp. 196–201.
Date: Ca. 1878.

114

Portrait of Cézanne's son, on a sheet with a small sketch of the head and shoulders of a female figure. Art Institute of Chicago.

Ink on white paper; page XLIV in a sketchbook measuring 12.4 × 21.7 cm. (Rewald, *Carnet II*).
Verso: No. 115.
Literature: Rewald, *Carnet II,* p. XLIV; Schniewind, Vol. I, p. 15, and Cat. No. XLIV; Wayne V. Andersen, ''Cézanne's Sketchbook in the Art Institute of Chicago,'' *The Burlington Magazine*, CIV, 1962, pp. 196–201.
Date: Ca. 1878.

115

Two portraits of Cézanne's son wearing a hat. Art Institute of Chicago.

Pencil on white paper; page XLIV verso in a sketchbook measuring 12.4 × 21.7 cm. (Rewald, *Carnet II*).
Verso: No. 114.
Literature: Rewald, *Carnet II,* p. XLIV verso; Schniewind, Cat. No. XLIV verso; Wayne V. Andersen, ''Cézanne's Sketchbook in the Art Institute of Chicago,'' *The Burlington Magazine*, CIV, 1962, pp. 196–201.
Date: Ca. 1878.

116

Two portrait sketches of Cézanne's son, in one of which he is wearing a hat. Art Institute of Chicago.
Pencil on white paper; page XLV in a sketchbook measuring 12.4 × 21.7 cm. (Rewald, *Carnet II*).
Verso: Back view of a figure seated in a chair, perhaps Madame Cézanne (not catalogued).
Literature: Rewald, *Carnet II*, p. XLV; Schniewind, Vol. I, p. 15, and Cat. No. XLV; Wayne V. Andersen, "Cézanne's Sketchbook in the Art Institute of Chicago," *The Burlington Magazine*, CIV, 1962, pp. 196–201.

The lower drawing has not previously been identified, but it is Cézanne's son wearing a hat with an adaptable brim. In this sketch and in one on p. XXX (No. 106, also a previously unidentified image of the child), the brim is pulled down, whereas in No. 115 the brim is up.

Date: Ca. 1878.

117

Portrait sketch of Cézanne's son, on a sheet with a sketch of an unidentified object, arithmetical notations in Cézanne's hand with the numerals "029" and their underscoring in the hand of the child. Art Institute of Chicago.
Pencil on white paper; page XLVI in a sketchbook measuring 12.4 × 21.7 cm. (Rewald, *Carnet II*).
Verso: Study for an erotic theme, or perhaps a murder.
Literature: Rewald, *Carnet II*, p. XLVI; Schniewind, Cat. No. XLVI; Wayne V. Andersen, "Cézanne's Sketchbook in the Art Institute of Chicago," *The Burlington Magazine*, CIV, 1962, pp. 196–201.

The numerals written by the child provide a *terminus ante quem* of 1878 for the unidentified study, which they overlap.

Date: Ca. 1878.

118 fac.

Portrait of Cézanne's son sleeping. Art Institute of Chicago. Pencil on white paper; page XLVII in a sketchbook measuring 12.4 × 21.7 cm. (Rewald, *Carnet II*).
Verso: No. 119.
Literature: Rewald, *Carnet II*, p. XLVII; Schniewind, Vol. I, p. 15, and Cat. No. XLVII; Wayne V. Andersen, "Cézanne's Sketchbook in the Art Institute of Chicago," *The Burlington Magazine*, CIV, 1962, pp. 196–201.
Date: Ca. 1878.

119 fac.

Portrait of Cézanne's son sleeping, on a sheet with a sketch
of a hat. Art Institute of Chicago.
Pencil on white paper; page XLVII verso in a sketchbook
measuring 12.4 × 21.7 cm. (Rewald, *Carnet II*).
Verso: No. 118.
Literature: Rewald, *Carnet II,* p. XLVII verso; Schniewind,
Vol. I, p. 15, and Cat. No. XLVII verso; Wayne V. Andersen,
"Cézanne's Sketchbook in the Art Institute of Chicago,"
The Burlington Magazine, CIV, 1962, pp. 196–201.
Date: Ca. 1878.

120 fac.

Two portraits of Cézanne's son; in one he is asleep. Art
Institute of Chicago.
Pencil on white paper; page XLVIII in a sketchbook measuring 12.4 × 21.7 cm. (Rewald, *Carnet II*).
Verso: No. 121.
Literature: Rewald, *Carnet II*, p. XLVIII; Schniewind, Vol. I,
p. 15, and Cat. No. XLVIII; Wayne V. Andersen, "Cézanne's
Sketchbook in the Art Institute of Chicago," *The Burlington
Magazine*, CIV, 1962, pp. 196–201.
Date: Ca. 1878.

121 fac.

Two portraits of Cézanne's son, on sheet with the name
"paul" in the hand of the child. Art Institute of Chicago.
Pencil on white paper; page XLVIII verso in a sketchbook
measuring 12.4 × 21.7 cm. (Rewald, *Carnet II*).
Verso: No. 120.
Literature: Rewald, *Carnet II*, p. XLVIII verso; Schniewind,
Vol. I, p. 15, and Cat. No. XLVIII verso; Wayne V. Andersen,
"Cézanne's Sketchbook in the Art Institute of Chicago,"
The Burlington Magazine, CIV, 1962, pp. 196–201.
Date: Ca. 1878. For discussion see pp. 20–21.

122 fac.

Two portraits of Cézanne's son. Art Institute of Chicago. Pencil on white paper; page XLIX in a sketchbook measuring 12.4 × 21.7 cm. (Rewald, *Carnet II*).
Verso: Portrait of Madame Cézanne with the words "Madame Cézanne" written by Cézanne's son (No. 38).
Literature: Rewald, *Carnet II*, p. XLIX; Schniewind, Vol. I, p. 15, and Cat. No. XLIX; Wayne V. Andersen, "Cézanne's Sketchbook in the Art Institute of Chicago," *The Burlington Magazine*, CIV, 1962, pp. 196–201.
Date: 1878. For discussion see pp. 20–21.

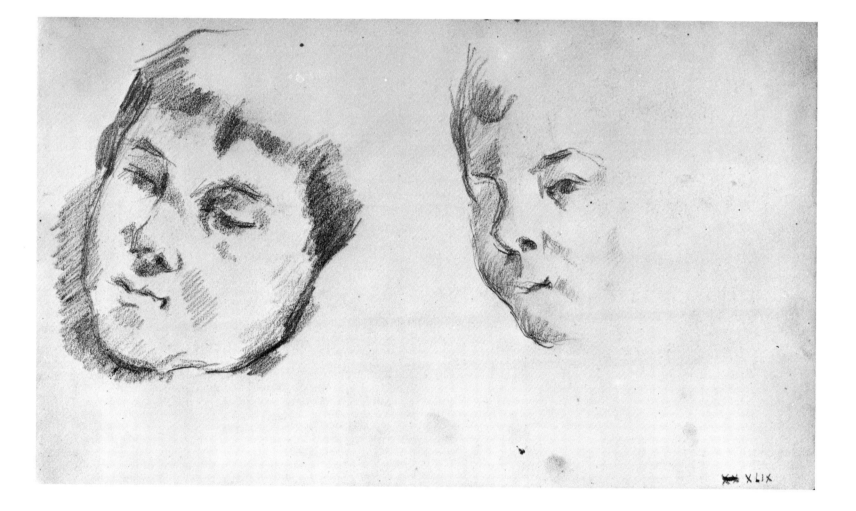

123

Portrait of Cézanne's son on a sheet with a composition inspired by Millet and figure and bather studies. Museum Boymans-van Beuningen, Rotterdam.
Pencil on white paper; 31.0 × 44.2 cm.
Verso: A commercial lithograph by Toussaint Duchemin after a painting by J. B. Greuze, *Le Coucher*.
Literature: Vollard, p. 176 (detail) and p. 184 (detail); Julius Meier-Graefe, *Cézanne und sein Kreis*, Munich, 1922, p. 33 (detail) and p. 63 (detail); Venturi, Cat. No. 1218, dated "1873(?)"; Basel, Kunsthalle, *Paul Cézanne*, 1936, No. 170; The Hague, Gemeentemuseum, *Paul Cézanne*, 1956, No. 102; Zurich, Kunsthaus, *Paul Cézanne*, No. 157; Munich, Haus der Kunst, *Paül Cézanne*, 1956, No. 120; John Rewald, *Paul Cézanne*, London, n. d., p. 65 (detail); Hoetink, Cat. No. 18, dated 1877–1878.

The central motif in this drawing is a study for the painting V. 248, which Reff has dated 1875–1877.[1] The pose of the female nude at the bottom of the sheet depends on the woman in Cézanne's *Tentation de Sainte Antoine* (V. 240) of about 1875 and may date from the same year or a little later. The two other sketches of kneeling figures are studies for V. 243, dating from about 1875–1876. The child seems to be a little younger in this portrait than in the majority of drawings in the Chicago Sketchbook; compare it, for example, with No. 112.

Date: Ca. 1876–1877.

1 See Theodore Reff, "Cézanne's Bather with Outstretched Arms," *Gazette des beaux-arts*, ser. 6, LIX, 1962, p. 184.

124 fac.

Portrait of Cézanne's son, on a sheet with the upper part of a female bather in a three-quarter view from the back. Albertina, Vienna.
Pencil on white paper, 15.2 × 10.2 cm., cut from a larger sheet; watermark "Michallet." (For the same watermark see Nos. 148, 173.)
Verso: Couple in a landscape from the back. Unpublished.
Literature: Unpublished.

In this drawing the child seems to be a little older than in the Chicago sketchbook, yet there is a very close point-by-point relationship with the left image on Chicago XLVIII verso (No. 121); the rendering of the lips, especially, would make it difficult to date this drawing with certainty later than 1879.

The bather study probably dates from the same time; see the figures at the left of V. 381.

Date: 1878–1879. For discussion see pp. 20–21.

125 n.r.

Portrait sketch of Cézanne's son. Collection Sam Salz, New York. Formerly Collections Ambroise Vollard, August Pellerin, René Lecomte, all of Paris.
Pencil on white paper; 20 × 12 cm.
Verso: Watercolor of a blue vase with plants (Venturi 1539A).
Literature: Columbia University, Department of Art History and Archaeology, *Cézanne Watercolors*, ed. Theodore Reff, New York, 1963, mentioned at Cat. No. 8.

Not examined.

126 fac. detail

Portrait of Cézanne's son, on a sheet with a self-portrait (No. 10). Art Institute of Chicago.
See No. 10.
Date: Ca. 1879–1880. For discussion see pp. 21–22, 25, 28, 30.

127

Portrait of Cézanne's son. Albertina, Vienna.
Pencil on white paper; 27.2 × 22.9 cm.
Verso: Blank.
Literature: Alfred Stix, *Von Ingres bis Cézanne,* Vienna, 1927,
No. 32; *Correspondance,* No. 25, dated ca. 1882–1883; John
Rewald, *Cézanne,* New York, 1948, p. 99; Neumeyer, Cat.
No. 38 (description in error), dated 1880–1882.
Date: Ca. 1880–1881. For discussion see p. 28.

128

Sketch of Cézanne's son, on a sheet with a study of a
candlestick and a copy of a bathing soldier in Michel-
angelo's *Battle of Cascina.* Present location unknown.
Formerly Collection Sir Kenneth and Lady Clark, London;
acquired from Cézanne *fils* through the dealer Paul Guil-
laume in 1934; sold by Sir Kenneth Clark through Galerie
Motte, Geneva, November 23, 1957.
Pencil on beige paper, approximately 15 × 23 cm.
Verso: Studies of Cézanne's son (No. 129).
Literature: Venturi, Cat. No. 1484, dated 1879–1882;
Galerie Motte, Geneva *Vente aux enchèzes publiques* [*cata-
logue*], November 23, 1957, No. 113; Berthold, Cat. No. 259.

The style of the child's head is problematic; the hatching is
mechanical and does not correspond to that in other drawings of the child at the same age (cf. Nos. 124, 127). The
dark outlines of the copy after Michelangelo (for others see

V. 1217, 1224, 1225, 1297, 1298) seem to have been either
added by another hand or traced by Cézanne, perhaps to
transfer or to reverse the image.

Date: 1879–1881.

129 n.r.

Studies of Cézanne's son. Present location unknown.
See No. 128.
Not examined.

130 fac.

Portrait of Cézanne's son asleep. Collection Sir Kenneth and Lady Clark, London.
Pencil on coarse, textured, white paper, 15.5–16.0 × 23.5 cm. Same paper as V. 1481, Chappuis 67 and 85. The indicia "5E" appear at the upper left corner.
Verso: Landscape sketch, similar in style to the verso of V. 1481 and to Chappuis 86.
Literature: Venturi, Cat. No. 1244, dated ca. 1880.
Date: 1880–1881. For discussion see pp. 28, 30.

131

Two portraits of Cézanne's son, on a sheet with a study for the standing male bather with outstretched arms, a study of a drinking glass, and a copy of a decorative figure on an eighteenth-century clock. Albertina, Vienna.
Pencil on white paper, 23.3 × 29.5 cm.
Verso: Studies perhaps of Madame Cézanne (No. 64) and perhaps of Cézanne's son, a pair of scissors, and a cooking pot.
Literature: Venturi, Cat. No. 1242 (detail of one of the studies of the child only, dated 1877–1882); Theodore Reff, "Cézanne's Bather with Outstretched Arms," *Gazette des beaux-arts,* ser. 6, LIX, 1962, p. 186 and note 41.

Venturi did not know this sheet and reproduced only a photoengraving of a detail.

Although Reff does not specifically date the sketch of the child, he suggests that the bather was drawn in the mid-seventies and that the still-life elements were added be-

tween 1880 and 1885. In my opinion all the drawings on the sheet are of the same date; the differences in rendering reflect the flexibility of Cézanne's style in relation to different subjects.

Date: Ca. 1881–1882.

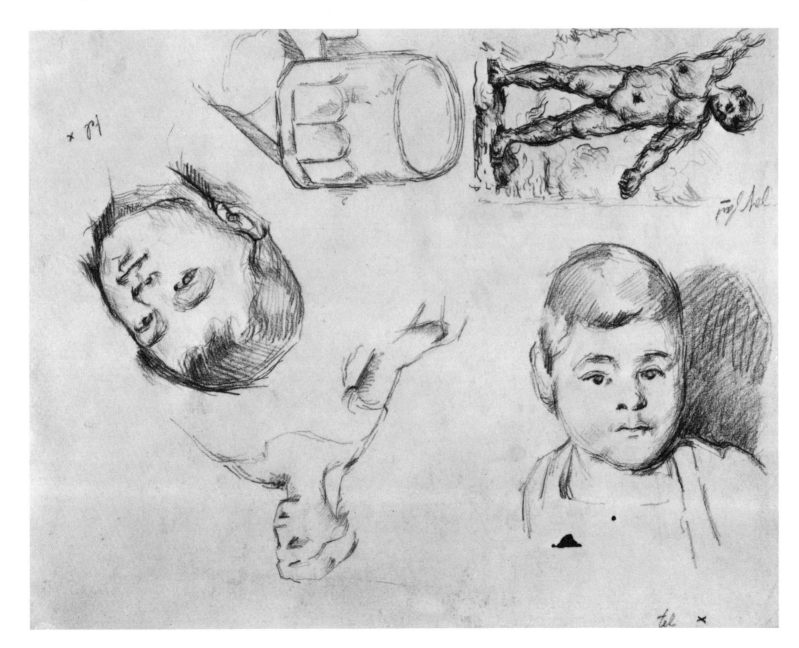

132 fac.

Portrait of Cézanne's son wearing a hat. Collection Mr. and
Mrs. Leigh Block, Chicago.
Pencil on white paper; page XLVI verso in a sketchbook
measuring 12.6 × 21.7 cm. (Rewald, *Carnet V*).
Verso: Portrait of Madame Cézanne (No. 54).
Literature: Rewald, *Carnet V*, p. XLVI verso.
Date: Ca. 1880–1882.

133 n.r.

Study of heads, probably Cézanne's son. Collection Mr. and
Mrs. Leigh Block, Chicago.
Pencil on white paper; page IX in a sketchbook measuring
12.6 × 21.7 cm. (Rewald, *Carnet V*).
Verso: Sketch of a house and trees.
Literature: Rewald, *Carnet V*, p. IX.

Not examined.

134 fac.

Portrait of Cézanne's son, on a sheet with a still life of a cup and drinking glasses on a table. Collection Mr. and Mrs. Leigh Block, Chicago.
Pencil on white paper; page XLIII verso in a sketchbook measuring 12.6 × 21.7 cm (Rewald, *Carnet V*).
Verso: Landscape study.
Literature: Rewald, *Carnet V,* page XLIII verso.

The cup on the table appears in another drawing, Collection Chappuis, described by Venturi under Cat. No. 1270, and reproduced in Chappuis, 1957, p. 95, dated 1878–1887.

Date: Ca. 1882. For discussion see pp. 30, 32.

135 fac.

Portrait of Cézanne's son. Collection Mr. and Mrs. Leigh Block, Chicago.
Pencil on white paper; page XLIX verso, detached from a sketchbook measuring 12.6 × 21.7 cm. (Rewald, *Carnet V*).
Verso: Study of a candlestick.
Literature: Rewald, *Carnet V*, p. XLIX verso; *idem, Paul Cézanne,* New York, 1968, Fig. 60, dated ca. 1880.
Date: Ca. 1882. For discussion see pp. 30, 32.

136

Sketch of Cézanne's son asleep. Collection Mrs. Ira Haupt, New York.
Pencil on white paper; page 2 verso of a dismantled sketchbook measuring approximately 12.7 × 21.6 cm. (Rewald, *Carnet I*).
Verso: Unidentified sketch.
Literature: Rewald, *Carnet I*, p. 2 verso, not reproduced.
Date: Ca. 1882.

137

Sketch of Cézanne's son sleeping. Collection Mrs. Ira Haupt, New York.
Pencil on white paper; page 3 verso in a dismantled sketchbook measuring approximately 12.7 × 21.6 cm. (Rewald, *Carnet I*).
Verso: No. 138.
Literature: Rewald, *Carnet I*, p. 3 verso, not reproduced.
Date: Ca. 1882.

138

Sketch of Cézanne's son asleep, on a sheet with a notation in Cézanne's hand: "Lambert, 17, rue de Loursine [sic]"[1]
Collection Mrs. Ira Haupt, New York.
Pencil on white paper; page 3 in a dismantled sketchbook measuring approximately 12.7 × 21.6 cm. (Rewald, *Carnet I*).
Verso: No. 137.
Literature: Rewald, *Carnet I*, p. 3.
Date: Ca. 1882.

1 A misspelling of Rue de l'Ourcine in Paris. In 1890 its name was changed to Rue Broca.

139

Sketch of Cézanne's son asleep. Collection Mrs. Ira Haupt, New York.
Pencil on white paper; page 10 in a dismantled sketchbook measuring approximately 12.7 × 21.6 cm. (Rewald, *Carnet I*).
Verso: No. 140.
Literature: Rewald, *Carnet I*, p. 10, not reproduced.
Date: 1882–1884.

140

Cézanne's son asleep, on a sheet with a study of a hand. Collection Mrs. Ira Haupt, New York.
Pencil on white paper; page 10 verso in a dismantled sketchbook measuring approximately 12.7 × 21.6 cm. (Rewald, *Carnet I*).
Verso: No. 139.
Literature: Rewald, *Carnet I*, p. 10 verso, not reproduced.
Date: 1882–1884.

141 n.r.

Sketch of Cézanne's son asleep, on a sheet with a study of foliage. Collection Mrs. Ira Haupt, New York.
Pencil on white paper; page 11 in a dismantled sketchbook measuring approximately 12.7 × 21.6 cm. (Rewald, *Carnet I*).
Verso: Study after the *Venus accroupie* in the Louvre.
Literature: Rewald, *Carnet I*, p. 11, not reproduced.
Date: 1882–1884.

142

Sketch of Cézanne's son sleeping. Collection Mrs. Ira Haupt, New York.
Pencil on white paper; page VI in a dismantled sketchbook measuring 12.7 × 26.6 cm. (Rewald, *Carnet IV*).

See No. 188.

143 n.r.

Portrait of Cézanne's son, partially effaced. Collection Mrs. Ira Haupt, New York.
Pencil on white paper; page XLVII in a dismantled sketchbook measuring 12.7 × 26.6 cm. (Rewald, *Carnet IV*).
Verso: Study of a collar on a man's shirt or coat.
Literature: Rewald, *Carnet IV*, p. XLVII, not reproduced.

The drawing is unavailable for study.

144

Three sketches of Cézanne's son asleep. Collection Sir Kenneth and Lady Clark, London.
Pencil on white paper; 35.6 × 49.2 cm.
Verso: Sketch of foliage, heightened with watercolor.
Literature: Venturi, Cat. No. 1471, dated 1878–1882.
Date: Ca. 1882–1883. For discussion see p. 32.

145 n.r.

Portrait of Cézanne's son, on a sheet with a study for an outdoor genre scene and a copy of a bathing soldier after Michelangelo. Present location unknown. Originally Collection Vollard.
Pencil on paper (genre scene in ink wash); measurements unknown.
Verso: Unknown.
Literature: Venturi, Cat. No. 1225, dated 1872–1883; Reff, "Studies," p. 40, the portrait dated ca. 1878.

Venturi's date is for the entire sheet: "Il semble que les motifs de cette page aient été dessinés à différentes époques." He apparently allowed the early date for the genre motif, a study for the right half of *Le Déjeuner sur l'herbe*, V. 234 (see also V. 876), and the later date for the portrait of the child, who appears to be eight or nine years old. In my opinion the genre scene dates from about 1878–1882.

Date: Ca. 1882.

146

Four heads of Cézanne's son in different states of completion, on a sheet with a copy after Jean de Parega's *Vocation of Saint Matthew*. Kunstmuseum, Basel.
Pencil on white paper; 32.5 × 25 cm.
Verso: Three heads of Cézanne *fils* and a study of a sleeve (No. 149).
Literature: Venturi, Vol. I, p. 352, not reproduced; Berthold, Cat. No. 311; Chappuis, Cat. No. 90, dated 1877–1882; Douglas Cooper, review of Chappuis, *Les Dessins de Cézanne au Musée de Bâle*, in *Master Drawings*, I, No. 4, 1963, p. 56, dated ca. 1879.

Chappuis, who identified the source of the group motif, suggests that it predates the sketches of the child; for these his date span is about 1880–1882. Cooper believes the child to be about seven years old.

Date: Ca. 1882.

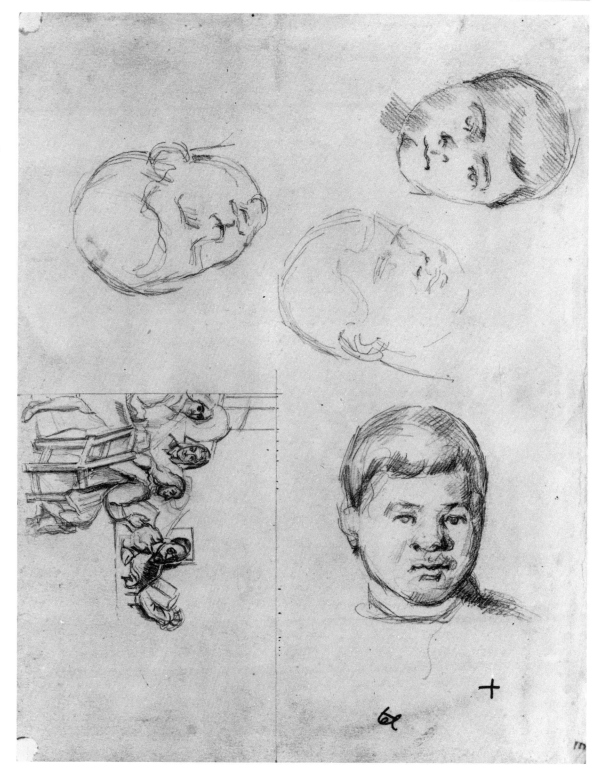

147 fac.

Portrait of Cézanne's son. Kunstmuseum, Basel; acquired
from Cézanne *fils* through the dealer Werner Feuz in 1934.
Pencil on white paper; 17.1 × 16.6 cm.
Verso: Fragment of an academic study of a nude male
(Chappuis, Cat. No. 20, dated 1867–1870).
Literature: Venturi, Cat. No. 1572, dated 1880–1887;
Chappuis, Cat. No. 99, dated 1880–1882.
Date: 1882–1883. For discussion see p. 32.

148 fac.

Portrait of Cézanne's son, on a sheet with a study of a chair and a small sketch of an unidentified head. Kunstmuseum, Basel.
Pencil on white paper, 31.3 × 47.3 cm.; "Michallet" watermark. (For the same watermark see Nos. 124, 173.)
Verso: Landscape sketch with houses and trees (Chappuis, Cat. No. 86, dated 1870–1874).
Literature: Venturi, Cat. No. 1590, dated 1882–1885; Chappuis, Cat. No. 101, dated 1882–1884 (reproduction inverted).

Reproduced here (148a) is a photograph of Cézanne's son in what I believe to be his confirmation suit. According to custom in the late nineteenth century, he would have been confirmed at the age of eleven.

Date: Ca. 1883. For discussion see p. 32.

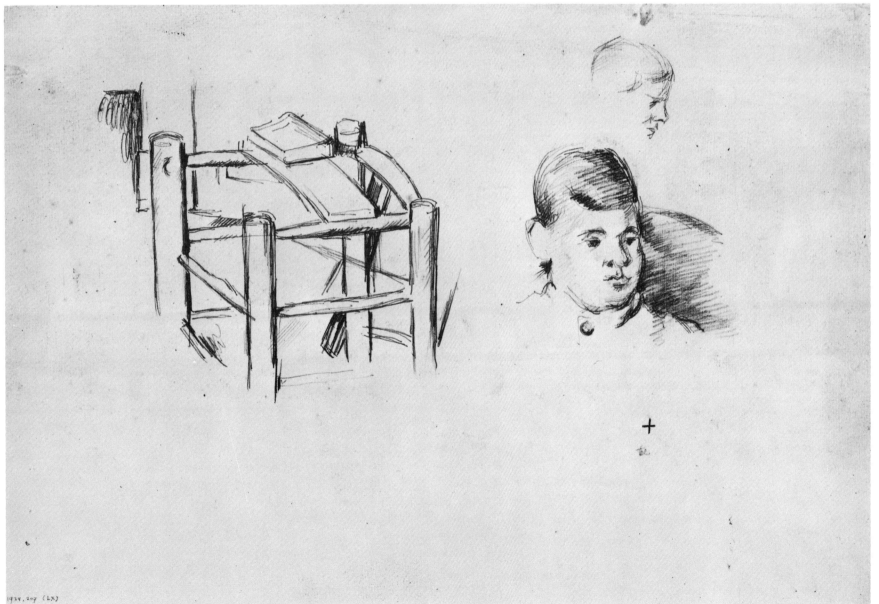

149

Three heads of Cézanne's son, on a sheet with a study of a sleeve. Kunstmuseum, Basel.
Pencil on white paper; 25 × 32.5 cm.
Verso: Four heads of Cézanne's son (No. 146), on a sheet with a copy after Jean de Pareja's *Vocation of Saint Matthew* (Berthold Cat. No. 331; Chappuis Cat. No. 90).
Literature: Venturi, Vol. I, p. 352, not reproduced; Chappuis, Cat. No. 92, dated 1877–1882. Douglas Cooper, review of Chappuis, *Les Dessins de Cézanne au Musée de Bâle,* in *Master Drawings,* I, No. 4, 1963, p. 56, dated ca. 1879.

Venturi identified each of the three heads as Cézanne's son. Chappuis failed to find his likeness in the one at the lower right, which he thought might be a female head. My identification relies on a comparison of this image with the uppermost head on the verso, which is similarly treated (it too is inclined forward) and is certainly that of Cézanne's son.

Date: Ca. 1882–1883.

150 (reproduced at No. 15)

Portrait sketch of Cézanne's son asleep in an armchair, on a sheet with a self-portrait (No. 15) and a copy after Pajou's *Psyche abandonné* in the Louvre. Museum Boymans-van Beuningen, Rotterdam.
See No. 15.

Although not previously identified, the sleeping youth is almost certainly Cézanne's son. The face and graphic traits correspond very closely with those in the drawing of the child in the Petit Palais (No. 161), and the armchair is the one in which Madame Cézanne posed for several oil portraits, V. 291 and 292, for example. In the latter even the upholstery button, so apparent in the drawing, is discernible; in the former, we see the same slight swelling of the chair arm just before it dips into its terminal spiral. Cézanne would not have found this intimate motif in a pictorial source, and the pose is not one in which he would have placed a model.

Date: Ca. 1882–1884.

151

Portrait of Cézanne's son àsleep. Kunstmuseum, Basel.
Pencil on white paper, 25.5 × 19.8 cm.; watermark
''HALLINES.''
Verso: Sketch of three bathers in a landscape, a seated male
in oriental costume, and an unfinished sketch of a head
(No. 25).
Literature: Venturi, Vol. I, p. 352, not reproduced; Chappuis, Cat. No. 100, dated ca. 1882, Douglas Cooper, review
of Chappuis, *Les Dessins de Cézanne au Musée de Bâle*, in
Master Drawings, I, No. 4, 1963, pp. 54–57, dated ca. 1878.
Date: Ca. 1882–1884.

152

Three portrait sketches of Cézanne's son, on a sheet with
studies after Pedro de Moya[1] and Tintoretto.[2] Collection
Lazarus Phillips, Montreal. Formerly Collection Sir Kenneth
and Lady Clark, London, acquired in 1934 from Cézanne
fils through the dealer Paul Guillaume.
Pencil on white paper; approximately 25 × 32 cm.
Verso: Portrait of Cézanne's son, on a sheet with a copy
after Marcantonio's *Caryatides* (No. 162).
Literature: Venturi, under Cat. No. 1475, mentioned only;
Berthold, under Cat. No. 336, mentioned only; Adrien
Chappuis, ''Cézanne dessinateur: copies et illustrations,''
Gazette des beaux-arts, ser. 6. LXVI, 1965, p. 297, Fig. 9,
dated 1879–1880.
Date: 1882–1884.

153 n.r.

Sketch of Cézanne's son (?), incomplete. Collection Adrien
Chappuis, Tresserve (Savoie).
Pencil on white paper; page V in a sketchbook measuring
12.6 × 21.5 cm. (Chappuis II).
Verso: Portrait of Cézanne's son, on a sheet with a sketch
of a book on a table (No. 168).
Literature: Venturi, under Cat. No. 1282, not reproduced.
Date: Ca. 1883.

154 n.r.

Sketch of Cézanne's son, incomplete. Private collection,
Paris; formerly Collection Adrien Chappuis, Paris.
Pencil on white paper; page VII verso from a sketchbook
measuring 12.6 × 21.5 cm. (Chappuis II).
Verso: Landscape.
Literature: Venturi, under Cat. No. 1283, not reproduced.
Date: Ca. 1883.

1   Identification by Robert Ratcliffe. See Adrien Chappuis, ''Cézanne dessinateur: copies et illustrations,'' *Gazette des beaux-arts,* ser. 6, LXVI, 1965, p. 297.

2   Identification by Chappuis in ''Cézanne dessinateur.''

155 fac.

Portrait of Cézanne's son. Collection Adrien Chappuis
Tresserve (Savoie).
Pencil on white paper; page X verso in a sketchbook mea-
suring 12.6 × 21.5 cm. (Chappuis II).
Verso: Sketch of Zola writing (No. 238).
Literature: Venturi, under Cat. No. 1284, not reproduced;
Chappuis, 1938, p. 23; Neumeyer, Cat. No. 39, dated
1880–1882.

Neumeyer has based his date on an estimate of the child's
age in this drawing as about ten years.

Date: Ca. 1883. For discussion see pp. 28, 32.

156 fac.

Portrait of Cézanne's son, on a sheet with a sketch of a formally attired man greeting a woman, a nude male bather seated next to a tree, and a standing female bather. Collection Adrien Chappuis, Tresserve, (Savoie).
Pencil on white paper; page XVII verso in a sketchbook measuring 12.6 × 21.5 cm. (Chappuis II).
Verso: Self-portrait (No. 20).
Literature: Vollard, p. 118 (female bather only); Venturi, Cat. No. 1288 (female bather only); Chappuis, 1938, No. 2.

Although he did not reproduce the child's head, Venturi commented on it and identified it as Cézanne's son, ''âgé de douze ans,'' dating it therefore 1884.

Date: Ca. 1883. For discussion see pp. 28, 32.

157 n.r.

Portrait of Cézanne's son, on a sheet with an unidentified female head. Collection Adrien Chappuis, Tresserve (Savoie).
Pencil on white paper; page XXIX verso in a sketchbook measuring 12.6 × 21.5 cm. (Chappuis II).
Verso: Blank.
Literature: Venturi, Cat. No. 1290 (catalogued in error as page XXVIII verso).
Date: Ca. 1883. For discussion see pp. 28, 32.

158 n.r.

Venturi (Vol. I, p. 307) catalogued in error page XXXIII in Chappuis II as a portrait of Cézanne's son on a sheet with an unidentified head. Actually, page XXXIII contains a portrait of Madame Cézanne and a sketch of an orange (61).

159 fac.

Portrait of Cézanne's son, with the date "1877," on a sheet with a study of a running female bather and a copy of a female head from an unidentified source. Collection Adrien Chappuis, Tresserve (Savoie).
Pencil on white paper; page XXXV verso in a sketchbook measuring 12.6 × 21.5 cm (Chappuis II).
Verso: Landscape sketch with houses.
Literature: Venturi, under Cat. No. 1290, dated 1884, not reproduced; Chappuis, 1938, Cat. No. 28; Berthold, Cat. No. 319.

The date "1877" that appears on this sheet is not in Cézanne's hand. Venturi was the first to question the date, "vu l'âge du petit Paul," and estimated that the child was twelve years old. (See No. 168 for other portraits of the son in this sketchbook that Venturi has dated on the same basis.)

Date: Ca. 1883. For discussion see p. 32.

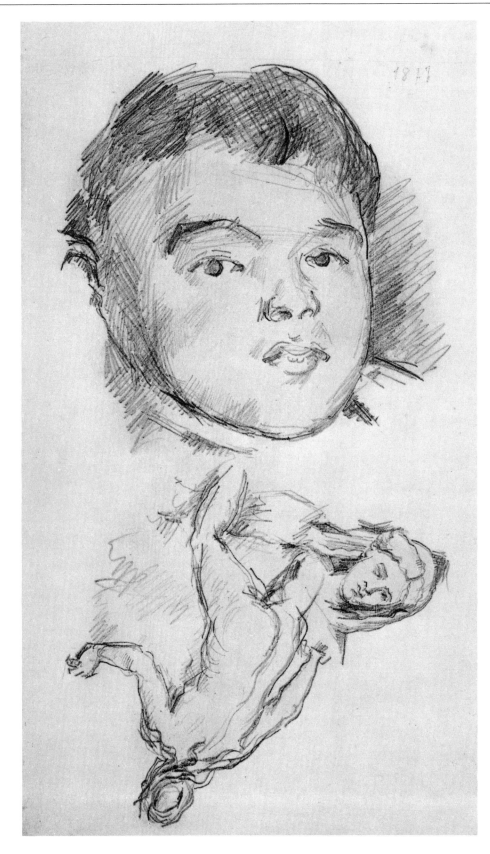

160

Portrait of Cézanne's son, on a sheet with accounting notes.
Collection Adrien Chappuis, Tresserve (Savoie).
Pencil on white paper; on the inner face of the back cover of
a sketchbook measuring 12.6 × 21.5 cm. (Chappuis II).
Literature: Venturi, under Cat. No. 1299, not reproduced;
Chappuis, 1957, No. 34, dated 1884.

Both Venturi and Chappuis have suggested that the son
here is twelve years old; the sketch would thus date from
1884.

Date: Ca. 1884. For discussion see pp. 28, 32.

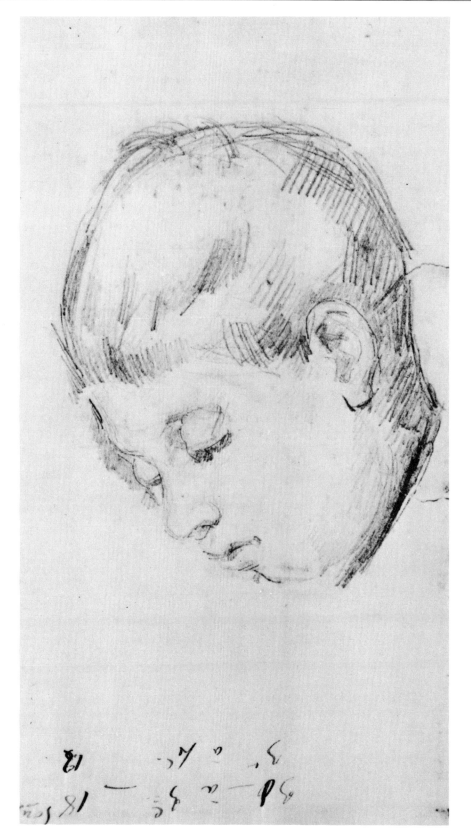

161 fac.

Portrait of Cézanne's son. Musée Nationale de la Ville de Paris (Petit Palais); gift of Adrien Chappuis, 1958.
Pencil on white paper; page XXXII verso from a sketchbook measuring 12.6 × 21.5 cm. (Chappuis II).
Verso: Copy after Antonin Mercié's *David* in the Louvre (Berthold, Cat. No. 176).
Literature: Venturi, under Cat. No. 1291, not reproduced.

Berthold's date of 1872–1873 for the verso of this drawing reflects her tendency to associate the dates of copies too closely with the *terminus post quem* established by the acquisition of the models and their availability to Cézanne. (Mercié's *David* was first exhibited in 1872) Cézanne's copy is well within the range of his style from ca. 1882 to 1884.

Date: Ca. 1884. For discussion see pp. 28, 32.

Portrait of Cézanne's son, on a sheet with a study after Marcantonio's *Caryatides* and a sketch of drapery. Collection Lazarus Phillips, Montreal. Formerly Collection Sir Kenneth and Lady Clark, London, who acquired it in 1934 from Cézanne *fils* through the dealer Paul Guillaume. Pencil on paper; approximately 25 × 32 cm.
Verso: Three portrait studies of Cézanne's son and copies after Pedro De Moya and Tintoretto (No. 152).
Literature: Venturi, Cat. No. 1475, dated 1880–1885; Berthold, Cat. No. 263, the copy dated second half of the 1880's.
Date: Ca. 1883–1885. For discussion see p. 32.

Portraits of Cézanne's son, on a sheet with two portaits of Madame Cézanne (No. 65), a study of a decorative female figure on an eighteenth-century clock (V. 1474 verso, not reproduced; Berthold, Cat. No. 328), a copy of a figure by Pedro de Moya,[1] and other sketches. Collection Sir Kenneth and Lady Clark, London.
Pencil on coarse textured, white paper, deckle edges; 31.1–32.0 × 49.5 cm., folded in half.
Verso: Self-portrait (No. 21), on a sheet with a drawing after a self-portrait by Goya, a study of an apple, a running female bather, and other studies.
Literature: Venturi, mentioned at Cat. No. 1474; Berthold, Cat. No. 328 (the copy after Pedro de Moya reproduced but not identified).
Date: Ca. 1885. For discussion see pp. 32, 34.

1 Identification by Robert Ratcliffe. See Adrien Chappuis, "Cézanne dessinateur: copies et illustrations," *Gazette des Beaux-Arts,* ser. 6, LXVI, 1965, p. 297.

164 fac.

Two portraits of Cézanne's son, in one of which he is asleep. Collection Adrien Chappuis, Tresserve (Savoie). Pencil on white paper; page XXXVI in a sketchbook measuring 12.6 × 21.5 cm (Chappuis II).
Verso: Sketch of a head, probably of Cézanne's son, and a study for *Leda and the Swan* (No. 165).
Literature: Venturi, under Cat. No. 1290, not reproduced.
Date: Ca. 1884–1886. For discussion see p. 32.

Study of a head, probably of Cézanne's son, on a sheet with a study for *Leda and the Swan*. Collection Adrien Chappuis, Tresserve (Savoie).
Pencil on white paper; page XXXVI verso in a sketchbook measuring 12.6 × 21.5 cm. (Chappuis II).
Verso: Two portraits of Cézanne's son (No. 164).
Literature: Venturi, under Cat. No. 1290, not reproduced; Chappuis, 1938, No. 9.

Neither Venturi nor Chappuis has suggested that this study represents the head of Cézanne's son. My conclusion is based on a comparison with Nos. 160 and 164. For a similar study of *Leda and the Swan* see Rewald, *Carnet I*, p. 6. For the painting see V. 550, 551, where the motif is dated 1886–1890.

Date: Ca. 1884–1886. For discussion see p. 32.

Portrait of Cézanne's son, on a sheet with arithmetical notations. Collection Adrien Chappuis, Tresserve (Savoie).
Pencil on white paper; page XLII verso in a sketchbook measuring 12.6 × 21.5 cm. (Chappuis II).
Verso: Study of a male bather with outstretched arms and a related sketch of a clothed figure (V. 1294).
Literature: Venturi, Cat. No. 1300; Paris, Musée de l'Orangerie, *Cézanne*, 1936, Cat. No. 153, dated ca. 1880.
Date: 1884–1886. For discussion see p. 32.

Bust of Cézanne's son (?), on a sheet with an unidentified male head. Collection Adrien Chappuis, Tresserve (Savoie).
Pencil on white paper; page XLVI verso in a sketchbook measuring 12.6 × 21.5 cm. (Chappuis II).
Verso: Touches of watercolor.
Literature: Venturi, under Cat. No. 1295, not reproduced; Theodore Reff, ''Cézanne's Bather with Outstretched Arms,'' *Gazette des beaux-arts,* ser. 6, LIX, 1962, p. 179 and Fig. 9, dated 1885–1886.

Reff believes that this head of Cézanne's son is a study for the standing male bather in V. 549, which he dates 1885–1886 according to his estimate of the child's age in this drawing as about thirteen or fourteen.

Date: 1884–1886.

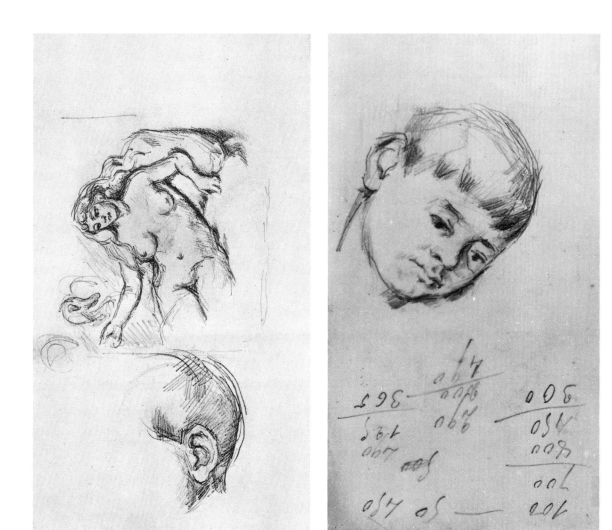

168 fac.

Portrait of Cézanne's son, on a sheet with a sketch of a book on a table. Collection Adrien Chappuis, Tresserve (Savoie). Pencil on white paper; page IV verso in a sketchbook measuring 12.6 × 21.5 cm. (Chappuis II).
Verso: Portrait of Cézanne's son (No. 153).
Literature: Venturi, under Cat. No. 1282, dated ca. 1884, not reproduced; Chappuis, 1938, No. 8.

Venturi estimated the age of the child in this sketchbook on pp. IV verso, XVII verso, XXXV verso, and on the inside face of the back cover as twelve years, thus assigning these drawings to 1884.

Date: Ca. 1884–1886.

169

Portrait of Cézanne's son standing with right hand on hip.
Collection Hillman Periodicals, Inc., New York. Originally
Collection Cézanne *fils,* Paris.
Pencil on paper, 49 × 31 cm.
Verso: Watercolor: a scene from *Faust* after Delacroix.
Literature: Venturi, Cat. No. 1469, dated ca. 1885; Wilden-
stein & Co., New York, *Cézanne Loan Exhibition,* 1959,
No. 66, dated ca. 1885.

Meyer Schapiro has pointed out to me the remarkable
similarity between this pose and that in the *Boy in a Red
Vest* (V. 682, Paul Mellon Collection).

The back wall in the portrait, which was drawn in the
studio, appears also in a contemporary drawing of a nude
model.[1] The floral motif to the right of the child's left hand
in the background is similar to that in the *fond à tapisserie
de fleurs* used as evidence in dating several paintings from
1879 to 1882.[2] Its presence here strengthens the possibility
that the design was portable backdrop material used by
Cézanne in his studio, rather than a wallpaper pattern in
one of his residences.

Date: Ca. 1886. For discussion see pp. 32, 34.

1 Fogg Museum of Art, Harvard University. For a reproduction see Neumeyer,
Cat. No. 24.

2 See the discussion in Wayne V. Andersen "Cézanne, Tanguy, Choquet,"
The Art Bulletin, XLIX, 1967, pp. 137–139.

170

Portrait of Cézanne's son standing with right hand on hip. Present location unknown. In 1936, part of a private collection in Berlin.
Pencil on beige paper, 49 × 31 cm.
Verso: Unknown.
Literature: Venturi, Cat. No. 1470, dated ca. 1885.
See No. 169.
Date: Ca. 1886.

171

Portrait of Cézanne's son writing at a table. Collection Werner Feuz, Zurich; probably acquired from Cézanne *fils* in 1934.
Pencil on white paper, 22.5 × 31 cm.
Verso: Not known.
Literature: Venturi, Cat. No. 1468, dated ca. 1885.
Date: Ca. 1887–1888. For discussion see pp. 32, 34.

Full-length study for Harlequin in the composition known as *Mardi Gras* (V. 552), modeled by Cézanne's son. Collection Mrs. Ira Haupt, New York.
Pencil and bistre wash, 18.2 × 11.6 cm.; page 18 from a sketchbook (Rewald, *Carnet I*).
Verso: Study of an antique statue.
Literature: Rewald, *Carnet 'I*, p. 18 verso; Meyer Schapiro, *Paul Cézanne*, New York, 1952, p. 19, dated 1888–1890; Chicago, Art Institute, *Cézanne: Paintings, Watercolors, and Drawings*, 1952, Pl. 39, dated 1888; Columbia University, Department of Art History and Archaeology, *Cézanne Watercolors*, ed. Theodore Reff, New York, 1963, Cat. No. 23, dated 1888.

The catalogue of the Columbia University exhibition suggests that this wash drawing is the earliest in the series of many studies for Harlequin in the *Mardi Gras* composition, as it has "the roughness, but also the freshness, of a first attempt to seize an idea." The complete series was almost certainly accomplished within a short period of time, and it seems reasonable that the compositions progressed from the establishment of the pose of the complete figure to the details of the head. The first study, however, may be the watercolor in the Javal collection in Paris; there the baton is held in Harlequin's left hand, whereas in this drawing it is in the right hand, corresponding to the final painting. In fact, of the several studies in oil, watercolor, and pencil, this alone indicates the parted curtain behind Harlequin, and it may be the only study specifically for the final version (V. 552) in which Harlequin appears with Clown. (In V. 553–555 Harlequin is standing still, whereas in V. 552 he is striding forward, but these versions give no hint of the larger composition and need not be considered as studies.) Although it is true that the pose in this drawing is tentative and that the legs are unrelated to the pose of the final version, the head is placed on the shoulders exactly as in Harlequin's final appearance. In the other studies the head is cocked slightly in the opposite direction. I would therefore assume that this drawing comes later in the sequence than my No. 173.

According to Cézanne *fils, Mardi Gras* was painted in 1888 in Paris, in Cézanne's atelier in the rue du Val-de-Grâce.[1] Martha Conil, Cézanne's niece, has written that it was painted in the grand salon of the Jas de Bouffan in Aix,[2] but as the Clown was modeled by Louis Guillaume, who lived in Paris, the correct account is probably that given by Cézanne's son.

Date: Ca. 1888. For discussion see pp. 32, 34.

1 See the remarks under V. 552.

2 Martha Conil, "Quelques souvenirs sur Paul Cézanne par une de ses nièces," *Gazette des Beaux-Arts*, ser. 6, LVI, 1960, pp. 299–302.

173

Full-length study for Harlequin (V. 552), modeled by Cézanne's son. Art Institute of Chicago. Formerly Collection W. Halvorsen; acquired from Cézanne *fils*; later, the Thannhauser Gallery, Berlin (exhibited January–February 1927).
Pencil on white paper, 47.0 × 30.1 cm.; watermark ''Michallet'' (for the same watermark see Nos. 124, 148).
Verso: Blank.
Literature: Julius Meier-Graefe, *Cézanne und sein Kreis,* Munich, 1922, Pl. 76; Göran Schildt, *Riktlinjer för en enhetlig psykologisk Tolkning av Paul Cezannes Personlighet och Konst mot Bakgrund av den allmänna romantiska Livkon-flikten,* Stockholm, 1947, Fig. 10; Venturi, Cat. No. 1486, dated ca. 1888; Philadelphia, Museum of Art, *Masterpieces of Drawing,* 1950, dated ca. 1888; Chicago, Art Institute, *Cézanne: Paintings, Watercolors, and Drawings,* 1952, Cat. No. 72, dated 1888; Neumeyer, Cat. No. 23, dated 1888; Paris, Musée de l'Orangerie, *De David à Toulouse-Lautrec,* 1955, No. 56; Chappuis, 1957, No. 16; Wildenstein & Co., New York, *Master Drawings from the Art Institute of Chicago,* 1963, No. 108.

See No. 172 and an almost identical study in watercolor, V. 1079 (color reproduction in Georg Schmidt, ed., *Water-Colours by Paul Cézanne,* New York, 1953, Pl. 28).

Date: Ca. 1888. For discussion see pp. 32, 34.

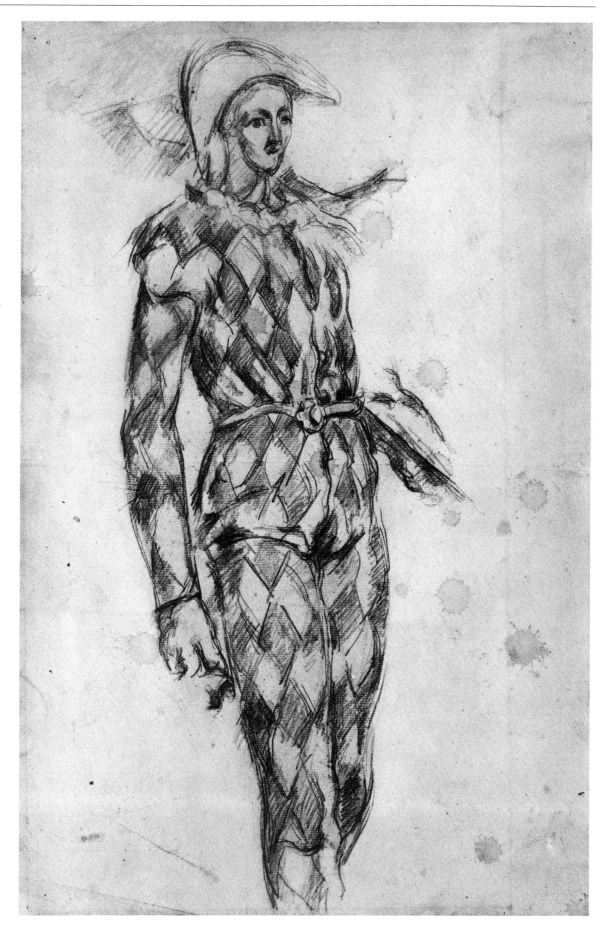

Three studies for Harlequin in the composition known as *Mardi Gras* (V. 552), modeled by Cézanne's son: two studies of the head, one of the right ear. Present location unknown. Formerly Collection Antonin Personnaz, Bayonne.
Pencil on paper.
Literature: Vollard, p. 148; Julius Meier-Graefe, *Cézanne und sein Kreis,* Munich, 1922, p. 210; Atzouji Zeisho, *Paul Cézanne* [Tokyo?], 1921, Pl. 20; Venturi, Cat. No. 1473, dated ca. 1888.

See No. 172.

Date: Ca. 1888. For discussion see pp. 32, 34.

Two studies for Harlequin in the composition known as *Mardi Gras* (V. 552), modeled by Cézanne's son: one of the head and shoulders, the other of the face. Collection Robert von Hirsch, Basel.
Pencil on white paper, 19.0 × 25.5 cm.
Verso: Unavailable for examination.
Literature: Venturi, Cat. No. 1622, dated ca. 1888; Neumeyer, Cat. No. 41, dated 1888.

See No. 172. For discussion see pp. 32, 34.

Date: Ca. 1888.

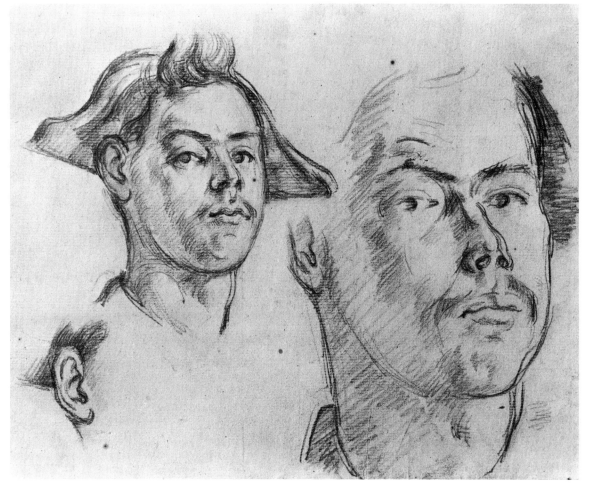

176

Study of Cézanne's son reading a book. Collection Adrien Chappuis, Tresserve (Savoie).
Pencil on white paper; page III in a sketchbook measuring 15 × 23.8 cm. (Chappuis III).
Verso: Copy after Puget's *Milon de Crotone* in the Louvre (Berthold, Cat. No. 106).
Literature: Venturi, under Cat. No. 1301, not reproduced; Chappuis, *Album,* Cat. No. III, dated 1885–1890, not identified.
Date: Ca. 1892–1894. For discussion see pp. 35, 40.

177

Head of Cézanne's son, on a sheet with a still life of a cup and a loaf of bread. Collection Adrien Chappuis, Tresserve (Savoie).
Pencil on white paper; page VIII in a sketchbook measuring 15 × 23.8 cm. (Chappuis III).
Verso: Sketch of an oil lamp.
Literature: Venturi, under Cat. No. 1303, neither reproduced nor identified; Chappuis, *Album,* Cat. No. VIII, dated 1888–1892, not identified.
Date: Ca. 1892–1894. For discussion see pp. 35, 40.

178

Portrait of Cézanne's son, on a sheet with a second head, perhaps also Cézanne's son. Collection Adrien Chappuis, Tresserve (Savoie).

Pencil on white paper; page IX in a sketchbook measuring 15 × 23.8 cm. (Chappuis III).

Verso: Portrait of Madame Cézanne (No. 78).

Literature: Venturi, under Cat. No. 1306, not reproduced; Chappuis, *Album,* Cat. No. IX, dated 1886–1889, not identified.

Date: Ca. 1892–1894. For discussion see pp. 35, 40.

179 fac.

Sketch of Cézanne's son writing. Collection Adrien
Chappuis, Tresserve (Savoie).
Pencil on white paper; page XVII verso in a sketchbook
measuring 15 × 23.8 cm. (Chappuis III).
Verso: Portrait of Madame Cézanne (No. 85).
Literature: Venturi, Cat. No. 1305; Fritz Novotny, *Cézanne,*
Vienna, No. 118, dated ca. 1885; Chappuis, *Album,* Cat.
No. XVII verso, dated 1885–1888.
Date: Ca. 1892–1894. For discussion see pp. 35, 40.

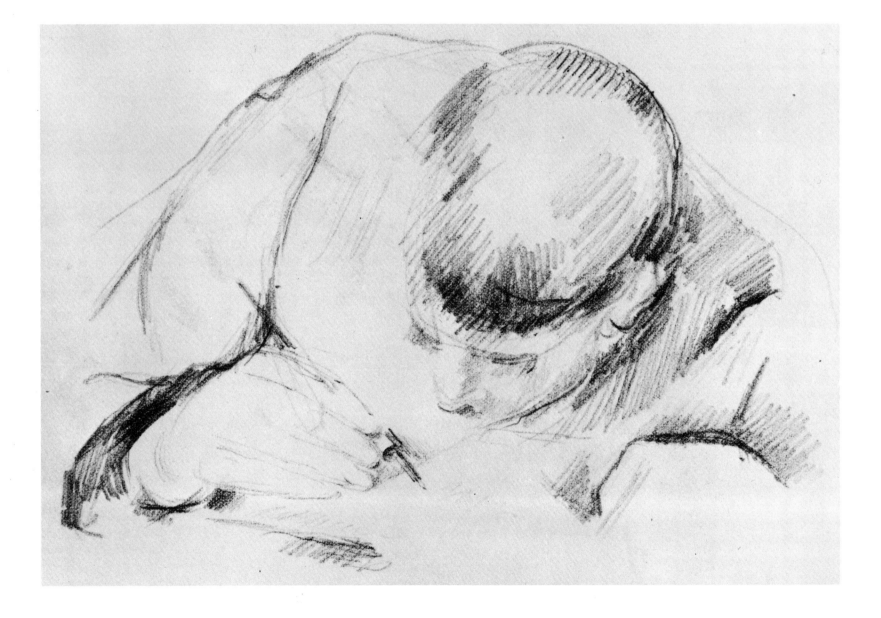

180 fac.

Portrait of Cézanne's son. Collection Adrien Chappuis, Tresserve (Savoie).

Pencil on white paper; page XVIII in a sketchbook measuring 15 × 23.8 cm. (Chappuis III).

Verso: Cézanne's son writing (No. 181).

Literature: Venturi, Cat. No. 1306; Chappuis, *Album,* Cat. No. XVIII, dated 1885–1888.

Date: Ca. 1892–1894. For discussion see pp. 35, 40.

181 fac.

Portrait sketch of Cézanne's son. Collection Adrien Chap-
puis, Tresserve (Savoie).
Pencil on white paper; page XVIII verso in a sketchbook
measuring 15 × 23.8 cm. (Chappuis III).
Verso: Portrait of Cézanne's son (No. 180).
Literature: Venturi, under No. 1306, not reproduced;
Chappuis, *Album,* Cat. No. XVIII verso, dated 1889–1893,
not identified.
Date: Ca. 1892–1894. For discussion see pp. 35, 40.

182

Portrait of Cézanne's son, three-quarter view from the back. Collection Adrien Chappuis, Tresserve (Savoie).
Pencil on white paper; page XIX in a sketchbook measuring 15 × 23.8 cm. (Chappuis III).
Verso: Sketch for *Carnaval*.
Literature: Venturi, under Cat. No. 1306, not reproduced; Chappuis, *Album,* Cat. No. XIX, dated ca. 1885, not identified.
Date: Ca. 1892–1894. For discussion see pp. 35, 40.

183

Portrait of Cézanne's son. Collection Adrien Chappuis, Tresserve (Savoie).
Pencil on white paper; page XXI verso in a sketchbook measuring 15 × 23.8 cm. (Chappuis III).
Verso: Sketch of a female head and the address of a model, "Antonio Franchi, Avenue de Maine, 124."
Literature: Venturi, under Cat. No. 1306, not reproduced; Chappuis, *Album,* Cat. No. XXI verso, dated 1886–1889, not identified.
Date: Ca. 1892–1896. For discussion see pp. 35, 40.

184

Portrait sketch of Cézanne's son. Kunstmuseum, Basel.
Pencil on white paper, 23.6 × 15 cm.; page XX from a sketchbook. (Chappuis III).
Verso: Study for *Carnaval* (Chappuis, Cat. No. 124, dated 1885–1890).
Literature: Chappuis, Cat. No. 91, dated 1876–1880.

Chappuis did not catalogue this as a drawing of Cézanne's son. My decision is based on the general conformation and attitude of the head, as well as its similarity to the head in my No. 177.

Date: Ca. 1892–1894.

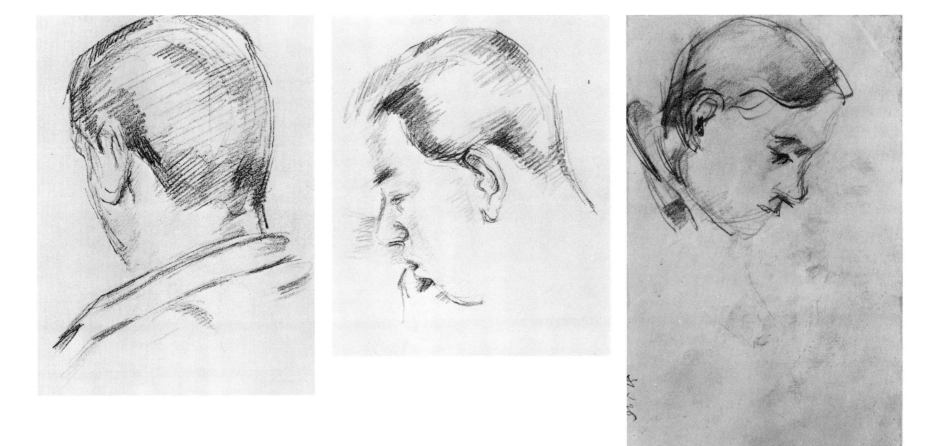

185

Head, shoulder, and hand of Cézanne's son. Collection Adrien Chappuis, Tresserve (Savoie).
Pencil on white paper; page XXIII verso in a sketchbook measuring 15 × 23.8 cm. (Chappuis III).
Verso: Sketch of two male bathers.
Literature: Venturi, under Cat. No. 1306, not reproduced; Chappuis, *Album,* Cat. No. XXIII verso, dated ca. 1882, not identified.
Date: Ca. 1894–1896. For discussion see pp. 35, 40.

186

Head of Cézanne's son, on a sheet with a portrait of Madame Cézanne (No. 90). Collection Adrien Chappuis, Tresserve (Savoie).
Pencil on white paper; page XXIV in a sketchbook measuring 15 × 23.8 cm. (Chappuis III).
Verso: Blank.
Literature: Venturi, under Cat. No. 1306, not reproduced; Chappuis, 1938, No. 11; Chappuis, *Album,* Cat. No. XXIV, dated 1891–1895.
Date: Ca. 1894–1898. For discussion see pp. 35, 40.

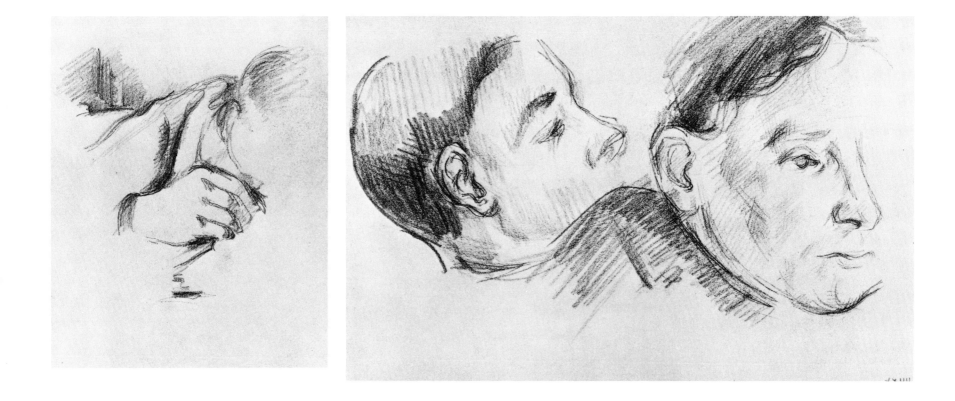

187

Study of the head of Cézanne's son, on a sheet with a portrait of Madame Cézanne (No. 80) and an unidentified figure. Collection Adrien Chappuis, Tresserve (Savoie). Pencil on white paper; page XXXI bis in a sketchbook measuring 15 × 23.8 cm. (Chappuis III).
Verso: Unidentified sketches.
Literature: Venturi, under Cat. No. 1309, not reproduced; Chappuis, *Album,* Cat. No. XXXI bis, portrait of Madame Cézanne dated 1877–1882, portrait of Cézanne's son dated 1882–1885.
Date: Ca. 1894–1896. For discussion see pp. 35, 40.

188

Sketch of Cézanne's son, perhaps sleeping. Collection Mrs. Ira Haupt, New York.
Pencil on white paper; probably p. VI from a sketchbook measuring 12.7 × 26.6 cm. (Rewald, *Carnet IV*).[1]
Verso: Uncertain.
Literature: Unpublished (Rewald, *Carnet IV,* p. VI?).
Date: Ca. 1894–1896.

1   As the drawing is framed, it is not possible to determine its original position in the sketchbook.

188 bis

Sketch of Cézanne's son, perhaps reading. Collection
Mrs. Ira Haupt, New York.
Pencil on white paper; p. XLVII from a sketchbook mea-
suring 12.7 × 26.6 cm (Rewald, *Carnet IV*).
Verso: Sketch of a collar.
Literature: Rewald, *Carnet IV*, p. XLVII (not reproduced).
Date: Ca. 1894–1896.

189

Study of Cézanne's son. Collection Adrien Chappuis,
Tresserve (Savoie).
Pencil on white paper; page XXXIV verso in a sketchbook
measuring 15 × 23.8 cm (Chappuis III).
Verso: Blank.
Literature: Venturi, under Cat. No. 1309, not reproduced;
Berthold, Cat. No. 271, not reproduced; Chappuis, *Album*,
Cat. No. XXXIV verso, dated 1883–1886, not identified.
Date: Ca. 1894–1896. For discussion see pp. 35, 40.

190 fac.

Sketch of Cézanne's son perhaps writing or reading. Collection Adrien Chappuis, Tresserve (Savoie).
Pencil on white paper; page XXXII in a sketchbook measuring 15 × 23.8 cm. (Chappuis III).
Verso: Sketch of a house in mountains.
Literature: Venturi, under Cat. No. 1309, not reproduced; Chappuis, *Album*, Cat. No. XXXII, dated 1885–1890, not identified.
Date: Ca. 1894–1896. For discussion see pp. 35, 40.

191 fac.

Portrait sketch of Cézanne's son, on a sheet with a study of a male bather descending into the water. Collection Colin Clark, New York. Formerly Collection Sir Kenneth and Lady Clark, London; acquired from Cézanne *fils* through the dealer Paul Guillaume in 1934.
Pencil on white paper, approximately 12 × 19.5 cm.; page from a sketchbook (probably Chappuis I; compare No. 194).
Verso: Watercolor, sketch of foliage (unpublished).
Literature: Unpublished.

This bather appears in several of Cézanne's drawings. As the source of his pose, Neumeyer (Cat. No. 15) has suggested the front left figure in Marcantonio's engraving after Michelangelo's *Battle of Pisa*. Berthold (Cat. No. 273) believes it to be the figure of Christ in Alonso Cano's *Dead Christ*; Cézanne made a copy of this figure from an engraving in Charles Blanc's *Histoires des peintres de toutes les écoles*, Paris, 1861–1876. Berthold's hypothesis is the more convincing of the two, although it too must admit to con-

siderable latitude in the representation of the model (the position of the legs, for example, is reversed). For variations of the bather see V. 541, 581, and 1110.

Date: Mid-1890's. For discussion see pp. 35, 40.

192

Study of a male head leaning forward, probably Cézanne's son. Collection Adrien Chappuis, Tresserve (Savoie). Pencil on white paper; page XXX in a sketchbook measuring 12 × 19.5 cm (Chappuis I).
Verso: Seated male bather (reproduced in Chappuis, 1938, No. 20; catalogued in error by Venturi under No. 1282).
Literature: Unpublished.
Date: Mid-1890's. For discussion see pp. 35, 40.

193

Portrait study of Cézanne's son. Musée du Louvre, Paris; acquired in 1951 as a gift from the dealer Sam Salz, who had purchased it in 1950 from Maurice Renou. Originally Collection Cézanne *fils*, who sold it to an anonymous Lyon collector in 1934 through the dealer Paul Guillaume. Pencil on white paper; page 6 verso in a sketchbook measuring 11.6 × 18.2 cm. (Rewald, *Carnet III*).
Verso: Copy after Coysevox's *Buste de Le Brun* in the Louvre (identification by Rewald).
Literature: Rewald, *Carnet III,* p. 6, described as ''tête d'enfant (le fils de l'artiste?).''
Date: Mid-1890's. For discussion see pp. 35, 40.

194 fac.

Portrait sketch of Cézanne's son sleeping. Collection Adrien Chappuis, Tresserve (Savoie).
Pencil on white paper; page XLIII verso in a sketchbook measuring 12 × 19.5 cm. (Chappuis I).
Verso: Drawing of a child writing (erroneously catalogued by Venturi, under No. 1275, as XLII).
Literature: Unpublished.
Date: Mid-1890's. For discussion see pp. 35, 40.

195 fac.

Head of Cézanne's son asleep. Collection Adrien Chappuis, Tresserve (Savoie).
Pencil on white paper; page LI verso in a sketchbook measuring 12 × 19.5 cm. (Chappuis I).
Verso: Blank.
Literature: Venturi, under Cat. No. 1280, neither reproduced nor identified.
Date: Mid-1890's. For discussion see pp. 35, 40.

196

Beginning of a study of a head, probably of Cézanne's son. Collection Adrien Chappuis, Tresserve (Savoie).
Pencil on white paper; page XLIV in a sketchbook measuring 12 × 19.5 cm. (Chappuis I).
Verso: Copy of a bust of the Roman Emperor Lucius Verus.
Literature: Venturi, under No. 1275, described as "traits vagues," not reproduced.
Date: Mid-1890's. For discussion see pp. 35, 40.

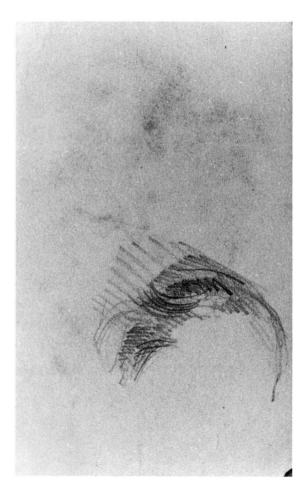

197

Male figure seated at a table, head supported by left arm, on a sheet with the legs of a standing male bather. Private collection, Paris.
Pencil on medium-grain white paper, 11.2 × 14.5 cm., part of a larger sheet.
Verso: Study of a standing male bather, from the back; at the right center are indications of another drawing.
Literature: Unpublished.

This drawing appeared on the Paris art market in the early 1960's, identified as a portrait of Cézanne's son, but in my opinion it is a forgery that utilizes a hitherto unpublished drawing by Cézanne (197a). The paper and the verso drawing, however, are authentic. (For the same hand, see Nos. 29 and 92.)

Portraits of Cézanne's Father

198

Portrait sketch of Louis-Auguste Cézanne reading a news-
paper, on a sheet with a study for a lamentation and
arithmetical notations. Kunstmuseum, Basel.
Pen and ink on white paper (the study for the lamentation
in pencil); 17.6 × 23.5 cm.
Verso: Sketch of an unidentified male head and study for
L'Orgie, V. 92 (Chappuis, Cat. No. 12).
Literature: Venturi, Vol. I, p. 350, not reproduced;
Chappuis, Cat. No. 35, dated 1866–1871; Douglas Cooper,
review of Chappuis, *Les Dessins de Cézanne au Musée de
Bâle*, in *Master Drawings*, I, No. 4, 1963, pp. 54–57, dated
ca. 1866; Wayne V. Andersen, "Cézanne's Portrait Draw-
ings from the 1860's," *Master Drawings*, V, 1967, pp. 265–
280.

In a letter of November 2, 1866, from Antoine Guillemet to
Émile Zola, there is a reference to a portrait of Cézanne's
father in a large armchair (Fig. 4): "The father would look
like a pope on his throne were it not that he is reading *Le
Siècle*."[1] This statement has been interpreted as an error in
Guillemet's observation, since in the painting Louis-
Auguste is reading *L'Événement*. Zola had published some
articles in the latter on the 1866 Salon with favorable comments about certain Impressionists. Guillemet may have
been correct, however; it is probable that Cézanne's father
was reading *Le Siècle* and that Cézanne substituted the
title *L'Événement* as a jest to make his father appear as
completely absorbed in Zola's remarks as in the contents
of a bourgeois newspaper.

Date: Ca. 1866–1868. For discussion see p. 4.

1 *Correspondance*, p. 43.

199

Portrait of Louis-Auguste Cézanne dressed in coat and cap.
Present location unknown. Formerly Collection Cézanne
fils, Paris.
Charcoal on paper; approximately 22 × 25 cm.
Literature: Venturi, Cat. No. 1234, dated 1872–1879; Reff,
"Studies," p. 76, dated "early seventies."
Date: Ca. 1874. See discussion on pp. 9, 10.

200 fac. detail

Portrait of Louis-Auguste Cézanne dressed in cap and
coat, on a sheet with a sketch of Madame Cézanne (No. 41).
Art Institute of Chicago.
Pencil on white paper; page XIX verso in a sketchbook
measuring 12.4 × 21.7 cm. (Rewald, *Carnet II*).
Verso: Study of an *écorché.*
Literature: Rewald, *Carnet II*, p. XIX verso, not reproduced;
Schniewind, Cat. No. XIX verso.
Date: 1878–1880.

201 fac.

Portrait of Louis-Auguste Cézanne dressed in cap and coat.
Art Institute of Chicago.
Pencil on white paper; page XXIX in a sketchbook measuring 12.4 × 21.7 cm. (Rewald, *Carnet II*).
Verso: Study of a running youth attacked by rats.
Literature: Rewald, *Carnet II,* p. XXIX; Schniewind, Cat. No. XXIX; Neumeyer, Cat. No. 40, dated 1880–1886.
Date: 1878–ca. 1880.

202 fac. detail

Portrait of Louis-Auguste Cézanne asleep, on a sheet with a portrait sketch probably of Madame Cézanne (No. 45). Art Institute of Chicago.

Pencil on white paper; page XXXVIII verso in a sketchbook measuring 12.4 × 21.7 cm (Rewald, *Carnet II*).

Verso: Two studies for figures in an erotic theme and a faint, unidentified portrait sketch (No. 256).

Literature: Rewald, *Carnet II,* p. XXXVIII verso; Schniewind, Cat. No. XXXVIII verso.

Date: 1878–ca. 1880.

203

Full-length portrait of Louis-Auguste Cézanne seated in a chair reading a newspaper. Collection Robert von Hirsch, Basel.

Pencil on white paper; page III verso from a sketchbook, measuring 12.5 × 20.5 cm. (Basel III).

Verso: Sketch of male bathers, V. 1402.

Literature: Venturi, Cat. No. 1403; John Rewald, *Cézanne et Zola,* Paris, 1936, No. 48, dated ca. 1880; *idem, Paul Cézanne,* New York, 1948, p. 112, dated ca. 1880; Neumeyer, Cat. No. 27, dated 1868–1870; John Rewald, *Paul Cézanne,* New York, 1968, p. 112, dated ca. 1880.

Rewald's date is disputed by Neumeyer, who relates this sketch to V. 91, the painted portrait of Cézanne's father generally dated from 1866 to 1868. Neumeyer points out the "undulating 'baroque' line which stands in so strange a contrast to the 'classical' nature of his later compositions." The style of this drawing, however, is foreign to Cézanne in the late sixties; rather, it represents a rapid sketch style of the late seventies and early eighties. The over-all alternation of hatching with light areas, the regularity in the direction of hatching, and the complex, unacademic chiaroscuro all point to 1879–1881. An identical style characterizes a portrait drawing of Zola, which I have dated about 1881 (No. 237), and also drawings such as V. 1404–1407, 1413, and 1417, all of which were close to this drawing in a sketchbook, now dismantled, Basel III, which Chappuis has dated, I think correctly, ca. 1880 to the mid-nineties.

Date: Ca. 1879–1881.

204 detail

Portrait sketch of Louis-Auguste Cézanne with cap, on a
sheet with a portrait of Madame Cézanne (No. 59). Fogg
Art Museum, Harvard University.
See No. 59.
Date: 1882–1884.

205

Portrait sketch of Louis-Auguste Cézanne at a table, on a
sheet with a second portrait sketch, probably of either
Cézanne's wife or son, overlaid by a sketch of a furniture
detail. Collection Adrien Chappuis, Tresserve (Savoie).
Pencil on white paper; page XXXIV verso in a sketchbook
measuring 12.6 × 21.5 cm. (Chappuis II).
Verso: Landscape sketch, Valley of the Arc near Aix.
Literature: Venturi, under Cat. No. 1290, not reproduced.

Venturi has not identified this figure nor has he detected
the second portrait drawing overlaid by the furniture detail.
The only evidence that it is the artist's father is the characteristic cap and pose.

See No. 201.

Date: Ca. 1882–1886.

206

Portrait sketch of Louis-Auguste Cézanne, on a sheet with sketches of a clock and flower pots. Collection Adrien Chappuis, Tresserve (Savoie).
Pencil on white paper; page XL verso in a sketchbook measuring 12.6 × 21.5 cm (Chappuis II).
Verso: Self-portrait (No. 19).
Literature: Venturi, Vol. I, under Cat. No. 1293, mentioned only.
Date: 1882–1886.

207

Portrait of Cézanne's mother sleeping. Present location unknown.
Pencil on paper.
Literature: John Rewald, *Paul Cézanne,* New York, 1948, Fig. 26; *Paul Cézanne Letters,* ed. John Rewald, 2d ed., London [1944], No. 33, dated ca. 1885; Reff, "Studies," Fig. 2.

See No. 208.

Date: 1881–1885.

208

Two portrait sketches of Cézanne's mother sleeping. Present location unknown. (Photograph courtesy Thannhauser Gallery, Paris.)
Pencil on paper.
Literature: Unpublished.

The identification of the subject as Cézanne's mother depends on No. 207. The close correspondence in character, pose, and style between these drawings suggests that they date from about the same time.

Date: 1881–1885.

Portrait of Gustave Boyer. Collection Sir Kenneth and Lady Clark, London.

Pencil on beige paper, trimmed at the bottom and right edge, 13.8 × 13.2–7 cm.; page from a sketchbook.

Verso: The number "12" written in blue pencil at upper left corner (same style of lettering and color as the number "2" on the verso of No. 2); impression from the drawing of a left hand on the verso of the following page, similar to the hand on Chappuis 3, perhaps from the same sketchbook, but not from *Carnet 18 × 24 cm.*[1]

Literature: Vollard, p. 26; Paris, Musée de l'Orangerie, *Cézanne*, 1936, Cat. No. 181, dated ca. 1870; Venturi, Cat. No. 1236, dated 1873–1877; Chappuis, 1957, Frontispiece, dated 1873–1877; Reff, "Studies," p. 48, dated 1873–1874; Wayne V. Andersen, "A Cézanne Self-Portrait Reidentified," *The Burlington Magazine*, CVI, 1964, pp. 284–285, dated "not later than 1872."

The first recorded mention by Cézanne of Gustave Boyer, one of his boyhood comrades, is in a note appended to a letter he wrote to Zola in 1858;[2] nothing is known about their subsequent relationship. Three oil portraits have been identified as Boyer: V. 130, 131, 132; Venturi dated them 1870–1871, no doubt feeling that Manet's technique and color had guided Cézanne's hand and that the style is clearly pre-Impressionist. Gerstle Mack (*Paul Cézanne*, New York, 1935) assigned the most important Boyer portrait, V. 131 (Fig. 7), then known as *L'Homme au chapeau de paille,* to Cézanne's stay at Auvers, 1872–1874, and retained this date even in the later edition of his study (*The Life of Cézanne,* Paris, 1938, p. 16), which was generally adjusted to Venturi's chronology. Rivière (*Le Maître Paul Cézanne,* Paris, 1923, p. 200) dated the portrait 1873. Charles Sterling in the Orangerie catalogue (p. 62) disputed Rivière's date and suggested 1870–1871, on the basis of the stylistic similarity between the Boyer portraits, particularly V. 131, and *Melting Snow à L'Estaque* (V. 51), which dates from the end of the 1870–1871 winter. (Cézanne spent that winter in L'Estaque evading conscription into the Franco-Prussian war. The armistice was signed on January 28, 1871, and Cézanne returned to Paris shortly afterward.)

The drawing of Boyer was first published as a self-portrait by Ambroise Vollard in 1914 and this identification has since been upheld by Charles Sterling, Lionello Venturi, Adrien Chappuis, and Theodore Reff. With the exception of Sterling (whose opinion that the drawing dates from ca. 1870 preceded Venturi's publication, all others have dated it between 1873 and 1877 on evidence drawn from comparisons with photographs and painted portraits of Cézanne that can be assigned to the early and mid-seventies. Sterling's date was based less on the subject's age than on the style of the drawing, which indicates a date prior to Cézanne's submission to Pissarro's influence in 1872. Although there is no need to assume that the drawing was contemporary with the paintings of Boyer, this stylistic *terminus ante quem* is equally acceptable for the drawing. Comparisons with other drawings from this period (Chappuis, Cat. Nos. 55 and 56, for example, dated 1870[3]) suggest that a date of 1870–1871 for the drawing would be

accurate. By this time, Cézanne had reached the limit at which his media and techniques could embody his intense romantic imagery. The heavy blacks of his canvases were produced in this drawing by repeated lines of forcefully applied soft lead; in the denser areas light is still reflected from the graphic surface that was brightly polished by repeated strokes. During the execution the pencil was sharpened and then applied with such force that it plowed deep furrows through already darkened areas, at times damaging the surface of the paper: the hair near each ear, the corners of the mouth, and the tip of the nose are gouged and scuffed, as is one eye (its glazed expression is therefore accidental).

It is not surprising that this drawing was assumed to be a portrait of Cézanne. Before Georges Rivière identified the sitter in the three oil portraits as Boyer,[4] they had also been mistaken for self-portraits: in 1910 Julius Meier-Graefe published V. 131 as a portrait of the artist, an error he re-

peated in 1920 in the case of both V. 131 and 132.[5] Cézanne and Boyer shared certain physiognomic traits: both were nearly bald by 1870, and both had a full round head, strong eyes, and a heavy nose. The striking difference between them was in the style of their beards. Cézanne's beard had, one might say, no style; from a letter he wrote to Zola we know that his periodic haircuts were the result not of his vanity but of his wish to keep children from teasing him and throwing rocks.[6] On the other hand, we can tell from Cézanne's painted portraits of Boyer that the latter's beard did follow a style: a thin, wispy mustache, a few longer hairs at the corners of the mouth, and a dense, well-defined beard parted sharply beneath a clean-shaven chin.[7] This style is evident in the drawing of Boyer, but to discern it the preliminary soft lines of the original drawing must be distinguished from the dark lines that more accurately define the characteristic features of the sitter: the chin is found to be clean-shaven, the mustache rendered by two preliminary lines and one final stroke, and the beard deftly

---

1 For an argument that Chappuis, Cat. No. 3 is not a page from *Carnet 18 × 24 cm.,* see my review of Chappuis, *Les Dessins de Cézanne au Musée de Bâle,* in *The Art Bulletin,* XLV, 1963, pp. 79 ff.

2 *Paul Cézanne, Letters,* ed. John Rewald, 3rd ed., London, 1946, pp. 24, 27, 33. Cf. Gerstle Mack, *Paul Cézanne,* London, 1935, p. 411.

3 The painting, V. 104, for which these are studies is dated 1870.

4 *Le Maître Paul Cézanne,* Paris, 1923, p. 200.

5 *Paul Cézanne,* Munich, 1910, p. 48; *Cézanne und sein Kreis,* Munich, 1920, pp. 102–103.

6 Letter of April 14, 1878; *Paul Cézanne Letters,* ed. Rewald, 3rd ed., p. 115.

7 This style of beard is clearly defined in Guillaumin's self-portrait in the Louvre. Reproduction in *Bulletin des Musées de France,* 1950, opp. p. 8.

parted below the chin. Further, the hair rolls under, carrying through the style of the beard—a characteristic clearly related to the painted portraits of Boyer. Whereas in the drawing and the painted portraits of Boyer, especially V. 131 (Fig. 7), the line of the beard drops abruptly at mid-cheek to pass under the chin, all the portraits of Cézanne show the conformation of a natural beard.

Date: 1870–1872. For discussion see pp. 7–8, 10, 12–13, 17, 22.

210 fac.

Portrait of Victor Chocquet. Baltimore Museum of Art (Mrs. Adelyn D. Breeskin Collection). Formerly Collection Ambroise Vollard.
Pencil on white paper; approximately 14 × 10 cm.
Verso: Blank.
Literature: Venturi, Cat. No. 1241, dated 1877–1886; Theodore Reff, ''Cézanne's Drawings, 1875–1885,'' *The Burlington Magazine*, CI, 1959, p. 172, dated 1875–1876.

Chocquet was a chief supervisor in the Paris customs administration; though of modest means, he collected pottery and furniture, as well as paintings by Delacroix and by the young Impressionists.[1] Through his defense of the Impressionists at the Hôtel Druot sale of March 24, 1875, Chocquet made the acquaintance of Renoir, who later introduced him to Cézanne. According to Renoir, he first took Chocquet to Tanguy's shop, where Chocquet immediately purchased one of Cézanne's paintings.[2] Tanguy's records, which I have examined at Jean-Pierre Cézanne's in Paris and published elsewhere,[3] indicate sales of Cézanne's canvases only on the following dates: October 25, November 1, and December 30, 1875; therefore, at least six months must have elapsed between the Hôtel Druot sale and Chocquet's meeting with Cézanne.

As Chocquet promptly responded to his meeting with Renoir by commissioning a portrait of Madame Chocquet and, soon afterwards, two of himself, we might assume that Cézanne's first portrait of Chocquet was made soon after they were introduced. A letter of February 4, 1876, from Monet to Chocquet, proves that by that time Chocquet and Cézanne were in touch;[4] and a letter from Cézanne to Pissarro, writte in Aix, April, 1876, mentions that he had received correspondence from Chocquet.[5] These do not, however, provide, a date for the portrait of Chocquet. Rivière was the first to conclude that the portrait exhibited in 1877 was the oil painting (20 × 15 cm.) in the Pellerin collection, and he was the first to date it 1875. He reported in the newspaper *L'Impressionniste*, ''Un journal appelait le portrait d'homme exposé cette année 'Belloir en Chocolat' .... C'était le portrait de M. Chocquet, le premier fait de lui par Cézanne.''[6] If Cézanne painted this portrait in 1875, he must have done it very late that year, for, as Tanguy's records show, Chocquet did not purchase a Cézanne canvas before October 25.

Date: Ca. 1876–1877. For discussion see p. 20.

1 See the catalogue of the Madame Veuve Chocquet sale at Galerie Georges Petit, July 1–4, 1899.

2 See Vollard, Ch. VIII; and Maurice Denis, *Nouvelles théories*, Paris, 1922, pp. 115–116. For a full account of this event, see John Rewald, *History of Impressionism*, New York, 1961, pp. 354–358.

3 ''Cézanne, Tanguy, Chocquet,'' *The Art Bulletin*, II, 1967, pp. 135–139.

4 Published in Jules Joëts, ''Les Impressionnistes et Chocquet,'' *L'Amour de l'art*, XVI, 1935, p. 121.

5 *Correspondance*, p. 124.

6 See the account given by Georges Rivière in *Le Maitre Paul Cézanne*, Paris, 1923, p. 89.

Portrait of Victor Chocquet. Present location unknown. Formerly Collection Sir Kenneth and Lady Clark, London. Pencil on coarse, textured, white paper.
Literature: *Paul Cézanne Letters,* ed. John Rewald, 3rd ed., New York, dated ca. 1877–1882; Wayne V. Andersen, ''Cézanne, Tanguy, Chocquet,'' *The Art Bulletin,* XLIX, 1967, pp. 137–139.

When Venturi catalogued the oil portrait of Chocquet, now in the collection of Étienne Bignou, New York, he noted ''Selon une tradition acceptée par M. Rivière, ce portrait aurait été peint en 1902, d'après une photographie.''[1] But he added, ''Le dessin [V. 1240, my No. 212] montre que Cézanne a fait une étude d'après Chocquet, qui est très ressemblante à ce portrait, et contemporaine à une étude de Mme Cézanne de 1877 environ.'' This question can be resolved because I have found the photograph that Cézanne used (211a). It served for four of the nine likenesses of Chocquet: the painting V. 532, a small oil in the Lecomte

collection (mentioned under V. 532 but not catalogued, and two drawings.[2] Rivière was correct, then, in maintaining that Cézanne had painted V. 532 from a photograph; it is also possible that Cézanne was working from the photograph in 1902, even though Chocquet had died in 1899. The photograph was probably given to Cézanne shortly after he met Chocquet. See also No. 212.

Date: Ca. 1877–1878. For discussion see p. 20.

1 Venturi 532, dated 1883–1887.

2 See my article cited at this entry.

212 detail

Portrait of Victor Chocquet, on a sheet with two portraits of Madame Cézanne (No. 33). Collection Benjamin Sonnenberg, New York.
Literature: Wayne V. Andersen, "Cézanne, Tanguy, Chocquet," *The Art Bulletin,* XLIX, 1967, pp. 137–139.

See Nos. 33, 211.

Date: Ca. 1877–1878. For discussion see p. 20.

213 n.r.

Portrait sketch of Victor Chocquet, on a sheet with an outdoor genre scene. Collection Robert van Hirsch, Basel. Formerly Collections Werner Feuz, Zurich, and Cézanne *fils,* Paris.
Literature: Georges Rivière, *Le Maître Paul Cézanne,* Paris, 1923, p. 127; Venturi, Cat. No. 1200, the complete sheet dated 1871–1877. The portrait has not been reproduced.

Not examined.

214 fac.

Portrait of Achille Emperaire, on a sheet with a partial sketch of a female figure in a long dress or coat, carrying a lantern. Atelier Cézanne, Aix-en-Provence; gift of Lucien Blanc, Aix, in 1954.
Pencil on white paper (partial sketch in pen with bistre ink); 11.7 × 12.4 cm.
Verso: Bistre ink sketch of a seated female nude, one arm extended toward a partial figure on the left. The same ink and technique can be seen on a sheet in Basel, Chappuis, Cat. No. 35.
Literature: Wayne V. Andersen, "Cézanne's Portrait Drawings from the 1860's," *Master Drawings,* V, 1967, pp. 265–280.
Date: Ca. 1866–1870.

215

Portrait of Achille Emperaire seated in an armchair. Kunstmuseum, Basel.
Charcoal on gray paper; 30.6 × 24.1 cm.
Verso: Blank.
Literature: Venturi, Vol. I, p. 352, not reproduced; Chappuis, Cat. No. 49, dated 1867–1870.

Venturi has suggested that this image of Emperaire is a vague and confused counterproof of a very beautiful drawing. Although Chappuis has not refuted this completely, he has added that if it is a counterproof, it was taken with great care. In my opinion it is simply a smudged drawing; the pose and the direction of the hachures are correct as they appear here and cannot be inverted. It is probably a preliminary study for the large painted portrait of Emperaire that Cézanne tried to enter in the Salon of 1870 (Fig. 6). In the painting, however, the viewer's eye level is differently aligned: in this drawing it is at Emperaire's knees, whereas in the painting it is on a line with his eyes.

Emperaire, also a painter, was a childhood friend of Cézanne's from Aix.[1] His strange appearance was due to the stunted growth of his legs. Joachim Gasquet described him as "a dwarf, but with a magnificent cavalier's head, like a Van Dyck, nerves of steel, an iron pride in a deformed body, a flame of genius on a warped hearth, a mixture of Don Quixote and Prometheus."[2]

Date: 1868–1870. For discussion see pp. 4–5.

1   On Cézanne's relationship with Achille Emperaire see John Rewald, "Achille Emperaire ami de Paul Cézanne," *L'Amour de l'art*, XIX, 1938, pp. 151 ff.

2   *Cézanne*, Paris, 1921, pp. 38–39. See also the description by Émile Bernard in *Souvenirs sur Paul Cézanne*, Paris, 1912, pp. 49–50.

216

Portrait of Achille Emperaire, on a sheet with three studies of a male head. Kunstmuseum, Basel.
Pencil on white paper (the three studies in India ink); 28.9 × 24.9 cm.
Verso: Head and torso of a male academic model (Chappuis, Cat. No. 18).
Literature: Venturi, described as verso of Cat. No. 1584, not reproduced; Chappuis, Cat. No. 51, dated 1867–1870; Wayne V. Andersen, "Cézanne's Portrait Drawings from the 1860's," *Master Drawings*, V, 1967, pp. 265–280.

The two ink studies on this sheet are of a lay-figure head and are partly similar to the ink sketches on the Rotterdam sheet with the profile of Guillaumin (226). Both sheets show evidence of practice with tilted heads in a manner suggesting that the Basel sketches may be contemporary with three studies of foreshortened male nudes dating from the second half of the sixties (V. 1166, 1167, 1193). One of these, V. 1167, is rendered in precisely the same technique as the portrait drawing of Emperaire owned by Chappuis (218). This similarity in itself proves nothing, but V. 1167 corresponds in technique to an early drawing of a reclining nude woman (216b) that is related, in turn, to a painting of a nude woman reclining on a couch that Cézanne submitted, along with the portrait of Emperaire, to the Salon of 1870. The painting of the nude woman is known only through a caricature by Stock of Cézanne's entries (216a). The figure as shown in the caricature corresponds in detail, even though its position is reversed, to that of the reclining woman in the drawing V. 1227 (216b); the pose of the latter is the same as

in Stock's caricature, and, in both, the anatomy is rather lumpy, the breasts sag, and the hip is very high. The arm of the couch in V. 1227 has an exact counterpart in the caricature. In addition, the graphic style of V. 1227 is the same as that of Chappuis's portrait drawing of Emperaire (218). Although the evidence is inconclusive, the stylistic associations between the drawings just described and the studies on this Basel sheet suggest that the latter also date from about 1868–1870.[1]

Date: Ca. 1868–1870.

1 For a more complete discussion see my article cited at this entry.

217

Portrait of Achille Emperaire. Kunstmuseum, Basel; acquired in 1951 from Lucas Lichtenhan. Formerly Collection Cézanne *fils*.
Charcoal on white paper, 43.2 × 31.9 cm.; watermark ''D & C BLAUW.''
Verso: Blank.
Literature: Vollard, p. 161; Venturi, Cat. No. 1194, dated 1867–1870; Paris, Musée de l'Orangerie, *Cézanne*, 1936, Cat. No. 149, dated ca. 1877 (date suggested by Cézanne *fils*); Reff, ''Studies,'' p. 70, dated 1866–1867; Chappuis, Cat. No. 50, dated 1867–1870.

See also Nos. 215, 218.

The dating of this remarkable drawing has followed that of the painted portrait (Fig. 6) for which it is a study. Chappuis has pointed out that, considering the facture alone, it resembles the studies in the same medium that Cézanne made from posed models at the Académie Suisse (V. 1584, for example). Reff has drawn a stylistic parallel with other life drawings, including V. 1167, 1171–75. In my opinion, this drawing is more advanced than academic studies such as V. 1584 and was done later than 1865, the date of our latest documentation for Cézanne's studies at the Académie Suisse.[1]

Date: 1868–1870. For discussion see pp. 4–5, 8–10, 12–13.

1 See Cézanne's letter to Pissarro of March 15, 1865, in *Correspondance*, p. 91. This does not mean that Cézanne did not continue working there beyond this date.

218

Portrait of Achille Emperaire. Collection Adrien Chappuis, Tresserve (Savoie).
Charcoal on white paper; 49 × 31 cm.
Verso: Blank.
Literature: Vollard, p. 17; Julius Meier-Graefe, *Cézanne und sein Kreis,* Munich, 1922, p. 91; Paris, Musée de l'Orangerie, *Cézanne,* 1936, Cat. No. 141, dated ca. 1867; Venturi, Cat. No. 1195, dated 1867–1870; Fritz Novotny, *Cézanne,* London, 1937, dated 1867–1870; Giorgio Nicodemi, *Paul Cézanne, 76 disegni,* Milan, 1944, No. XIV, dated 1867–1870; Reff, "Studies," p. 70, 1866–1867.

Probably a study for V. 88 (Fig. 6). See also Nos. 215, 217.

Date: 1868–1870. For discussion see pp. 4–5, 12, 14, 17.

219 n.r.

Three male heads: one resembling Cézanne, another, Achille Emperaire. Private collection, Switzerland. See No. 26.

220 n.r.

Head and hand studies from an academic model. Collection Elvira B. Reilly, New York. Formerly Collections David Lederer, New York; Paul Franke, Munich, acquired in 1925.
Charcoal on tan paper; 31–43 × 48.9 cm.
Literature: Julius Meier-Graefe, *Cézanne und sein Kreis,* Munich, 1922, p. 90; Venturi, Cat. No. 1193, dated 1867–1870; Chicago, Art Institute, *Cézanne: Paintings, Watercolors, and Drawings,* 1952, No. 9, dated 1867–1869; Chappuis, 1957, No. 3 (referred to); Reff, "Studies," p. 69; Neumeyer, No. 26, dated 1867–1869.

Venturi has catalogued these drawings as studies of Achille Emperaire. The identification was first questioned in the 1952 exhibition catalogue of the Chicago Art Institute where, under No. 8, it is called a study for *The Autopsy* (V. 105, dated 1867–1869); both Chappuis and Reff have concurred with this. Neumeyer, while agreeing that these studies are for *The Autopsy,* has claimed that the model was Emperaire. Citing Gasquet's description of Emperaire, "a dwarf, but with a magnificent cavalier's head, like a Van Dyck . . ." he overlooks the fact that a second sheet of studies for *The Autopsy,* also in charcoal on buff paper, shows the model full-length with a body of normal proportions.[1]

In my opinion the model was not Emperaire.

Date: Ca. 1867–1869.

1 Venturi has not catalogued this sheet. For reproduction see Chicago, Art Institute, *Cézanne: Paintings, Watercolors, and Drawings,* 1952, Cat. No. 8.

221

Portrait of Achille Emperaire. Present location unknown. This drawing is based on No. 218. In my opinion it is not in Cézanne's hand.

222

Portrait of Dr. Paul Gachet painting. Musée du Louvre, Paris; donated in 1951. Formerly Collection Paul Gachet, Paris.
Charcoal on beige paper; 32.5 × 21.5 cm.
Literature: Venturi, Vol. I, p. 347 (medium inaccurately described); Paul Gachet, *Le Docteur Gachet et Murer,* Paris, 1956, Fig. 3, dated 1873.

Dr. Paul F. Gachet (1828–1909), famous for his sympathetic treatment of van Gogh, was an amateur artist and a devoted friend of several of the Impressionist painters.[1] In April 1872 he purchased a house at Auvers-sur-Oise. Pissarro had a house in the neighboring village of Pontoise, and in the autumn of 1872 he invited Cézanne to join him there and to paint with him out of doors; Cézanne moved to Auvers in November and remained there until the spring of 1874.[2]

Cézanne had met Dr. Gachet much earlier, in 1858, when Gachet had come to Aix to meet Cézanne's father, to whom he had been referred as a possible source of capital to assist him in starting a medical practice. Perhaps out of sentiment engendered by that event, Gachet took extra trouble to arrange for Cézanne's stay at Auvers (Cézanne at that time had a newborn son). In 1872 Gachet wrote to Cézanne's father, recalling his visit in 1858 and impressing him with Cézanne's need for a reasonable pension.[3]

See No. 224.

Date: Ca. 1873–1874. For discussion see pp. 9–10, 12–14.

1 For the most reliable biography of Dr. Gachet, see Paul Gachet, *Le Docteur Gachet et Murer,* Paris, 1956, pp. 13 ff.

2 See *Correspondance,* pp. 117–118.

3 Gachet, *Le Docteur Gachet et Murer,* pp. 28–29.

223

Portrait sketch of Dr. Gachet, on a sheet with a study for *Un après-midi à Naples*. Kunstmuseum, Basel.
Pencil on white paper, 10.3 × 16.8 cm.; page from *Carnet 10.3 × 17*.
Verso: A picnic scene of three men, a woman, and a dog (No. 247).
Literature: Chappuis, Cat. No. 69, dated 1872–1874.

This figure was first identified by Robert Ratcliffe[1] and later discussed by Chappuis, who has quite correctly suggested that as the erotic theme overlaps the portrait of Dr. Gachet, it must postdate it. Chappuis' date is based on the length of time Cézanne spent in close contact with Dr. Gachet at Auvers, from the autumn of 1872 to the spring of 1874.

Date: 1873–1874. For discussion see p. 13.

224 n.r.

Portrait of Dr. Gachet. Collection Paul Gachet, Auvers-sur-Oise.

Venturi described this drawing as "portrait du Docteur Gachet. Au fusain" (Vol. I, p. 347), but did not catalogue it. Because it is neither reproduced nor mentioned in Paul Gachet's *Le Docteur Gachet et Murer* (Paris, 1965), which includes all visual material related to Gachet and his artist friends, we can assume that the drawing was either inaccurately described by Venturi or is now lost. A third possibility might be that, because Venturi cited my No. 222 as a drawing in pencil rather than charcoal, he may have compounded his error by assuming that there was a separate charcoal drawing in Gatchet's collection.

225

Dr. Gachet and Cézanne preparing the acid bath for etching a plate. Collection Paul Gachet, Auvers-sur-Oise.
See No. 28.

1 Cited by Chappuis, Vol. 1, p. 125, note 29. For images of Dr. Gachet see Paul Gachet, *Le Docteur Gachet et Murer*, Paris, 1956, Figs. 23, 25.

226

Portrait of Armand Guillaumin. Museum Boymans-van Beuningen, Rotterdam.
Pencil on fine-grained white paper; 23.5 × 17.2 cm.
Verso: Sketch of an angel in flight (V. 1185), identified by Hoetink, Cat. No. 21, as a copy of Veronese's *Jupiter Destroying the Vices.*
Literature: Venturi, Cat. No. 1196, dated 1870–1877; Wayne V. Andersen, "Cézanne's Portrait Drawings from the 1860's," *Master Drawings,* V, 1967, p. 269, identified and dated 1866–1868; Hoetink, Cat. No. 21.

My identification of the sitter as Armand Guillaumin is based in part on a comparison with Guillaumin's self-portrait in the collection of V. W. Van Gogh, Laren,[1] and in part on Cézanne's etching of Guillaumin, V. 1159.

Venturi placed this drawing in the seventies, perhaps because of the virgules in the beard that are characteristic of Cézanne's brushstroke at that time. If one compares it with the portrait heads of Valabrègue, however, which have similar lines in the beard and are somewhat rectangular in shape, it appears to be of no later date than 1866. The same type of stroke occurs in the beard of *Père Rouvel le Vieux* (V. 17), a painted portrait dated 1866 on external evidence.[2]

Date: 1866–1868. For discussion see pp. 3, 5.

1 For a reproduction of the self-portrait see John Rewald, *The History of Impressionsim,* rev. ed., New York, 1961, p. 363.

2 Rodolphe Walter, "Cézanne à Bennecourt en 1866," *Gazette des beaux-arts,* ser. 6, LIX, 1962, pp. 106–107.

227

Portrait of Armand Guillaumin seated on the ground. Two exemplars: 1. Present location unknown. Formerly Weyhe Gallery, New York. 2. Present location unknown. Formerly Collection Pellerin, Paris; sold at the Hôtel Druot on May 7, 1926.
Etching (sanguine); 26 × 20.5 cm.
Literature: *L'Amour de l'art*, 1921, p. 29; Venturi, Cat. No. 1159, dated 1873.
Date: 1873. For discussion see p. 13.

228

Portrait of Louis Guillaume as Clown. Kunstmuseum, Basel.
Pencil on white paper; 31.4 × 24.3 cm.
Verso: Arithmetical notations.
Literature: Venturi, Cat. No. 1573; Chappuis, 1957, p. 18, dated ca. 1888; *Le Dessin français au XIXe siècle,* ed. René Huyghe, Lausanne, 1948, p. 102. Chappuis, Cat. No. 154, dated ca. 1888.

Preparatory drawing for the group portrait of Louis Guillaume and Cézanne *fils* (V. 552). Guillaume was the son of Cézanne's neighbor and friend, Antoine Guillaume, who is mentioned in the letters from Cézanne to Zola of July 29 and November 4, 1878, and in a letter of October 15, 1906, from Cézanne to his son.[1] According to Cézanne *fils,* V. 552 was painted in Cézanne's atelier in the rue de Val-de Grâce in 1888.[2]

Date: Ca. 1888. For discussion see p. 34.

1   *Correspondance,* pp. 144, 151, 297.

2   See Paris, Musée de l'Orangerie, *Cézanne,* 1936, Cat. No. 72. For a conflicting statement by Cézanne's niece, Martha Conil, see my No. 172.

229

Portrait of Fortuné Marion(?), on a sheet with a study of an
écorché and of the lower portion of a seated man. Kunstmuseum, Basel.
Pencil and ink on white paper; 23 × 17.7 cm.; page from a
sketchbook (*Carnet 18 × 24*).
Verso: Copies after earlier artists (Berthold, Cat. No. 286
and Fig. 33; Chappuis, Cat. No. 24).
Literature: Venturi, mentioned under Cat. No. 1579;
Berthold, Cat. No. 81; Chappuis, Cat. No. 52, dated 1869–
1874.

Chappuis was the first to suggest that this image is perhaps
of Fortuné Marion, one of Cézanne's Aixois friends. The
drawing compares quite closely in appearance with a
photograph of Marion dating from about 1866–1868 (229a).

Date: 1866–1870. For discussion see p. 3.

230 fac.

Portrait of Camille Pissarro. Collection Mr. and Mrs. John Rewald, New York. Originally Collection Camille Pissarro. Pencil on white paper, 10.0 × 8.0 cm.
Verso: Blank.
Literature: John Rewald, *Paul Cézanne*, Paris, 1939, No. 34; *Camille Pissarro, Letters to His Son Lucien*, ed. Rewald, New York, 1943, No. 49; Rewald, *Paul Cézanne*, 1948, No. 44; Wildenstein & Co., New York, *Cézanne*, 1947, No. 87; Neumeyer, Cat. No. 28, dated ca. 1873; John Rewald, *Paul Cézanne*, New York, 1968, Fig. 41, dated ca. 1873.
Date: Ca. 1874. For discussion see pp. 9, 13, 14, 17.

231 fac.

Portrait sketch of Pissarro seated in a chair. Collection Robert von Hirsch, Basel. Formerly Collections Tanner, Zurich, and Camille Pissarro, Paris.
Pencil on paper; 12.5 × 15 cm. Notation in a later hand. Signature not in Cézanne's hand.
Verso: Not examined.
Literature: Galerie Georges Petit, Paris, *Collection Camille Pissarro* [Catalogue of sale], December 3, 1928, No. 61; Venturi, Cat. No. 1226, dated 1872–1877.

The identification of the sitter depends on No. 230.

Date: Ca. 1874. For discussion see pp. 9, 13, 18.

232 fac.

Full-length portrait of Camille Pissarro, out of doors with walking stick and knapsack. Musée du Louvre, Paris; acquired in 1928 by the *Société des Amis du Louvre*. Originally Collection Camille Pissarro.

Pencil on white paper; 19.5 × 11.3 cm.

Verso: Blank.

Literature: Galerie Georges Petit, Paris, *Collection Camille Pissarro* [Catalogue of sale], December 3, 1928, No. 62; Bucharest, Musée des Beaux-Arts, *Le Dessin français aux XIXᵉ et XXᵉ siècles*, 1931, No. 63; Paris, Musée de l'Orangerie, *Les Achats du Musée du Louvre et les dons de la Société des Amis du Louvre, de 1922 à 1932*, 1933, No. 132; *La Renaissance*, 1928, p. 507; *Parnassus*, I, 1929, p. 13; John Rewald, "Les Sources d'inspiration de Cézanne," *L'Amour de l'art*, XVII, 1936, p. 192, Figs. 96 and 97; John Rewald, *Cézanne et Zola*, Paris, 1936, Fig. 34; Venturi, Cat. No. 1235, dated 1872–1876; Wildenstein & Co., London, *Homage to Paul Cézanne*, 1939, Cat. No. 77; Fritz Novotny, *Cézanne*, Vienna, 1937, No. 119, dated ca. 1877; John Rewald, *Cézanne*, New York, 1948, Fig. 42; Neumeyer, Cat. No. 29, dated 1872–1876; Theodore Reff, "Cézanne's Drawings, 1875–1885," *The Burlington Magazine*, CI, 1959, p. 172, dated ca. 1877; John Rewald, *Paul Cézanne*, New York, 1968, Fig. 39, dated ca. 1873.

This portrait was drawn from a photograph of the 1870's.

Date: 1875–1877.

Portrait of Camille Pissarro at his easel, on a sheet with a portrait of Madame Cézanne (No. 50) and a head of a peasant woman. Collection Mr. and Mrs. Leigh Block, Chicago. Pencil on white paper; page II verso in a sketchbook measuring 12.6 × 21.7 cm. (Rewald, *Carnet V*).

Verso: Sketch of two trees.

Literature: Rewald, *Carnet V*, p. II verso; Neumeyer, Cat. No. 30, dated ca. 1881.

Date: Ca. 1881–1882. For discussion see p. 30.

Two portrait sketches of Antoine Valabrègue, on a sheet with studies of a standing male from the back. Kunstmuseum, Basel.

Pencil on white paper (upper portrait drawing heightened with India ink); 23.5 × 17.6 cm.; page from a sketchbook (*Carnet 18 × 24*).

Verso: Studies of male heads and a man kneeling (Chappuis, Cat. No. 39, dated 1873–1880).

Literature: *Correspondance*, Fig. 8, dated ca. 1866; Chappuis, Cat. No. 8, dated 1866, Wayne V. Andersen, "Cézanne's Portrait Drawings from the 1860's," *Master Drawings*, V, 1967, pp. 265–280, dated 1866; John Rewald, *Paul Cézanne*, New York, 1968, p. 46, identified as Fortuné Marion, dated ca. 1866.

Rewald has identified the portrait sketches as probably of Marion. Chappuis, on comparing these with V. 126–129, has concluded that they are of Valabrègue. He concurs with Alfred Barr, who, in 1937, identified V. 126 (Fig. 5) as Valabrègue rather than Marion.[1] See V. 127–129.

Chappuis' identification of the verso of this sheet as studies for the *Apothéose de Delacroix* (V. 245) is erroneous. It may be that this sheet served as an exemplar for the kneeling figure in the *Apothéose de Delacroix;* perhaps they depend on a common pictorial source. This drawing almost certainly dates from the second half of the sixties, probably 1866–1868.

Date: 1866–1868. For discussion see pp. 3–5, 12.

1 "Cézanne d'après les lettres de Marion à Morstatt, 1865–1868," *Gazette des Beaux-Arts*, ser. 6, XVII, 1937, p. 47.

ensemble
les 2 têtes

1934. 161. (XIV).

235

Portrait of Ambroise Vollard. Fogg Art Museum, Harvard University; gift of Mr. and Mrs. Frederick Deknatel in 1961. Soft pencil on white paper; 43.0 × 33.0 cm., folded edges.
Verso: Blank.
Literature: Vollard, p. 103, dated 1899; Venturi, Cat. No. 1480, dated 1899; Berthold, p. 154; Neumeyer, Cat. No. 46, dated 1899; Maurice Serrullaz, *French Impressionists (Drawings of the Masters,* ed. Ira Moskowitz), New York, 1962, No. 100.

This drawing is related to and is probably a study for the portrait of the Paris art dealer Vollard (Fig. 35). The date 1899 is based not only on Vollard's own account[1] but also on an entry by Maurice Denis in his journal, October 21, 1899: "Vollard pose tous les matins chez Cézanne, depuis un temps infini."[2] Vollard had given Cézanne an exhibition in 1895 but did not meet him until 1896.[3]

Date: 1899. For discussion see p. 40.

---

1 Chapter VIII in his book *Paul Cézanne,* Paris, 1914, is devoted to his experience of posing for *Cézanne.*

2 *Théories, 1890–1910,* Paris, 1913.

3 See Vollard's account of this meeting in his *Paul Cézanne,* Ch. VI.

236 fac.

Two portraits of Émile Zola writing. Collection Mr. and
Mrs. Leigh Block, Chicago.
Pencil on white paper; page XV in a sketchbook measuring
12.6 × 21.7 cm. (Rewald, *Carnet V*).
Verso: Vase with flowers (similar to V. 1492).
Literature: Rewald, *Carnet V*, p. XV, dated 1879–1885.
Date: 1881–1882. For discussion see pp. 26, 28, 30.

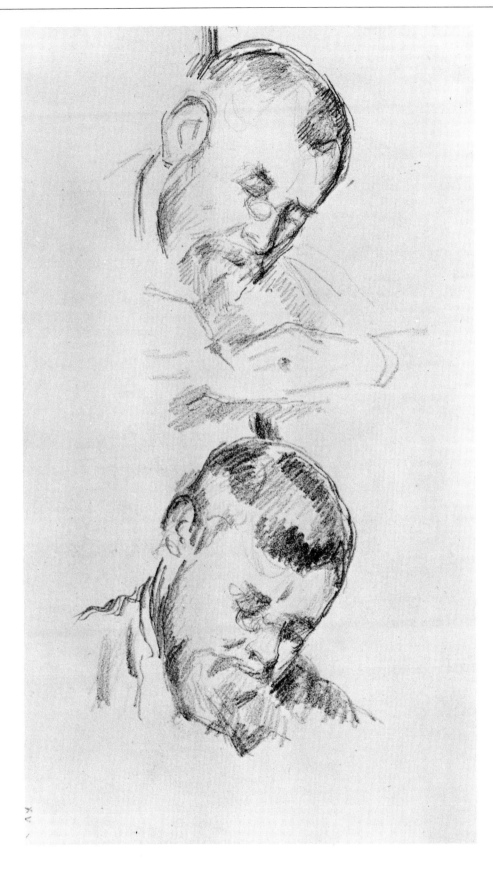

237

Portrait of Émile Zola, on a sheet with a copy after an unidentified source (Berthold Cat. No. 318) and a standing male bather. Collection Mr. and Mrs. Leigh Block, Chicago. Pencil on white paper; page XVI verso in a sketchbook measuring 12.6 × 21.7 cm. (Rewald, *Carnet V*).
Verso: Study of a marble sculpture presumably in Zola's house at Médan (Rewald, *Carnet V*, p. XV and Fig. 70, dated 1879–1885).
Literature: Rewald, *Carnet V*, p. XVI verso.

Rewald has stated that the marble sculpture sketched on the verso was at Zola's house at Médan. I have not been able to verify this, but, in any case, it would not be of much help in dating this sheet, since Cézanne visited Zola at Médan on several occasions between 1879 and 1885;[1] moreover, it is possible that Zola had the sculpture before moving to Médan.

A drawing of the head and shoulders of a woman, copied from an unidentified pictorial source, appears also on a sheet in the sketchbook owned by Leigh Block (Berthold, Cat. No. 305). Both copies probably date from the early eighties.

The sketch of the standing male bather also seems to be of this period. Its history in Cézanne's oeuvre of bathers goes back at least to 1876, when this pose appears in a composition of four male bathers (V. 273, V. 274, V. 276),[2] for which the model was a photograph that Cézanne owned.[3] The pose reappears in the mid-eighties as *Le grand baigneur* (V. 548). The attitude of the standing bather in the Block drawing differs slightly, however, from that in the other two examples: this is the only case where his head is turned slightly to the side and his left foot is not noticeably advanced. In general, the pose is casual, and the bather does not seem to be in deep thought. Reff has demonstrated Cézanne's renewed interest during the early eighties in the single standing male that he had developed in the mid-seventies.[4] I believe that this drawing can be associated with that circumstance.

Date: 1881–1882. For discussion see pp. 26, 28, 30.

1 *Correspondance*, p. 138.

2 On the history of this bather see Melvin Waldfogel, ''Caillebotte, Vollard and Cézanne's 'Baigneurs au Repos,''' *Gazette des beaux-arts*, ser. 6, LXV, 1965, pp. 113–120.

3 See Alfred Barr, *Masters of Modern Art*, New York, 1954, p. 22.

4 Theodore Reff, ''Cézanne's Bather with Outstretched Arms,'' *Gazette des beaux-arts*, ser. 6, LIX, 1962, p. 178.

238 fac.

Portrait of Émile Zola writing. Collection Adrien Chappuis, Tresserve (Savoie).
Pencil on white paper; page X in a sketchbook, measuring 12.4 × 21.7 cm. (Chappuis II).
Verso: Portrait of Cézanne's son (No. 155).
Literature: Paris, Musée de l'Orangerie, *Cézanne,* 1936, Cat. No. 163, dated 1894–1895; Venturi, under Cat. No. 1290, not reproduced; Chappuis, 1938, No. 38, dated 1894–1895; Reff, "Studies," p. 84, dated 1879–1882.

First identified as a portrait drawing of Gustave Geffroy, this drawing was associated with the oil portrait of Geffroy (V. 692) and dated 1894–1895. The correct identification was made by Reff.

See also No. 237 and, for a second portrait of Zola from this sketchbook, No. 239.

Date: 1882–1883. For discussion see pp. 26, 28.

239 fac.

Portrait of Émile Zola. Collection Harold Gershinowitz, Paris. Formerly Collection Adrien Chappuis, Tresserve (Savoie).
Pencil on white paper; page XI verso from a sketchbook; 12.4 × 21.7 cm. (Chappuis II).
Verso: Study of an armchair.
Literature: Venturi, under Cat. No. 1284, not reproduced. Chappuis, 1938, No. 40, dated 1890–1895.

Venturi did not identify the subject as Zola. See also No. 237 and, for a second portrait of Zola from this sketchbook, No. 238.

Date: 1882–1883. For discussion see pp. 26, 28.

240 n.r.

Portrait sketch of Émile Zola, on a sheet with a study of a male bather modeled by Cézanne's son. Collection Adrien Chappuis, Tresserve (Savoie).
Pencil on white paper; page XLVI verso in a sketchbook measuring 12.4 × 21.7 cm. (Chappuis II).
Verso: Touches of watercolor.
Literature: Venturi, under Cat. No. 1295, neither identified nor reproduced; Theodore Reff, "Cézanne's Bather with Outstretched Arms," *Gazette des Beaux-Arts,* ser. 6, LIX, 1962, pp. 179, 182, Fig. 9 (the bather study only, dated 1885–1886), and note 18 where he states that the portrait of Zola was done earlier than 1885.
Date: 1882–1883.

241

Sketch of Marion and Valabrègue, full-length in a landscape setting, in a letter to Zola. Collection Jacques Émile Zola, Paris.

Ink on white paper.

Literature: *Correspondance,* p. 97 and Pl. 10, dated ca. October 19, 1886; Wayne V. Andersen, "Cézanne's Portrait Drawings from the 1860's," *Master Drawings,* V, 1967, pp. 265–280, dated 1866; John Rewald, *Paul Cézanne,* New York, 1968, p. 63, dated 1866.

The letter to Zola in which this sketch appears does not bear a date. Rewald's date is supported by a note Cézanne appended to a letter from A. Guillemet to Zola, dated November 2, 1866: ". . . as you feared, my big picture of Valabrègue and Marion has not been done."[1]

Perhaps the painting was never realized. Today we have only a sheet of pencil sketches (242), now in Basel, and a small oil sketch (241a), which preceded this drawing. The probable sequence of the studies on the Basel sheet is from the hesitant sketch at the lower left to the composition of figures at the upper left. The gradual change of Valabrègue's pose away from a three-quarter view shows that these drawings were preparatory to the oil sketch, in which he is facing directly forward.

It is unlikely that Cézanne's friends posed for these studies. In the pencil sketch (242) there is an obvious discrepancy in their positions: Marion's feet are placed as if he were standing on the side of a hill, while Valabrègue's right arm and the angle of his pose indicate that Cézanne had made a separate study of him before joining the figure arm in arm with that of Marion. The evidence for this comes from a rather strange and unexpected source. One of the earliest of Cézanne's sketchbooks, the *Carnet de jeunesse,* contains a drawing of a well-dressed couple on an afternoon stroll who have chanced upon the decaying carcass of a dog (242b)—a motif recently identified by Chappuis as an illustration for Baudelaire's *Une Charogne.*[2] On this and on a second page of the sketchbook the figure of the woman, nude and slightly modified in pose, has been repeated several times. It seems that Cézanne's experience of drawing this man and woman helped to determine the composition of the portrait of Marion and Valabrègue. The position of Marion's legs and feet and the general attitude of his body correspond exactly to one study of the woman in Figure 242b, where she is standing on an inclined terrain and leaning slightly to the left. Valabrègue's pose seems to derive from that of the male figure. Seen from a three-quarter view, the man is standing on flat ground with his head tilted slightly forward and his right arm extended; Valabrègue appears in a corresponding pose at the beginning of the progression of sketches on the Basel sheet (242); both figures are identically dressed, and their hats and hair are rendered in the same way.[3]

Date: 1866. For discussion see pp. 3–4.

---

1 *Correspondance,* p. 302.

2 Adrien Chappuis, "Cézanne dessinateur: copies et illustrations," *Gazette des beaux-arts,* ser. 6, LXVI, 1965, pp. 294–308.

3 For further discussion of this see my article cited at this entry.

242

Studies for a full-length group portrait of Marion and Vala-
brègue. Kunstmuseum, Basel.
Pencil on white paper, 28 × 19 cm.
Verso: Blank.
Literature: Chappuis, Cat. No. 5, dated 1866; Wayne V.
Andersen, ''Cézanne's Portrait Drawings from the 1860's,''
Master Drawings, V, 1967, 265–280.

See No. 241.

Date: 1866. For discussion see p. 3.

243 fac.

Group portrait of five persons, out of doors. Kunstmuseum, Basel.
Pencil on gray paper; 12.5 × 22.6 cm.
Verso: Fragmentary sketch of a house.
Literature: Venturi Vol. I, p. 351, *Déjeuner sur l'herbe,* not reproduced; Chappuis, Cat. No. 53, dated 1870–1877; Douglas Cooper, review of Chappuis, *Les Dessins de Cézanne au Musée de Bâle,* in *Master Drawings,* I, 1963, p. 56, dated ca. 1868.

Chappuis' date depends on an erroneous comparison (also made by Venturi) of this sketch with my No. 222, which dates from ca. 1873–1874. Chappuis has also related this sketch to the composition *La Lecture chez Zola* (see No. 247), although there is no affinity between them, other than a stylistic one, that would assure a date of 1869–1870. An accurate description of this group portrait is given in a letter from Marion to Morstatt, dated 1868: "Cézanne projette un tableau auquel il fera servir les portraits. L'un de nous, au milieu d'un paysage, parlera, tandis que les autres écouteront."[1]

See also Nos. 244 and 245.

Date: Ca. 1867–1868. For discussion see p. 5.

1   Alfred Barr, "Cézanne d'après les lettres de Marion à Morstatt, 1865–1868," *Gazette des beaux-arts,* ser. 6. XVII, 1937, p. 44. Letter of May 24, 1868. Chappuis cites this letter but does not accept it as evidence in dating the drawing.

244

Group of men around a table, out of doors. Collection
Henry Roland, London. Formerly Collection Sir Leigh
Ashton, who acquired it from Sir Kenneth Clark, London.
Pencil on white paper; 17.8 × 24.1 cm.
Verso: Sketches of a tiger, a flying female figure, and a male
head.
Literature: Unpublished.

This drawing represents, as do Nos. 243 and 245, the group,
or genre, portrait idea that Cézanne developed in 1868.

Date: 1868–1869. For discussion see p. 5.

245 fac.

Group portrait in a wooded setting: four figures, including Pissarro. Kunstmuseum, Basel.

Pencil on white paper; 10.3 × 16.8 cm.; page from a sketchbook (*Carnet 10.3 × 17*).

Verso: Portrait of Dr. Gachet (Cat. No. 223).

Literature: Vollard, p. 15; Georges Rivière, *Le Maître Paul Cézanne,* Paris, 1923, p. 93; Venturi, Cat. No. 1204, dated 1871–1877; Chappuis, 1957, p. 7, dated 1871–1877; Chappuis, Cat. No. 59, dated 1871–1877; Douglas Cooper, review of Chappuis, *Les Dessins de Cézanne au Musée de Bâle,* in *Master Drawings,* I, No. 4, 1963, p. 55.

Venturi entitled this composition *Déjeuner sur l'herbe;* Rivière, *Les Brigands;* Chappuis, *Quatre hommes assis sous un arbre;* and Cooper, *Three Men and a Woman.* A fifth sitter has been overlooked: to the right of the woman there is a large dog also seated on his haunches, with his muzzle behind the woman's shoulder and his ear just to her right; his shoulder, flank, and tail are clearly discernible. It may be the same dog as in Chappuis, Cat. No. 95 and V. 245, which date from about 1876.

This composition was no doubt made during Cézanne's stay at Auvers, and the bearded man in the Barbizon hat may be Pissarro. Although it is a simple genre scene of three artists, the wife of one of them, and a dog resting in the shade, it can be considered a group portrait in that it illustrates a concept of genre portraiture peculiar to Impressionism. It recalls Cézanne's group portraits of the late 1860's and looks ahead to the Card–Player compositions of the early nineties. See the quotation at No. 243 from a letter from Marion to Morstatt describing Cézanne's idea for a genre painting using portraits of Cézanne's friends. This group demonstrates the same concept and composition: one person is speaking while the others are listening.

Date: 1873. For discussion, see p. 13.

246 fac.

Group portrait of Émile Zola dictating to Paul Alexis. Collection Sir Kenneth and Lady Clark, London.
Pencil on beige paper; present mat opening 8.0 × 10.7 cm.
(Venturi's measurements: 13.5 × 10.5 cm.)
Verso: Not examined.
Literature: Vollard, p. 61; Venturi, Cat. No. 1199, dated 1869–1870; Wayne V. Andersen, "Cézanne's Portrait Drawings from the 1860's" *Master Drawings*, V, 1967, pp. 265–280, dated 1869–1870.

A study for *Zola dictant . . .* , V. 118 (248a). See also Nos. 247, 248.

The identification of the figure on the left as Alexis has been rejected by Jean Adhémar, who has dated the drawing 1864–1865.[1] Adhémar's wish to assign the composition this early date may have forced him to question the identification. Neither in the oil painting nor in the three pencil studies now known has the identification of the figure as Alexis been considered doubtful; the head in one study (248), in fact, corresponds exactly to Alexis' head in the painting *La Lecture chez Zola* (V. 117), with the same conformation of the hair and mustache. Both Zola and the other figure are somewhat caricatured in the latter painting, but the deviation from Alexis' appearance, as portrayed in *La Lecture chez Zola*, is no greater than the deviation from Zola's. If the figure at the right in *La Lecture chez Zola* is Zola, certainly the one at the left is Alexis. See Nos. 247 and 248.

Date: Mid-September 1869–August 1870. For discussion see pp. 5, 7, 13.

1   In "Le Cabinet de travail de Zola," *Gazette des beaux-arts*, ser. 6, LVI, 1960, p. 286, and previously in Paris, Bibliothèque Nationale, *Émile Zola*, 1952, p. 8, Cat. No. 53.

247 fac.

Group portrait of Émile Zola dictating to Paul Alexis.
Kunstmuseum, Basel.
Pencil on white paper; 14.3 × 19.6 cm.
Verso: Sketch of a garden path (Chappuis, Cat. No. 102).
Literature: Venturi, Vol. I, p. 351, *Homme écrivant,* not
dated; Chappuis, Cat. No. 54, dated 1869–1870; Wayne V.
Andersen, "Cézanne's Portrait Drawings from the 1860's,"
Master Drawings, V, 1967, pp. 265–280, dated 1869–1870.

Studies for V. 118 (248a). Cézanne first sketched Zola standing, perhaps employing a pose from another source (see
the pose and attitude of the man in Chappuis, Cat. No. 76).

See Nos. 246, 248.

Date: Mid-September 1869–August 1870. For discussion
see pp. 5, 7.

Group portrait of Émile Zola dictating to Paul Alexis.
Present location unknown. Formerly Collection Bollag,
Zurich.
Pencil on paper; 13 × 15.5 cm.
Verso: Unknown.
Literature: Zurich, *Vente Bollag*, April 3, 1925, No. 38, Pl.
XVIII; Venturi, Cat. No. 1198, dated 1869–1870; Wayne V.
Andersen, "Cézanne's Portrait Drawings from the 1860's,"
Master Drawings, V, 1967, pp. 265–280, dated 1869–1870.

A study for V. 118 (248a). See also Nos. 246, 247.

Date: Mid-September 1869–August 1870. For discussion
see pp. 5, 7.

249

Miscellaneous portrait sketches: head and shoulders of a bearded man with wide-brimmed hat, two incomplete male figures, head of a youth with a cap, and a seated man. Art Institute of Chicago.

Pencil and ink on white paper; page XLII verso in a sketchbook measuring 12.4 × 21.7 cm. (Rewald, *Carnet II*).
Verso: Numbers in the hand of Cézanne's son.
Literature: Rewald, *Carnet II,* p. XLII verso; Schniewind, Cat. No. XLII verso, dated 1869–1870; Reff, ''Studies,'' p. 75, dated 1869–1870; Chappuis, under Cat. No. 54, dated 1869–1870 (the seated figure only).

Reff has identified the seated male figure as Alexis and as a study for the oil painting known as *Zola dictant . . .* (V. 118); he has dated the drawing 1869–1870, although its style precludes this date. It seems doubtful that this figure is Alexis, as even in general appearance there is only a superficial resemblance to the figure in the oil painting, and in details there is no relationship at all. In the painting, the right arm is shown in the act of writing and has been momentarily raised from the paper while the writer listens to the reader's words; the forearm, just beyond the elbow, is resting on the table. The sketch in the Chicago sketchbook does not show a person writing, for the position of the arm is not related to the act of writing (the arm is resting on a surface) but, rather, to the act of painting or fishing, or to an expressive conversational gesture—like that of the seated male figure in *Déjeuner sur l'herbe* (V. 1204). Furthermore, the figure does not correspond to any known image of Alexis. In Cézanne's *Paul Alexis lisant à Zola* (V. 117), and the so-called *Lecture chez Zola* (248a), Alexis has a full beard with prominent sideburns, and his hair terminates in a tight inward roll across the base of his skull almost in line with the lower tip of his ears. The figure in the Chicago sketchbook has neither a beard (unless it is a very small one) nor sideburns; his hair, in a long, loose curve, falls below his collar. Even in rough sketches, Cézanne was attentive to the physiognomic characteristics of his subjects; he would hardly have devoted so much time to the surface modulation of the figure's coat while misrepresenting the beard, the mechanics of the arm, and the hair. This identification must be rejected, and the drawing should be re-dated according to its style.

Date: Ca. 1876.

250

Portrait of a man, seated; study for *Les Joueurs de cartes*.
Collection Mr. T. E. Hanley, Bradford, Pennsylvania, acquired through Knoedler and Company, New York. Formerly Collection Ambroise Vollard, sold through Matthiesen Gallery, London.
Pencil on white paper; approx. 53.3 × 43.2 cm.
Verso: Blank.
Literature: Maurice Serullaz, *French Impressionists (Drawings of the Masters,* ed. Ira Moskowitz), New York, 1962, No. 101; Kurt Badt, *The Art of Cézanne*, Berkeley, 1965, Pl. 15; Gallery of Modern Art, New York, *Selections from the Collection of Dr. and Mrs. T. Edward Hanley*, New York, 1967, pp. 23, 61, dated ca. 1890–1892.
Date: 1890–1892. For discussion see p. 39.

251

Portrait of a man. Present location unknown. Formerly Collections Ambroise Vollard, Adrien Chappuis, Paul Rosenberg, all of Paris.

Pencil on white paper; approx. 51 × 32 cm.

Verso: Watercolor study (V. 1088) for *Les Joueurs de cartes* (V. 557, 558).

Literature: Vollard, p. 146; Julius Meier-Graefe, *Cézanne und sein Kreis,* Munich, 1922, p. 38; Venturi, Cat. No. 1482, dated 1890–1892; John Rewald, *Paul Cézanne,* New York, 1968, p. 130, dated ca. 1890.

Study for *Les Joueurs de cartes,* V. 558 (Fig. 31).

Date: 1890–1892. For discussion see p. 39.

252

Portrait of a man seated at a table playing cards. Museum of Art, Rhode Island School of Design, Providence; gift in 1942 of Mrs. Murray S. Danforth, who had acquired it in 1934. Formerly Collections Ambroise Vollard, Paris, and Jacques Seligmann, Paris.

Pencil with traces of watercolor on white paper; 48.4 × 36.2 cm.

Verso: Blank.

Literature: Venturi, Cat. No. 1086, dated 1890–1892; Hans Tietze, *European Master Drawings in the United States,* New York, 1947, No. 51; *One Hundred Master Drawings,* ed. Agnes Mongan, Cambridge, 1949, p. 194, dated 1890–1892; Paul J.

Sachs, *Modern Prints and Drawings,* New York, 1954, Pl. 34, dated 1890–1892; Kurt Badt, *The Art of Cézanne,* Berkeley, 1965, Pl. 16, dated 1890–1892; Neumeyer, Cat. No. 43, dated 1890–1892.

Study of one version of *Les Joueurs de cartes,* V. 559 (Fig. 30).

See also Nos. 250, 253.

Date: 1890–1892. For discussion see p. 39.

253

Portrait of a man, seated. Kunstmuseum, Basel.
Pencil on white paper; 38 × 29 cm.
Verso: Landscape study (Chappuis, Cat. No. 173).
Literature: Venturi, Cat. No. 1587, dated 1890–1892; Neumeyer, Cat. No. 42, dated 1890–1892; *Le Dessins français au XIXᵉ siècle,* ed. René Huyghe, Lausanne, 1948, p. 99; Chappuis, Cat. No. 156, dated 1890–1892.

Although not a study, this portrait is related to V. 561, 563, and 565, as well as to the *Joueurs de cartes* compositions, V. 559 and 560 (Fig. 30).

Date: 1890–1891.

254

Portrait of a man. Museum Boymans-van Beuningen,
Rotterdam.
Pencil on medium-textured white paper; 50.2 × 31.3 cm.
(formerly folded to 26.5 × 27 cm.).
Verso: Blank.
Literature: Vollard, p. 107; Julius Meier-Graefe, *Cézanne und
sein Kreis*, Munich, 1922, p. 11; Rotterdam, Museum Boy-
mans, *Teekeningen van Ingres tot Seurat*, 1933, Cat. No. 6;
Basel, Kunsthalle, *Meisterzeichnungen französischer
Künstler van Ingres bis Cézanne*, 1935, Cat. No. 175; Basel,
Kunsthalle, *Paul Cézanne*, 1936, Cat. No. 140; Venturi, Cat.
No. 1483, dated 1890–1892; Amsterdam, Rijksmusem,
Fransche Meesters uit de XIXᵉ eeuw, 1938, Cat No. 24;
Amsterdam, Rijksmuseum, *Teekeningen van Fransche
Meesters*, 1946, Cat. No. 16; Paris, Musée du Louvre, *Le
Dessin français de Fouquet à Cézanne*, 1949, Cat No. 208;
Paris, Bibliothèque Nationale, *Dessins du XVᵉ au XIXᵉ siècle
du Musée Boymans de Rotterdam*, 1952, Cat No. 143; Rotter-
dam, Musée Boymans, *Dessins de Pisanello à Cézanne* (*Art
et style*, No. 23), 1952; Douglas Cooper, *The Courtauld
Collection*, London, 1954, p. 88; The Hague, Gemeente-
museum, *Paul Cézanne*, 1956, Cat. No. 125; Kurt Badt, *Die
Kunst Cézanne's*, Munich, 1956, pp. 66, 92, Fig. 14; Adrien
Chappuis, *Dessins de Paul Cézanne*, Lausanne, 1957, No. 25,
dated 1890–1892; Paris, Institut Néerlandais, *Le Dessin
français de Claude à Cézanne dans les collections hollandaises*,
1964, Cat. No. 204; L. Zahn, *Eine Geschichte der modernen
Kunst*, Berlin, 1958, p. 21; François Mathey, *The Impres-
sionists*, New York, 1961, p. 220; Kurt Badt, *The Art of
Cézanne*, Berkeley, 1965, Pl. 14, dated 1890–1892; Hoetink
Cat. No. 36, dated 1891–1892.

This drawing is related to the studies for *Les Joueurs de
cartes* (V. 556–558). See No. 249.

Date: 1890–1892. For discussion see p. 39.

255

Sketch of a man seated at a table. Collection Mrs. Ira Haupt,
New York.
Pencil on white paper; page VIII verso from a sketchbook
measuring 12.7 × 21.6 cm. (Rewald, *Carnet IV*).
Verso: Study after the *Mars Borghèse* in the Louvre.
Literature: Rewald, *Carnet IV,* p. VII verso, not reproduced.

Probably related to the *Les Joueurs de cartes* series.

Date: Ca. 1892–1894.

256

Portrait of a young girl. Original exemplar: present location unknown; formerly Weyhe Gallery, New York; sold at the Hôtel Druot on May 21, 1930.
Etching, black ink on brown paper; 32 × 23 cm. Signed on the plate "P. Cézanne."
Literature: Vollard, frontispiece; Gustave Coquiot, *Paul Cézanne*, Paris, 1919, p. 62; Philadelphia, Museum of Art, *Cézanne and French Painting*, 1934, No. 63; Venturi, Cat. No. 1160, dated 1873.

I believe that the model was the girl who posed for Guillaumin's pastel, *Head of a Young Girl*, originally Collection Durand-Ruel, New York (256a).

Date: 1873. For discussion see pp. 10, 12, 13.

257 n.r.

Head of a young girl, her hair covered with a kerchief.
Collection Paul Gachet, Auvers-sur-Oise.
Pencil on paper, approx. 22 × 17 cm.
Verso: Not examined.
Literature: John Rewald, *Cézanne et Zola*, Paris, 1936, p. 81; Paris, Musée de l'Orangerie, *Cézanne*, 1936, Cat. No. 145, dated 1873.
Date: 1873–1874.

258

Portrait of an unidentified man, seated. Present location unknown. Formerly Collection Ludovico Rodo Pissarro, Paris.
Pencil on paper.
Literature: Venturi, Cat. No. 1197, dated 1870–1877.
Date: Ca. 1873–1874. For discussion see p. 13.

259 n.r.

Unidentified head, probably female, lightly sketched, on a sheet with studies for an erotic theme. Art Institute of Chicago.
Pencil on white paper; page XXXVIII in a sketchbook measuring 12.4 × 21.7 cm. (Rewald, *Carnet II*).
Verso: Portrait drawings of Louis-August Cézanne (No. 202) and of Madame Cézanne (No. 45).
Literature: Rewald, *Carnet II*, XXXVIII; Schniewind, Cat. No. XXXVIII.

Neither Schniewind nor Rewald mentions this head. The other studies are identified erroneously as studies for *The Strangler*, V. 123, dated 1870–1872. The fact that the upper study overlaps the head, which is in an advanced graphic style that can be assigned to about 1878, assures a date for these drawings not earlier than 1878. Together with pages XLVI verso, XXIII, and XXXVIII of the same sketchbook, these are later versions of obsessive themes. The last is, in fact, a study for a composition such as V. 1266, which dates from about 1878.

Date: Ca. 1878.

260

Sketch of an unidentified man in a derby hat, seated. Collection Mrs. Ira Haupt, New York.
Pencil on white paper; page 31 in a sketchbook measuring 12.6 × 21.7 cm. (Rewald, *Carnet I*).
Verso: Sketch of a flying angel and a kneeling figure.
Literature: Rewald, *Carnet I*, p. 31; Chappuis, 1957, No. 10, dated 1870–1890.

Rewald does not identify this figure. Chappuis suggests that it is Ambroise Vollard, but this identification is too tenuous to accept Chappuis allows a date span of twenty years, which indicates the uncertainty of his stylistic criteria and proves his argument that the sitter is Vollard to be lacking in force. Cézanne did not meet Vollard until 1896,[1] and Cézanne's portrait of him dates from 1899 (see No. 235).

See also No. 261.

Date: Ca. 1882.

1 See Vollard's account of this meeting in his book *Paul Cézanne*, Paris, 1914, Ch. VI.

261 n.r.

Portrait of a man in a derby hat, on a sheet with a notation in Cézanne's hand: "Mlle Aimée Broquet, rue Ponchet, 45." Collection Mrs. Ira Haupt, New York.
Pencil on white paper; page 43 verso in a sketchbook measuring 12.6 × 21.7 cm. (Rewald, *Carnet I*).
Verso: Unidentifiable sketch.
Literature: Rewald, *Carnet I*, p. 43 verso; Chappuis, 1957, No. 13, dated 1870–1890.

The man in this sketch appears also in No. 260.

Date: ca. 1882.

262

Portrait of an unidentified man. Collection Werner Feuz, Zurich.
Pencil on coarse, textured, white paper; approximately 8.5 × 6 cm. part of a larger sheet.
Literature: Venturi, Cat. No. 1239, dated 1877–1882.

This drawing may be from the same original sheet as No. 57. For the same paper see also No. 130.

Date: Ca. 1882–1883.

263

Portrait of a girl in a straw hat. Museum Boymans-van Beuningen, Rotterdam.
Pencil on white paper; 37.4 × 30.3 cm.
Verso: Watercolor, study of tree branches.
Literature: Basel, Kunsthalle, *Paul Cézanne*, 1936, Cat. No. 172; Venturi, Cat. No. 1485; Amsterdam, Rijksmuseum, *Teekeningen van Fransche Meesters,* 1946, Cat. No. 6; J. Siblik, *Paul Cézanne, Dessins–Kresby*, Prague, 1968; Hoetink, No. 20.

Venturi's date is based on the watercolor of this child on the verso of V. 965, a watercolor entitled *Bords du lac*; the latter has the same motif as V. 762, *Le Lac d'Annecy*. Cézanne's stay in the Annecy region is documented from early June to the end of August 1896.[1]

For other studies of the same child see V. 698, 700, 1097, and 1098, and the frontispiece in Chappuis, 1938.

Date: 1896. For discussion see p. 39.

1 *Correspondance,* letter from Cézanne to Philippe Solari of July 23, 1896. On Cézanne's visit to Annecy see Wayne V. Andersen, "Cézanne's *Carnet violet-moiré,*" *The Burlington Magazine,* CVII, 1965, pp. 313–318.

264

Sketch of an unidentified male child on a sheet with a study
of a hand. Collection Mrs. Ira Haupt, New York.
Pencil on white paper; p. 9 in a sketchbook measuring
11.6 × 18.2 cm. (Rewald, *Carnet I*).
Verso: Sketch of a chair and an iron bed.
Literature: Rewald, *Carnet I*, p. 9 (not reproduced).
Date: Ca. 1882.

265

Head of an unidentified woman. Present location unknown.
Irregular measurements; cut from a larger sheet.
Verso: Miscellaneous unidentifiable sketches.

The drawing appeared on the Paris art market about 1963.
In my opinion it is not in Cézanne's hand but rather in the
same hand that rendered Nos. 29, 92, 197, and 221.

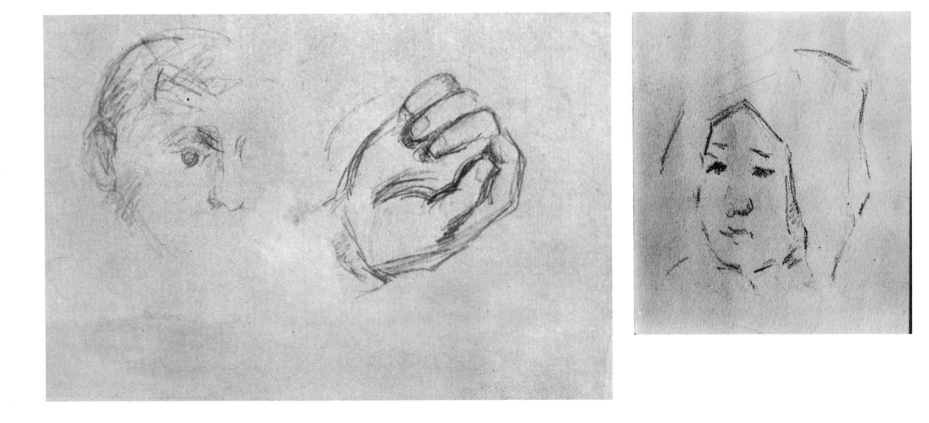

Provenance

Applicable unless noted otherwise at the catalogue entry

Art Institute of Chicago.
Acquired in 1951. Originally Collection Cézanne *fils*; sold in 1934 through the dealers Maurice Renou and Paul Guillaume, Paris, to a collector in Lyon. Acquired in 1950 by the dealers Maurice Renou and Sam Salz, New York.

Collection Mr. and Mrs. Leigh Block, Chicago.
Acquired in 1950 from a collection in Lyon through the dealers Maurice Renou and Sam Salz, New York. Originally Collection Cézanne *fils*, Paris; sold in 1934 through the dealers Maurice Renou and Paul Guillaume, Paris.

Collection Adrien Chappuis, Tresserve (Savoie).
Acquired from Cezanne *fils* through the dealer Paul Guillaume, Paris. (The sketchbook referred to in this work as Chappuis III is now in the collection of Mr. Paul Mellon, Upperville, Virginia).

Collection Sir Kenneth and Lady Clark, London.
Acquired in 1934 from Cézanne *fils* through the dealer Paul Guillaume, Paris.

Kunstmuseum, Basel.
Acquired in two lots. Originally Collection Cézanne *fils*; the first lot purchased from the dealers Maurice Renou and Paul Guillaume, Paris, through Werner Feuz, in February 1934; the second purchased through the same channel in the spring of 1935.

Collection Mrs. Ira Haupt, New York.
Acquired in 1950 from the dealers Maurice Renou and Sam Salz, New York. Originally Collection Cézanne *fils*; sold to a collector in Lyon in 1934 through the dealers Maurice Renou and Paul Guillaume, Paris.

Museum Boymans-van Beuningen, Rotterdam.
Formerly Collection F. Koenigs. Given to the museum in 1940 (for details see Hoetink).

Concordance of Catalogue Numbers

Lionello Venturi, *Cézanne, son art, son œuvre,* 2 vols., Paris, 1936

Adrien Chappuis, *Dessins de Paul Cézanne,* Paris, 1938.

Paul Cézanne, *Carnets de dessins,* preface and catalogue raisonné by John Rewald, 2 vols., Paris, 1951.

Venturi	Andersen	Venturi	Andersen	Chappuis	Andersen	Rewald		Andersen
						Carnet	Page	
1086	252	1295	60	1	19	I	2 v.	136
1100	66	1297	58	2	156	I	3	138
1158	24	1300	166	8	168	I	3 v.	137
1159	227	1303	70	9	165	I	9	264
1160	256	1305	179	11	90	I	10	139
1193	220	1306	180	14	188	I	10 v.	140
1194	217	1403	203	23	155	I	11	141
1195	218	1411	87	24	61	I	18 v.	172
1196	226	1434	73	26	72	I	31	260
1197	258	1466	67	28	159	I	42 v.	56
1198	248	1467	69	30	91	I	43 v.	261
1199	246	1468	178	32	70	II	II	95
1200	213	1469	169	34	78	II	VI v.	36
1204	245	1470	170	36	85	II	VII v.	9
1217	34	1471	144	38	238	II	VIII	37
1218	123	1472	35	40	239	II	XIII	102
1221	32	1473	174	47	23	II	XVI	103
1222	30	1474	21, 65			II	XVI v.	104
1225	145	1475	162			II	XIX v.	41
1226	231	1476	22			II	XXI	10
1234	199	1477	55			II	XXII	11
1235	232	1478	8			II	XXIV v.	105
1236	209	1479	15			II	XXVII v.	40
1237	7	1480	235			II	XXIX	201
1238	5	1481	46			II	XXX	106
1239	262	1482	251			II	XXXV	42
1240	33	1483	254			II	XXXV v.	43
1240 v.	99	1484	128			II	XXXVI v.	44
1241	210	1485	263			II	XXXVII	13
1242	131	1486	173			II	XXXVIII	259
1244	130	1572	147			II	XXXVIII v.	45
1246	57	1573	228			II	XXXIX	12
1251	3	1587	253			II	XXXIX v.	107
1280	74	1590	148			II	XL	108
1287	20	1622	175			II	XL v.	109
1288	156					II	XLI	110
1290	157					II	XLI v.	111
1293	19							

Paul Cézanne Sketchbook Owned by the Art Institute of Chicago, introductory text by Carl O. Schniewind, 2 vols., New York, 1951.

Adrien Chappuis, *Dessins de Paul Cézanne,* Lausanne, 1957.

Alfred Neumeyer, *Cézanne Drawings,* New York and London, 1958.

Adrien Chappuis, *Les Dessins de Paul Cézanne au Cabinet des Estampes du Musée des Beaux-Arts de Bâle,* Olten, 1962.

Adrien Chappuis, *Album de Paul Cézanne,* Paris, [1966].

Rewald *Carnet*	Page	Andersen
II	XLIII	112
II	XLIII v.	113
II	XLIV	114
II	XLIV v.	115
II	XLV	116
II	XLVI	117
II	XLVII	118
II	XLVII v.	119
II	XLVIII	120
II	XLVIII v.	121
II	XLIX	122
II	XLIX v.	38
II	L v.	39
III	6	193
IV	VI	142
IV	VII v.	255
IV	XLVII	143
V	I v.	49
V	II v.	50
V	III	51
V	V v.	52
V	IX	133
V	XIV v.	14
V	XV	236
V	XVI v.	237
V	XXXVII	53
V	XLIII v.	134
V	XLVI	54
V	XLVI v.	132
V	XLIX v.	135

Schniewind	Andersen
II	95
VI v.	36
VII v.	9
VIII	37
XIII	102
XVI	103
XVI v.	104
XIX v.	41
XXI	10
XXII	11
XXIV v.	105
XXVII v.	40
XXIX	201
XXX	106
XXXV	42
XXXV v.	43
XXXVI v.	44
XXXVII	13
XXXVIII	259
XXXVIII v.	45
XXXIX	12
XXXIX v.	107
XL	108
XL v.	109
XLI	110
XLI v.	111
XLIII	112
XLIII v.	113
XLIV	114
XLIV v.	115
XLV	116
XLVI	117
XLVII	118
XLVII v.	119
XLVIII	120
XLVIII v.	121
XLIX	122
XLIX v.	38
L v.	39

Chappuis	Andersen
Frontispiece	209
7	245
10	260
13	261
14	71
16	173
18	228
25	254
30	19
34	160
43	63

Neumeyer	Andersen
13	100
14	34
26	220
27	203
28	230
29	232
30	50
31	11
32	9
33	13
34	23
35	68
36	70
37	69
38	127
39	155
40	201
41	175
42	253
43	252
46	235

Chappuis	Andersen
5	242
8	234
35	198
43	31
49	215
50	217
51	216
52	229
53	243
54	247
59	245
69	223
80	25
83	94
82	96
90	146
91	184
92	149
93	8
96	109
98	3
99	147
100	151
101	148
130	73
154	228
156	253

Chappuis	Andersen
III	176
VII	70
VIII	177
IX	178
IX v.	71
X	23
XI v.	72
XII	75
XIII	91
XIV	77
XIV v.	78
XV	82
XVII	85
XVII v.	179
XVIII	180
XVIII v.	181
XIX	182
XXI	81
XXI v.	183
XXIII v.	185
XXIV	90
XXXI bis	80
XXXII	190
XXXIII	188
XXXIV v.	189
LI v.	79

Selected Bibliography

The following selection of books and articles on Cézanne's drawings is divided into two parts: items 1–13 are major sources for the study of the drawings and have been briefly annotated; items 14–28 are useful subsidiary references. In each part the items are listed in order of date of publication.

Major Sources

1 Venturi, Lionello. Cézanne, son art, son oeuvre. 2 vols., Paris, 1936. Of over twelve hundred drawings on about eight hundred sheets known today, Venturi catalogued and reproduced over three hundred and fifty and inventoried about three hundred others. The dates he assigned to the drawings were based largely on the stylistic evidence he had established for the paintings. Although it remains a fundamental source book, Venturi's chronology has been severely criticized in recent years. Reviewing Venturi's catalogue shortly after its publication, John Rewald ("A propos du catalogue raisonné de l'oeuvre de Paul Cézanne et de la chronologie de cette oeuvre," *La Renaissance*, XX, 1937, pp. 53–57) considered that of over eight hundred paintings, only one hundred and fourteen were dated with the help of external evidence (only six are dated on the canvas). The research of the past thirty years has resulted, ironically, in a decrease of established evidence. Robert Ratcliffe, who has reviewed all evidence pertinent to the chronology of Cézanne's paintings, concluded a few years ago that the number of securely dated canvases was at the most ninety ("Cézanne's Working Methods," unpublished Ph.D. dissertation, Courtauld Institute, University of London, 1960). More recently, Douglas Cooper has set the number of securely dated paintings even lower, suggesting that not more than fifty can be dated on other than purely stylistic evidence. ("Two Cézanne Exhibitions," *The Burlington Magazine*, XCVI, 1954, pp. 344–349, 378–383). For further commentary on Venturi's chronology see Lawrence Gowing's notes in Arts Council of Great Britain, *An Exhibition of Paintings by Cézanne*, London, 1954; Gowing, "Notes on the Development of Cézanne," *The Burlington Magazine*, XCVIII, 1956, pp. 185–192; Cooper, "Cézanne's Chronology," *ibid.*, pp. 449; and Theodore Reff, "Cézanne's Constructive Stroke," *The Art Quarterly*, XXV, 1962, pp. 214–227.

2 Novotny, Fritz. "Cézanne als Zeichner." Wiener Jahrbuch für Kunstgeschichte, XIV, 1950, pp. 225–240. A study of Cézanne's graphic style which, though responsive to the artist's development, does not establish a certain chronology.

3 Cézanne, Paul. Carnets de dessins. Preface and catalogue raisonné by John Rewald. 2 vols., Paris, 1951. Catalogue of the five Lyon sketchbooks containing over four hundred drawings, one hundred and sixty of which are reproduced in facsimile. Assigning dates to only a few of the individual drawings, Rewald dated the sketchbooks according to their periods of use: twenty, ten, two, thirty-three, and ten years respectively. His ten-year span 1875–1885 for *Carnet II* (Art Institute of Chicago) has been expanded to twenty-seven years by Theodore Reff (Bibl. 6 and 8) and reduced to eight to ten years by Wayne Andersen (Bibl. 9). Rewald's date 1880–1881 for the contents of *Carnet III* (Louvre) has been countered by Gertrude Berthold (Bibl. 5), who has assigned the sketchbook to the first half of the nineties.

4. Paul Cézanne Sketchbook Owned by the Art Institute of Chicago. Introductory text by Carl O. Schniewind. 2 vols. New York, 1951. Facsimile reproduction of the sketchbook, with preface and catalogue by Carl Schniewind, who assigns the contents to a period of seventeen years with specific dates for only a few of the drawings. For other opinions see Rewald (Bibl. 3), Reff (Bibl. 8), and Andersen (Bibl. 9).

5 Berthold, Gertrude. Cézanne und die alten Meister. Stuttgart, 1958. Although not primarily concerned with chronology, Berthold produced some valuable evidence of acquisition and installation dates for certain works that Cézanne had copied in the Louvre and the Trocadero. Regrettably, dates for only a few of the almost four hundred copies that she catalogued could be estimated with this type of evidence, and too often Berthold assigns dates too close to the limiting points. In a review of this publication, Theodore Reff ("New Sources for Cézanne's Copies," *The Art Bulletin*, XLII, 1960, pp. 147–149) augments Berthold's findings with a few additional copies and offers other evidence for dating some of the drawings. For an early study of Cézanne's copies, see John Rewald, "Cézanne au Louvre," *L'Amour de l'Art*, XVI, 1935, pp. 282–288.

6 Reff, Theodore. "Studies in Cézanne's Drawings." Unpublished Ph.D. dissertation, Harvard University, 1956. The first general consideration (other than Bibl. 2) of Cézanne's drawings, with important chapters on chronology and sources of Cézanne's copies. The most valuable external evidence for chronology is expanded in a later article (Bibl. 8). Reff's chapter on Cézanne's copies after sculpture by Puget is developed further in his article "Puget's Fortune in France," in *Essays in the History of Art Presented to Rudolf Wittkower,* London, 1967, pp. 274 ff.

7 Neumeyer, Alfred. Cézanne Drawings. New York, 1958. A selection of Cézanne's drawings presented by subject, with a sensitive introduction. The dates assigned to the portrait drawings are not dependable, as they are largely based on subjective interpretations of Cézanne's mood at different times of his life.

8 Reff, Theodore. "Cézanne's Drawings, 1875–1885." The Burlington Magazine, CI, 1959, pp. 171–176. A careful discussion of the development of Cézanne's graphic style between 1875 and 1885, using a combination of external and stylistic evidence.

9 Andersen, Wayne V. "Cézanne's Sketchbook in the Art Institute of Chicago." The Burlington Magazine, CIV, 1962, pp. 196–201.
A study of the sequence of the drawings in the Chicago sketchbook using external criteria and estimates of the age of Cézanne's son at the time he made some drawings in his father's sketchbook.

10 Chappuis, Adrien. Les Dessins de Paul Cézanne au Cabinet des Estampes du Musée des Beaux-Arts de Bâle. 2 vols. Olten, 1962. A superb catalogue of the two hundred and eleven drawings in Basel, the majority reproduced in facsimile. The drawings range in date from about 1857 to the late nineties. Chappuis found it possible to assign a precise date on the basis of external evidence to only three drawings. Forty others are assigned approximate dates, three are dated by a *terminus post quem*, six are not dated; the remaining one hundred and fifty-nine drawings are assigned to broad periods of five to sixteen years. Reviewed with some correction of dates by Wayne V. Andersen in *The Art Bulletin,* XLV, 1963, pp. 79–82; by Theodore Reff in *The Burlington Magazine,* CV, 1963, pp. 375–376; and Douglas Cooper in *Master Drawings,* I, No. 4, 1963, pp. 54–57.

11 Andersen, Wayne V. "Cézanne's Carnet violet-moiré." The Burlington Magazine, CVII, 1965, pp. 313–318. Presentation of evidence for the chronology and a catalogue of the drawings in a little notebook, published in a facsimile edition by Quartre Chemins-Editart, Paris, in 1954.

12 Chappuis, Adrien. Album de Paul Cézanne. 2 vols. Paris [1966]. Catalogue and excellent facsimile reproduction of one of the sketchbooks owned by Adrien Chappuis. Reviewed, with arguments against some of the dates Chappuis assigned, by Theodore Reff in *The Burlington Magazine,* CIX, 1967, pp. 652–653.

13 Andersen, Wayne V. "Cézanne's Portrait Drawings from the 1860's." Master Drawings, V, 1967, pp. 265–280. A discussion of Cézanne's graphic style in the 1860's, with reproductions of all Cézanne's portrait drawings datable before 1872.

Additional References

14   Bernard, Émile. "Le Dessin de Cézanne." L'Amour de l'art, V, January 1924, pp. 37–38.

15   Denis, Maurice. "Le Dessin de Cézanne." L'Amour de l'art, V, February 1924, pp. 37–38.

16   Salmon, André. "Dessins inédits de Cézanne." Cahiers d'art, I, 1926, pp. 263–265.

17   Raynal, Maurice. "Dessins de Cézanne." Arts et métiers graphiques, No. 54, 1936, pp. 46–52.

18   Chappuis, Adrien. Dessins de Paul Cézanne. Paris, 1938.

19   Chappuis, Adrien. "The Sketchbooks of Cézanne." XXe siècle, Nos. 5–6, 1939, pp. 34–35.

20   Nicodemi, Giorgio. Cézanne, 76 disegni. Milan, 1944.

21   Rewald, John. "Proof of Cézanne's Pygmalion Pencil." Art News, XLIII, October 1–14, 1944, pp. 17–20.

22.   Bouchot-Saupigue, Jacqueline. "Un Carnet de croquis de Cézanne." La Revue des arts, I, 1951, pp. 243-245.

23   Rewald, John. "The Louvre, 'Cézanne's Book to Consult': Models and Sketches." The Illustrated London News, May 9, 1956.

24   Chappuis, Adrien. Dessins de Paul Cézanne. Lausanne, 1957.

25   Andersen, Wayne V. "A Cézanne Copy after Couture." Master Drawings, I, No. 4, 1963, pp. 44–46.

26   Andersen, Wayne V. "A Cézanne Self-Portrait Re-identified." The Burlington Magazine, CVI, 1964, pp. 284–285.

27   Chappuis, Adrien. "Cézanne dessinateur, copies et illustrations." Gazette des beaux-arts, ser. 6, LXVI, 1965, pp. 294–308.

28   Andersen, Wayne V. "Cézanne, Tanguy, Chocquet." The Art Bulletin, XLIX, 1967, pp. 137–139.

Index of Identified Sitters

Alexis, Paul; with Zola, 246–248

Boyer, Gustave, 209

Cézanne, Elisabeth Aubert (Cézanne's mother), 207–208

Cézanne, Hortense (Madame Cézanne), 30–91;
not in Cézanne's hand, 92

Cézanne, Louis Auguste (Cézanne's father), 198–206

Cézanne, Paul, 1–24; wrongly identified, 25, 26;
not in Cézanne's hand, 27–29

Cézanne, Paul, *fils*, 93–196; not in Cézanne's hand, 197

Choquet, Victor, 210–213

Emperaire, Achille, 214–218; wrongly identified, 219, 220;
not in Cézanne's hand, 221

Gachet, Paul, 222–224; not in Cézanne's hand, 225

Guillaume, Louis, 228

Guillaumin, Armand, 226, 227

Marion, Fortuné, 229; with Valabrèque, 241, 242

Pissarro, Camille, 230–233; in group, 245

Valabrèque, Antoine, 234; with Marion, 241, 242

Vollard, Ambroise, 235

Zola, Émile, 236–240; with Alexis, 246–248